Out of the Whirlwind

Creation Theology in the Book of Job

HARVARD THEOLOGICAL STUDIES
61

CAMBRIDGE, MASSACHUSETTS

Out of the Whirlwind

Creation Theology in the Book of Job

Kathryn Schifferdecker

DISTRIBUTED BY

HARVARD UNIVERSITY PRESS

FOR

HARVARD THEOLOGICAL STUDIES

HARVARD DIVINITY SCHOOL

Out of the Whirlwind:
Creation Theology in the Book of Job

Harvard Theological Studies 61

Series Editors:
François Bovon
Francis Schüssler Fiorenza
Peter B. Machinist

© 2008 the President and Fellows of Harvard College

Managing editor: Margaret Studier
Copyeditor: Tom Wetzel
Typesetters: Anne Browder, Richard Jude Thompson
The foreign language fonts (New Jerusalem and Symbol GreekII) and transliteration fonts used in this book are available from Linguist's Software, Inc., PO Box 580, Edmonds, WA 98020-0580; tel: (425) 775-1130. Website: www.linguistsoftware.com

Schifferdecker, Kathryn, 1968–
    Out of the whirlwind : creation theology in the Book of Job / Kathryn Schifferdecker.
        p. cm. -- (Harvard theological studies ; 61)
    Includes bibliographical references and index.
    Summary: "Offers a close literary and theological reading of the book of Job--particularly of the speeches of God at the end of the book--in order to articulate the creation theology particularly pertinent in our environmentally conscious age"--Provided by publisher.
    ISBN 978-0-674-02597-4 (alk. paper)
    1. Creation--Biblical teaching. 2. Bible. O.T. Job--Theology. 3. Bible. O.T. Job--Criticism, interpretation, etc. I. Title. II. Series.

BS1415.6.C73S55 2008
223'.106--dc22
                                                          2007051977

For Doug, Esther, and Isaac

Table of Contents

Acknowledgments

This book is a revision of my dissertation. In its writing, I have benefited from the input and advice of a number of people. In particular, my thanks are due to the three members of my dissertation committee. Professor Jon Levenson served as my academic advisor during my studies at Harvard and was the director for the dissertation. He is a brilliant teacher, and was a wise and generous guide throughout my doctoral studies, not least during the time I wrote the dissertation. From the beginning of the project he has provided sage counsel, and I am indebted to him for many things, including his prompt and good-humored responses to whatever questions or issues I brought to him. I am also indebted to Professor Gary Anderson, the second member of my committee, who even after leaving Harvard for Notre Dame was willing to continue to guide the research and writing of my dissertation. I learned a great deal from him during my time at Harvard. His enthusiasm for scholarship and teaching is and will continue to be a model for me. Professor Ellen Davis has been a steadfast and discerning mentor for me for more than fifteen years now, from the time I entered Yale Divinity School. It was there, in a class she offered on wisdom literature, that I first became interested in the book of Job. Ellen graciously agreed to serve on my dissertation committee as an outside reader and was a constant source of encouragement during the writing process, reading the drafts I sent her with great care and providing insightful commentary. I am blessed by her friendship. I am very fortunate to have had these three brilliant scholars as guides and mentors during the process of writing the dissertation, and I thank them for their assistance.

Throughout my doctoral studies, I was fortunate to have colleagues who offered mutual support and encouragement. I am grateful in particular to Cathy Beckerleg, Greg Schmidt Goering, Martien Halvorson-Taylor, and Valerie Stein for the dinners we shared, for the many conversations we had about biblical scholarship, and for their friendship. I am also grateful to my to my colleagues for their support, and to the students in my Job classes, who have provided insightful comments and reflections on the book of Job. I have learned much already from both faculty colleagues and students.

Thanks to Margaret Studier and her staff in the Harvard Theological Studies office for their patience and help in revising and preparing the manuscript for publication. I am especially indebted to Tom Wetzel for his fine work in editing the book and to Michael Chan here at Luther Seminary for preparing the index. Any shortcomings in the book remain, of course, my own.

Finally, I thank my family for their support throughout the course of my academic studies. My parents, Jim and Carolyn Schifferdecker, have always encouraged my endeavors. They are models for me of faithful living and constant love. My sisters, Miriam Sutherland, Martha Ochoa, and Karen Schifferdecker, are among the greatest blessings in my life. My husband, Doug Steinke, enabled me to do the day-to-day work of writing and revising the book, even while enduring some Job-like struggles himself. For his love, his constancy, and his belief in me, it is to Doug and to our children Esther and Isaac that I dedicate this book.

Kathryn Schifferdecker
Saint Paul, Minnesota
October 11, 2007

Abbreviations

All other abbreviations throughout the text are taken from *The Society of Biblical Literature Manual of Style*.

AAR	American Academy of Religion
ANF	Ante-Nicene Fathers
ANRW	Aufstieg und Niedergang der römische Welt
BETL	Bibliotheca Ephemeridum Theologicarum Lovaniensium
CCSL	Corpus Christianorum Series Latina
Dummer	Epiphanius, *Panarion haer.* Berlin: Akademie-Verlag, 1980.
ET	English translation
FoC	Fathers of the Church
GCS	Die griechischen christlichen Schriftsteller
HTR	*Harvard Theological Review*
HTS	Harvard Theological Studies
JECS	*Journal of Early Christian Studies*
JSNTSup	Supplement to the Journal for the Study of the New Testament
JSOT	*Journal for the Study of the Old Testament*
JTS	*Journal of Theological Studies*
Lampe	G. W. H. Lampe, *A Patristic Greek Lexicon*. Oxford: Clarendon, 1961–1968.
LCL	Loeb Classical Library
LSJ	H. G. Liddell and R. Scott, *Greek-English Lexicon with a Revised Supplement*. Oxford: Clarendon, 1996.
NAPS	North American Patristics Society
NRSV	New Revised Standard Version
NTS	*New Testament Studies*
RSV	Revised Standard Version

SBL	Society of Biblical Literature
SBLDS	Society of Biblical Literature Dissertation Series
SC	Sources chrétiennes
Stud. Pat.	*Studia Patristica*
TDNT	Kittel, Gerhard, ed. *Theological Dictionary of the New Testament.* Trans. Geoffrey W. Bromiley. 10 vols. Grand Rapids, Mich.: Eerdmans, 1964–1973.
TLG	Thesaurus linguae graecae
Waszink	Jan H. Waszink, *Quinti Septimi Florentis Tertulliani* De anima. Amsterdam: J. M. Meulenhoff, 1947.
WUNT	Wissenschaftliche Untersuchungen zum Neuen Testament

Introduction

*"I read the book of Job last night–I don't think God comes
well out of it."*

Virginia Woolf[1]

The book of Job has given rise over the centuries to numerous
interpretations. There have been those who (like early Christian
interpreters) extol the book as a story of great piety and those who (like
Virginia Woolf) find within the book an unfavorable portrait of God. The
latter reaction arises in large measure from the speeches of God at the
end of the book, in which God appears to ignore the just complaints of
the suffering Job. Indeed, the interpretation of those divine speeches has
proved a conundrum for scholars and commentators through the centuries;
the speeches seem to have little to do with either the prose frame of the
book or the poetic dialogue of Job and his companions.

The prose frame and the poetic dialogue deal with issues of undeserved
suffering, divine justice, guilt and innocence, and disinterested piety. The
divine speeches describe the power of God as displayed in the phenomena
and creatures of the natural world. The divine speeches seem to address a
figure who has overreached his place, someone who has tried to storm the
gates of heaven. They do not appear to address the innocent but suffering
figure of Job. They do not in fact even mention Job's situation, nor do they
reference the "test" of Job's piety described in the book's prologue; least
of all do they address the problem of undeserved suffering. At first reading
then, the divine speeches seemingly offer no answer at all to Job's questions
or to Job's suffering. Gerhard von Rad writes of the divine speeches, "All

---

[1] Virginia Woolf, *The Letters of Virginia Woolf: Volume II: 1912–1922* (ed. Nigel Nicolson
and Joanne Trautmann; New York: Harcourt Brace Jovanovich, 1976) 585.

commentators find the divine speech highly scandalous, insofar as it bypasses completely Job's particular concerns, and because in it Yahweh in no way condescends to any kind of self-interpretation."[2] James G. Williams argues that the theology of the divine speeches is "poor theology" in comparison to the "good sociology of the dialogues."[3] William Safire writes of the divine speeches, "It's as if God appears in a tie-dyed T-shirt emblazoned with the words 'Because I'm God, That's Why.' "[4] In perhaps the most succinct statement of the problem of the divine speeches, S. B. Freehof writes, "Job cries, 'I am innocent.' And God responds, 'You are ignorant.' The answer seems not only irrelevant but even unfeeling and heartless."[5]

This book addresses such negative evaluations of the divine speeches in Job by examining closely the content of those speeches, specifically their portrait of creation and God's acts in creation. It is the argument of this book that the divine speeches in Job do indeed provide an answer to Job's situation. Moreover, they offer a view of creation–and of humanity's place in creation– that is fundamentally different from any other theology of creation in the Bible. The divine speeches depict creation as radically nonanthropocentric. At the same time, the divine speeches offer human beings (in the person of Job) a place in the created order not as the crown of creation, nor even as the caretakers of creation, but as participants in creation, along with the Sea, the celestial bodies, the animals, and the mythological beasts Behemoth and Leviathan. In the divine speeches God indeed "puts" Job "in his place." His "place," however, is one neither of servitude nor of mastery but of full and free relationship with the rest of God's creatures.

The problem of divine justice and innocent suffering–the source of Job's anguish–is related to the radically nonanthropocentric view of creation found in the divine speeches. God expands Job's vision of the world to include more

---

[2] Gerhard von Rad, *Wisdom in Israel* (trans. James Marton; London: SCM, 1972) 225.

[3] James G. Williams, "Job and the God of Victims," in *The Voice from the Whirlwind* (ed. Leo Perdue and W. Clark Gilpin; Nashville: Abingdon, 1992) 222. Williams goes on to say of the God revealed in the divine speeches: "his underlying savagery is great."

[4] William Safire, *The First Dissident: The Book of Job in Today's Politics* (New York: Random House, 1992) 22.

[5] S. B. Freehof, *Book of Job* (New York: Union of American Hebrew Congregations, 1958) 236. René Girard asserts that the God of the divine speeches is a charlatan [*Job, the Victim of His People* (trans. Yvonne Freccero; Stanford: Stanford University Press, 1987) 142]. For a list of similarly dissatisfied comments on the divine speeches by other biblical interpreters, see L. Alonso-Schökel, "God's Answer to Job," in *Job and the Silence of God* (ed. C. Duquoc and C. Floristan; New York: Paulist, 1983) 45.

fully the nonhuman realm and thereby teaches him about divine מִשְׁפָּט, that is, the divine order that governs and sustains God's creation. It is an order that includes the existence of chaotic forces like the Sea, Leviathan, and human wickedness, but that also limits these forces. While the divine speeches do not answer directly the problem of undeserved suffering, they do offer an answer to Job's assumptions and attitudes about creation, humanity's place in creation, and God's ordering of it. That answer enables Job to move out of despair into renewed participation in God's often-dangerous but beautiful world.

Previous Interpretations of the Divine Speeches

Before turning in more detail to the outline of this book, it is appropriate to provide an overview of what others have said about the divine speeches in Job, in order to articulate the contribution of this study.

Not all interpreters of Job find the speeches of God "highly scandalous" although most acknowledge the seeming incongruity between the speeches and what precedes them. Jewish and Christian biblical interpreters in the centuries before the rise of modern criticism generally found in the divine speeches a satisfactory and legitimate answer to Job's situation. They did not, however, always agree in their identification of the problem that the book is addressing or on what sort of "answer" the divine speeches offer.

Gregory the Great, in his sixth century *Moralia in Iob*, does not acknowledge any interpretive problem with the divine speeches. Rather, his allegorical interpretation makes the first speech a discourse on the creation and history of the church and on the way God works in the soul. The second speech then becomes a treatise on God's defeat of Satan, who is symbolized by Behemoth and Leviathan. The "problem" that the book of Job addresses through the divine speeches is not the issue of theodicy, according to Gregory, but that of how to overcome Satan's assaults.[6]

In the tenth century, the Jewish philosopher Saadiah ben-Joseph Al-Fayyumi produced an Arabic translation of the book of Job. In the accompanying commentary, he writes of the divine speeches, "[W]e know that people ask what sort of answer to Job this discourse on God's part represents, and what there is in it that responds to Job's request, 'Cause me

---

[6] Susan E. Schreiner, *Where Shall Wisdom Be Found? Calvin's Exegesis of Job from Medieval and Modern Perspectives* (Chicago: University of Chicago Press, 1994) 48–51.

to know wherefore Thou dost prosecute me' (10:2)."[7] Apparently even in
Saadiah's day, some readers found the divine speeches a puzzling answer
to Job's situation. Saadiah himself argues that God does not tell Job of the
test Job has endured thus far because Job must persevere without promise
of recompense. Instead, God speaks of three things to Job: creation as an
act of pure grace, the design of nature, and providence in nature. These
three topics are united under the category of divine sovereignty, which for
Saadiah means not that God can act arbitrarily or unjustly, but that he acts
with universal grace.[8]

Thomas Aquinas, writing in the thirteenth century, follows Gregory's
identification of Behemoth and Leviathan with Satan although Aquinas
gives a more naturalistic reading to the first divine speech. The first speech,
according to Aquinas, uses creation to demonstrate "His [i.e., God's] wisdom
and power so that from this demonstration it may be manifest that no man
can contend with God either in wisdom or in power."[9] The second speech,
on the other hand, "deals with the malice of Satan, which was the beginning
of Job's adversity and is the beginning of human damnation."[10] Job's ordeals
then are part of the story of God's redemption of humanity, a story that begins
with creation and culminates in Christ.[11]

John Calvin, three centuries after Aquinas, rejected the interpretation of the
second divine speech as referring to Satan and understood both speeches as
referring to the natural world. Calvin also judged Job more harshly than did
either Gregory or Aquinas. For Calvin, Elihu is the preeminent theologian of
the dialogue, and he agrees with Elihu's judgment that Job has tried to justify
himself while condemning God.[12] The divine speeches are the necessary
rebuke to Job's sin of self-justification, and they work by humbling Job with
the demonstration of God's overwhelming power and wisdom in creation.[13]

---

[7] Saadiah ben Joseph Al-Fayyumi, *The Book of Theodicy* (trans. and ed. Lenn E. Goodman; New Haven: Yale University Press, 1988) 384.

[8] Ibid., 123–27, 382–84, 393–97. See the discussion of these themes by Goodman on
99–106

[9] Thomas Aquinas, *The Literal Exposition on Job* (trans. Anthony Damico; Atlanta:
Scholars Press, 1989) 443.

[10] Ibid., 449.

[11] Schreiner, 89–90.

[12] John Calvin, *Sermons from Job* (trans. Leroy Nixon; Grand Rapids, Mich.: Eerdmans,
1952) 220–21. See Job 35:1–8 and Schreiner, 132, 139. Schreiner says, "There are few people
in the Bible Calvin admires more than Elihu" (131).

[13] Calvin, 287–300. See Schreiner, 140–41.

Behemoth and Leviathan, for Calvin, are simply the elephant and the whale; thus, the struggle at the end of the book is not between God and Satan but between God and human pride.[14]

Despite their differences, these pre-modern interpreters generally considered the divine speeches an essential part of the story of Job. By contrast, a group of writers in the twentieth century found the divine speeches so inadequate that they largely eliminated them from their works. The book of Job became the inspiration in the last century for some significant literary creations, including Archibald MacLeish's *J.B.* and Elie Wiesel's *Trial of God.*[15] The divine speeches suffer much the same fate in each of these works. That is, either God does not answer Job; or God's answer is disparaged as insufficient.

In Wiesel's play God is completely absent and the Job-like character cries out against that absent God, "I want no part of a justice that escapes me, diminishes me and makes a mockery out of mine! Justice is here for men and women—I therefore want it to be human, or let Him keep it!"[16] Wiesel's characters put God on trial and they have difficulty finding anyone who will speak on God's behalf. The mysterious stranger who is finally found to defend God is revealed at the end of the play to be none other than the Satan. The play ends with the Satan laughing while the human characters are killed in a pogrom. God remains completely absent and silent.

In the play-within-a-play *J.B.*, MacLeish has a "Distant Voice" quote the divine speeches at some length but the Satan figure disparages them:

> All he asks is reasons why–
> Why? Why? And God replies to him:
> God comes whirling in the wind replying–

[14] Schreiner, 143–44.

[15] Archibald MacLeish, *J.B.* (Boston: Houghton Mifflin, 1958); Elie Wiesel, *The Trial of God* (trans. Marion Wiesel; New York: Schocken Books, 1979). Note also two additional literary works based on the book of Job: H. G. Wells, *The Undying Fire* (New York: Macmillan, 1919) and Robert Frost, "A Masque of Reason," in *Robert Frost: Collected Poems, Prose, and Plays* (ed. Richard Poirier and Mark Richardson; New York: The Library of America, 1995) 372–88. Jon Levenson discusses the book of Job and the works of Wells, MacLeish, and Frost in *The Book of Job in Its Time and in the Twentieth Century* (Cambridge: Harvard University Press, 1972). Note that Wiesel's play does not make as explicit a connection with the book of Job as do the other three literary works. Nevertheless, *The Trial of God* addresses many of the same themes as Job: the problem of undeserved suffering, the absence of God, and the question of divine justice.

[16] Wiesel, 123

What? That God knows more than he does.
That God's more powerful than he!–
Throwing the whole creation at him!
Throwing the Glory and the Power!
What's the Power to a broken man
Trampled beneath it like a toad already?
What's the Glory to a skin that stinks![17]

At the end of the play, J.B. and his wife find the only "answer" to their suffering not in God's revelation but in human love: "Blow on the coal of the heart./ The candles in churches are out./ The lights have gone out in the sky./ Blow on the coal of the heart/ And we'll see by and by…"[18] The characters in the play, even the God-figure, find the divine speeches inadequate to J.B.'s situation.

Each of these twentieth-century literary works provides sensitive, nuanced readings of the book of Job, but in them the divine speeches play little or no part. Such literary reinterpretations of the book of Job reflect a modern dissatisfaction with the divine speeches as any sort of "answer" to Job's situation; a dissatisfaction that results, I would argue, from a superficial reading of those speeches.

In academic biblical scholarship–as opposed to literary readings of the book of Job–the divine speeches cannot be ignored; but the problem of how they function in the book is still very much present. Modern biblical scholars offer various solutions to this interpretive problem of the divine speeches.[19] Some downplay the importance of the divine speeches by saying that the "answer" to the problem of the book is found not in them, but earlier in the book: in chapter 19 (Job's appeal for a redeemer),[20] in chapter 28 (the poem

---

[17] MacLeish, scene 10, lines 54–63.

[18] Ibid., scene 11, lines 67–71

[19] For a succinct discussion of modern interpretation of the divine speeches, see Leo G. Perdue, *Wisdom in Revolt* (Sheffield: JSOT, 1991) 196–99. For a longer discussion of modern scholarship on the whole book of Job, see Carol Newsom *The Book of Job: A Contest of Moral Imaginations* (Oxford: Oxford University Press, 2003) 3–11.

[20] For a list of those commentators who argue that Job 19:25–27 refers to Job's resurrection or redemption, see Georg Fohrer, *Das Buch Hiob* (Gütersloh: Gütersloher Verlagshaus Gerd Mohn, 1963) 318.

on wisdom),[21] or in the speeches of Elihu, the young interlocutor who speaks right before the divine speeches.[22]

Even among those who do seek some sort of answer to the problems of Job in the divine speeches, no consensus has emerged. Some say that it is the *presence* of God at the end of the book, rather than God's *words*, that is the answer to Job's agonized questions. C. Kuhl, for instance, considers the event of the theophany (God appearing to Job in a whirlwind) an original part of the book of Job but argues that the verbal content of the theophany is a later addition.[23] Von Rad, while giving some attention to the content of the speeches, understands them primarily as a way in which "God has turned to Job" and so has answered Job's complaint that God is hidden.[24] Through the longed-for appearance of God, Job is enabled to put aside his questions and place the world (and his own destiny) into divine hands.[25]

Most recent scholarly works attempt to find the interpretive answer of the divine speeches in the content of the speeches, and not merely in the event of the theophany itself. Again, no consensus has been reached. The following interpretations are a sample of those offered by modern scholarship:[26]

[21] For citations and a discussion of this opinion, see C. Kuhl, "Neuere Literarkritik des Buches Hiob," *Theologische-Rundschau* 21 (1953) 163–205. A number of scholars who argue this position place chapter 28 at the end of the divine speeches. H. H. Rowley also argues that chapter 28, were it original to the book, "would render the Divine speeches unnecessary" because the two texts say essentially the same thing [*Job* (2d ed.; London: Marshall, Morgan & Scott, 1976) 179].

[22] Karl Budde, *Das Buch Hiob übersetzt und erklärt* (2d ed.; Göttingen: Vandenhoeck & Ruprecht, 1913) xlv–xlviii. See also Otto Eissfeldt, [*Einleitung in das Alte Testament* (2d ed.; Tübingen: Mohr, 1956) 561] for a discussion of the unusual argument that the Elihu speeches were the original climax of the book, and the divine speeches a later addition. I find this an untenable argument and agree with the scholarly consensus that the Elihu speeches are the work of a later redactor of the book of Job. See discussion below in chapter one.

[23] Kuhl, 270. Hans-Peter Müller similarly argues that the appearance of God, not the content of the speeches, is the important factor in the theophany [*Hiob und seine Freunde* (Zürich: EVZ, 1970) 42]. For strong arguments against this opinion, see M. Tsevat, "The Meaning of the Book of Job," *HUCA* 37 (1966) 79–82, and Georg Fohrer, "Gottes Antwort aus dem Sturmwind, Hi. 38–41," *TZ* 18:1 (1962) 4–8. Tsevat argues that the whole structure of the book leads one to expect an answer from the divine speeches. Fohrer, while questioning the authenticity of the second divine speech, still considers the *content* of the first speech, and not the *appearance* of God, to be decisive: "[N]icht die Vision, sondern das Wort ist entscheidend" (8).

[24] Von Rad, *Wisdom in Israel,* 226.

[25] Ibid., 221–26.

[26] One of the positions cited here has been adapted from Perdue's list (*Wisdom in*

■ In the divine speeches, God admits his own inability to stop evil in the world.[27]

■ To the contrary, the divine speeches reveal God as Creator of the world and "Lord of the Animals," like an ancient Near Eastern king. God controls the animals, who are enemies of civilization. God keeps the world from descending into chaos and at the same time destroys the evil represented by Behemoth and Leviathan.[28]

■ The divine speeches depict God as a parent who delights in the freedom and individual character of each of his creations. Unlike ancient Near Eastern kings who hunted wild animals as a sign of their sovereignty, God loves his creatures, delights in them, and allows them the freedom to develop into unique individuals. Through the divine speeches, God challenges Job to do the same.[29]

Revolt, 197–98).

[27] "God is not absolutely omnipotent: he rules the world he has created, but has little or no control over evil." Athalya Brenner, "God's Answer to Job," *VT* 31 (1981) 129. Brenner goes on to say that the divine speeches imply that evil is part of God's nature itself, that God "has not yet conquered his dark side," and is asking for human patience and understanding (135).

[28] Othmar Keel, *Jahwes Entgegnung an Ijob* (Göttingen: Vandenhoeck & Ruprecht, 1978). Keel argues for the integrity of the divine speeches by demonstrating that most of the animals listed in the first speech are associated in the Bible and in ancient Near East [ANE] iconography with demonic or chaotic forces. In Egyptian and Assyrian iconography, the king is portrayed defeating these animals as one would defeat foreign enemies. In a related motif, the king is pictured as "the Lord of the Animals," holding pairs of wild animals captive. This motif shares with the Joban dialogue all the animals listed in the first divine speech except the hawk and the raven. Keel interprets Behemoth and Leviathan as a similar pair of threatening animals, as seen in Egyptian art which depicts the king or Horus defeating the crocodile and the hippopotamus.

[29] William P. Brown, *Character in Crisis* (Grand Rapids, Mich.: Eerdmans, 1996) 89–103. Brown argues directly against Keel's characterization of the divine speeches. In Brown's view, God is more of a parent than a sovereign. The wild animals are a source of delight and beauty, not symbols of chaos and evil. See also Brown's later work, *The Ethos of the Cosmos* (Grand Rapids, Mich.: Eerdmans, 1999). In this book, he supplements and nuances Keel's iconographic examples with many Egyptian and Assyrian royal inscriptions related to wild animals (350–360). Brown considers the divine speeches to be addressed to Job's "patriarchal pride," which has been "nurtured and sustained at the expense of nature and community" (376). In the epilogue, Job learns how to govern his world as God governs his, delighting in and granting freedom to his children. Brown's interpretation of the divine speeches has much in common with that of J. Gerald Janzen [*Job* (Atlanta: John Knox, 1985)]. Janzen, too, emphasizes God's delight in creation and the freedom with which he endows it. Janzen contends that God challenges Job to act as God acts, to take up "the royal vocation

■ The divine speeches expand Job's vision from his own problems to the immensity of the universe. The questions of the speeches are not designed to humiliate Job but to remind him of what he already knows. They enable him to realize anew that God establishes order in the cosmos. Michael Fox holds this view: "God is saying to Job, You know very well that I and I alone created order and maintain it in the world, and I know that you know, and you know that I know that you know."[30] This order visible in the universe leads Job to trust God even when he does not understand why he suffers.

■ The divine speeches, like much of the rest of Job, are to be understood as having a forensic *Sitz im Leben*. That is, God is answering Job's legal case against him by testifying about his rule over creation. Job has challenged God's sovereignty and established himself as a rival to the Almighty. The divine speeches answer this challenge by reasserting God's sovereignty and humbling Job.[31]

■ The divine speeches reveal God as a capricious, jealous tyrant who abuses his power. Job's ambiguous responses to the divine speeches do not indicate repentance; rather, he renounces this God as a chaotic, malevolent ruler.[32]

---

of humanity," which corresponds to the "divine image" in humanity (257–58). For a similar argument, see Ellen F. Davis, "Job and Jacob: The Integrity of Faith," in *The Whirlwind* (ed. Stephen L. Cook et al.; New York: Sheffield, 2001) 100–20.

[30] Michael V. Fox, "Job 38 and God's Rhetoric," *Semeia* 19 (1981) 60. For a similarly cogent description of how the divine speeches expand Job's limited vision, see Robert Alter, *The Art of Biblical Poetry* (Edinburgh: T&T Clark, 1985) 85-110. Robert Gordis, among others, also emphasizes that the order and beauty of creation revealed in the divine speeches serve as an answer to Job's questions: "[T]he moral order which emanates from the same Divine source [as creation] must possess a meaning and rationality even in those aspects which are beyond man's comprehension" [*The Book of Job* (New York: Jewish Theological Seminary of America, 1978) 560. See also Edouard Dhorme, *A Commentary on the Book of Job* (trans. Harold Knight; London: Thomas Nelson, 1967) 645–46; and Rowley, 325–26.

[31] For variations on this argument, see Perdue, 200–32; Henry Rowold, "Yahweh's Challenge to Rival: The Form and Function of the Yahweh-Speech in Job 38–39," *CBQ* 47 (1985) 199–211; Sylvia Scholnick, "The Meaning of *Mishpat* in the Book of Job," *JBL* 101 (1982) 521–29; idem,"Poetry in the Courtroom: Job 38–41," in *Directions in Biblical Hebrew Poetry* (ed. E. R. Follis; Sheffield: JSOT, 1987) 185–204; and Edward L. Greenstein, "A Forensic Understanding of the Speech from the Whirlwind," in *Texts, Temples, and Traditions* (ed. Michael V. Fox; Winona Lake, Ind.: Eisenbrauns, 1996) 241–58.

[32] David Robertson, "The Book of Job: A Literary Study," *Soundings* 56 (1973) 446–69; James Williams, " 'You Have Not Spoken Truth of Me.' Mystery and Irony in Job," *ZAW* 83 (1971) 231–55. John Biggs Curtis, "On Job's Response to Yahweh," *JBL* 98 (1979) 495–511. This position is cited by Perdue, 198–99.

■ The world is amoral; God is neither just nor unjust. The book of Job (and its divine speeches, in particular) abolishes the doctrine of retribution and the corresponding belief in divine justice. It rejects the idea of collective retribution for sin and does not subscribe to the later doctrine of individual retribution for sin in the next life. Therefore, it contains the "purest moral theory in the Bible."[33] In other words, there is no reward for piety or punishment for wickedness so piety must be disinterested: one must be good simply for the sake of being good.

The foregoing list is by no means exhaustive. There are a myriad of works about the book of Job and many different interpretations of the divine speeches. Those listed here are simply some of the principal ones. As evidenced by the list, scholars do not agree on what sort of "answer" the divine speeches offer to Job. Some consensus has emerged in recent years, however, concerning the literary integrity of the divine speeches. Most scholars of the last twenty-five years resist excising parts of the divine speeches in the manner of earlier historical critics. Likewise, they do not emphasize the *event* of the theophany over its *content*. Generally speaking, recent scholarship treats the divine speeches as a whole, pays close attention to their content, and attempts to connect them with the rest of the book of Job.[34]

These characteristics are true of one of the most recent and significant interpretations of the divine speeches (as well as of the book of Job as a whole): Carol Newsom's *The Book of Job: A Contest of Moral Imaginations*. Newsom criticizes historical-critical readings of the book of Job for their inability to read the book as a whole and "final form" readings for their lack of attention to genre.[35] Newsom reads the final form of the book but also plays close attention to genre. She deals sympathetically with each discrete section of Job, highlighting the strengths of each "moral imagination" contained

---

[33] Tsevat, 104. See also James Crenshaw, *Old Testament Wisdom* (Atlanta: John Knox, 1981) 110–25.

[34] The connections most discussed by scholars are between the divine speeches, Job 3, and Job 29–31. For major examples of this sort of "final form" reading of the book of Job, including the divine speeches, see Janzen's *Job*; Norman C. Habel, *The Book of Job* (London: SCM, 1985); Francis I. Andersen, *Job* (Leicester, England: InterVarsity Press, 1976); and Alter, *The Art of Biblical Poetry*.

[35] Newsom, 6–11. Historical criticism, according to Newsom, never had an answer to "the problem of how such a multigenre, multiauthor composition [as Job] was to be read as a whole" (10). "Final form" and deconstructive readings both "have to minimize or ignore the rich textures of genre and style that historical criticism emphasized" (11).

therein. Basing her approach on the literary theory of Mikhail Bakhtin, Newsom imagines the book as a "polyphonic text" where each voice offers a different vision of reality, a text "in which a variety of different voice-ideas, embodied not only in characters but also in genres, engage one another without privilege."[36] According to this way of reading the book, no voice, not even God's, can be said to offer an "answer" to the questions raised in Job. More accurately, Newsom finds a different answer to Job's problems in every section of the book, but does not claim any of the answers as conclusive. Therefore, there can be "no end to the book, no end to its dialogue, and no end to the dialogue it provokes."[37]

Given the abundance of scholarly literature produced about the book of Job, I cannot argue with Newsom's statement that there is "no end to the dialogue it provokes." I do, however, find her final evaluation of the book and her interpretation of the divine speeches unsatisfactory. While the notion of a "polyphonic text" may be attractive and understandable in a modern context, the ancient Israelite reader must have understood the divine speeches to be the answer to Job's situation.[38] Indeed, Job's reply to the divine speeches and his restoration in the epilogue confirm the reader's sense that the divine speeches have engendered a change in the attitude and circumstances of the man from Uz. The book does indeed have an "end," whether contemporary readers appreciate it or not.

---

[36] Newsom, *Moral Imaginations*, 234. Newsom acknowledges that there is difficulty in maintaining this stance when it comes to the divine speeches: "When God speaks, it tends to bring conversation to an end." There is, however, such incongruity between the divine speeches and what follows them, according to Newsom, that the book "finds ways to evade the finalizing effect of the divine speeches."

[37] Ibid., 258; See also 234–35, 263–64.

[38] Jon D. Levenson makes this point in his review of Newsom's book in *JR* 84 (2004) 271–72. "Three centuries of secularization and historical criticism impel us to place God's words about himself on a plane with human speculations about him. There is ample reason to doubt that ancient Israelites felt the same agnostic impulse or evaluated interminable dialogue with no chance of resolution so highly" (272). Terence Fretheim also critiques Newsom's argument: "Does the author [of Job] think equally highly of each of the perspectives presented? . . . . Given the diversity of perspectives on suffering that the book presents, it seems unlikely that the author is so evenhanded or honors no theological move more than another" [*God and World in the Old Testament: A Relational Theology of Creation* (Nashville: Abingdon, 2005) 222].

An Overview

Like many of the works just discussed, this study attempts to understand how the divine speeches offer an answer to the problems and situation of Job. While no scholarly work on Job can claim to be conclusive, it is my hope that this study may offer some fresh perspective on the interpretive issues surrounding the divine speeches. It will do so by paying particular attention to the creation theology of those speeches, especially as it is articulated in comparison and contrast to the views of creation found in the rest of the book of Job. My assumptions are these: 1) because of their climactic position in the book and the identity of their speaker, the divine speeches must have been intended by the author and/or redactor of Job to be understood as containing the answer to the problems and situation of Job; 2) given the length of the divine speeches and the extraordinarily detailed vision of creation they articulate, that answer must be contained in their content, not simply in the event of the theophany; 3) the content of the divine speeches must be connected in some way to the rest of the book of Job, contrary to first impressions.

To see how the divine speeches are connected with the rest of Job, it will be fruitful to explore the views of creation found in earlier sections of the book. This discussion is taken up in chapter one of this study, with an overview of the different parts of the book of Job and an exploration of how each part addresses the issue of creation and humanity's place in creation. I find lacking in most modern scholarship just such a systematic exploration of the creation theologies of earlier chapters in Job. While attention often is paid to creation references in chapter 3 of Job and (to a lesser extent) in the Elihu speeches, the creation images in the rest of Job 1–37 are largely passed over without discussion.[39] Most modern scholars note the use in these chapters of imagery and language drawn from ancient legal traditions, to the neglect of the creation imagery found therein.

I move in chapter two of this book to articulate the creation theology of the divine speeches in comparison to the creation theologies found in the earlier chapters of Job. The work in this chapter is based on a close reading of the divine speeches, a reading detailed in the translation and commentary found in the appendix of this book. This second chapter also compares the

---

[39] For three significant exceptions to this general rule, see Alter, 85–110; Brown, *Ethos of the Cosmos*, 320–50; and Fretheim, 223–33.

creation theologies found in Job with those found in other biblical texts, particularly Genesis and Psalms.

Chapter three of this study relates the divine speeches specifically to what follows them: the second reply of Job and the epilogue. This chapter also includes a discussion of the concept of justice in the divine speeches and how this concept relates to Job's demands for justice in the dialogue. This last chapter summarizes the findings of the study and offers suggestions as to how the divine speeches function in the final form of the book of Job; that is, what sort of answer they offer to Job's situation.[40] Finally, this chapter explores some implications of this Joban creation theology for the modern environmental movement.

Excursus: The Date of the Book of Job

Before moving into the main arguments of this book, a word should be said here about the dating of the material in Job. Though the date of Job is not the primary concern of this study, an overview of the issues in question deserves some attention because it bears on the question of the content of the divine speeches. That is, why does the author/redactor of the book turn to creation theology for an answer to undeserved suffering, rather than to the covenant between God and Israel? It is generally agreed by scholars that the book was written by an Israelite to an Israelite audience.[41] The author uses the divine name YHWH, and alludes a number of times to other biblical texts. He does

---

[40] It has been suggested by Jon Levenson that the divine speeches were originally part of another composition, a story of a Prometheus-like man who challenges God's mastery over creation [*Creation and the Persistence of Evil: The Jewish Drama of Divine Omnipotence* (2d ed.; Princeton: Princeton University Press, 1994) 155]. See Siegfried Wagner, " 'Schöpfung' im Buche Hiob," *Die Zeichen der Zeit* 34 (1980) 95. Wagner considers some elements of the divine speeches to have arisen in other literary contexts although he does not specify which elements. If Levenson's theory is correct, then the book of Job can be understood as a kind of anthology of stories about the character Job, stories about both the patient Job and the Promethean Job. This study will delineate thematic and lexical connections between the divine speeches and the rest of the book. Given these connections, the term "anthology" does not seem to do justice to the nature of the book. Whatever the origin of the divine speeches, this study will address them within their current context: the prose frame and poetic dialogue of the book of Job in its final form.

[41] For a discussion and critique of alternate theories of authorship, see Robert Gordis, *The Book of God and Man: A Study of Job* (Chicago: University of Chicago Press, 1965) 209–18. Gordis lists many pieces of evidence for the claim that Job was written in Hebrew by a "Hebrew."

not, however, make any direct reference to Israel or to Israelite "salvation history." Instead, human suffering in Job is viewed from the perspective of creation and humanity's place in creation.

There is no consensus about the dating of Job. Many scholars of the last century date the final form of the book to postexilic times, while acknowledging that some parts of the book might be of earlier origin.[42] Some scholars argue for an exilic date for the composition of the majority of the book,[43] and a few favor a preexilic composition date.[44]

Rabbinic commentators on the book of Job are no less varied in their opinions as to the origins of the book. They do not, of course, speak so much about authorship as they do about the person of Job. *B. Baba Batra* 14b–16b argues that Job was a contemporary of Moses and that Moses himself wrote the book of Job.[45] Taking their cue from the character of Job in the prose prologue and epilogue, some rabbis place him in the period of the ancient Israelite patriarchs. *Genesis Rabbah* 57:4 places Job in the time of Abraham, while another tradition in *B. Baba Batra* 15b contends

---

[42] Rowley, 22; S. R. Driver and G. B. Gray, *A Critical and Exegetical Commentary on the Book of Job* (Edinburgh: T&T Clark, 1921) lxv–lxxi; Gordis, *The Book of God and Man*, 216–18; Dhorme, clxix–clxxi; Morris Jastrow, *The Book of Job* (Philadelphia: J. B. Lippincott Co., 1920) 34. H. L. Ginsberg, "Job and Patient and Job the Impatient," *Conservative Judaism* 21 (1967) 24. See Marvin H. Pope [*Job* (3d ed.; New York: Doubleday, 1973) xxxii–xl] for a comprehensive overview of scholarly opinions about the dating of Job and a learned discussion of the arguments.

[43] Janzen, *Job*, 5; N. H. Tur-Sinai, *The Book of Job* (Jerusalem: Turim Press, 1957) xxxvi–xxxviii. Tur-Sinai argues that Job was written in early exilic times in Aramaic by a Jew in Babylonia. Samuel Terrien dates the written form of the prose tale to between the eleventh and eighth centuries B.C.E., while he dates the rest of the book (excluding the Elihu speech and chapter 28) even more precisely to the period between Jeremiah and Deutero-Isaiah (i.e., the first half of the sixth century). He finds dependence in Job on Jeremiah, and in Deutero-Isaiah on Job [*Job: Poet of Existence* (New York: Bobbs-Merrill, 1957) 28–33]. See also Terrien, "Introduction and Exegesis of the Book of Job," *The Interpreter's Bible* (New York: Abingdon Press, 1954) 3:884–92. Gordis disagrees with Terrien and finds that the dependence runs the other way, from Deutero-Isaiah to Job [*The Book of God and Man*, 216].

[44] Yehezkel Kaufmann, *The Religion of Israel* (trans. Moshe Greenberg; New York: Schocken Books, 1972) 334–38. Cf. Pope, who asserts that "the evidence [for dating Job] is equivocal and inconclusive." Nevertheless, Pope assigns at least the poetic dialogue in a "best guess" to the seventh century B.C.E. (xl).

[45] *J. Sota* 20c. For these and other rabbinic references, see Judith R. Baskin, *Pharaoh's Counsellors: Job, Jethro, and Balaam in Rabbinic and Patristic Tradition* (Chico, Calif.: Scholars Press, 1983) 10–14.

that Job was a contemporary of Jacob and married his daughter Dinah.[46] Yet in anticipation of modern scholarship (though on the basis of different reasoning), some rabbis argue that Job was among those who returned from the Babylonian exile.[47]

The Septuagint appendix to Job continues to place the man from Uz in the age of the patriarchs. It identifies him with the Jobab of Gen. 36:33–34, a grandson of Esau.[48] The same genealogy is used in the pseudepigraphical *Testament of Job* but does not appear in rabbinic sources.[49] The patristic writers, for the most part, hold to the Septuagint tradition that Job was a descendant of Esau and a righteous Gentile--and thus a precursor to Gentile Christians.[50]

This wide variety of opinions concerning the origins of Job–both the character Job and the book itself–is the result of a distinct lack of clues in the book as to its date. There are no historical "markers" in the book, no references to specific kings or time periods. Its introduction has a "long ago and far away" character to it: "There was a man in the land of Uz whose name was Job."[51] If the original readers and listeners knew where to locate Uz, that information is long since lost.

The language of Job likewise makes it difficult to assign a particular date to the book. The Hebrew of the poetic core of the book is full of words that appear nowhere else in the Bible. There are many instances where the grammar or vocabulary of the Hebrew makes a verse difficult to understand.[52] This has led some scholars to propose a generous number of emendations to the text.[53] Others have noted "Aramaisms" in the text and have even argued

---

[46] Baskin, 13. Both traditions, as is often the case in rabbinic texts, are based on lexical connections between Genesis and Job: עוּץ in Gen. 22:21 and Job 1:1; and נְבָלוֹת / נְבָלָה in Gen 34:7 and Job 2:10.

[47] *B. Baba Batra* 15b (cited in Baskin, 13–14). This argument is based on the assumption that Job was an Israelite, not a righteous Gentile.

[48] Job 42:17b–17c (LXX).

[49] Baskin, 29. She argues that this connection of Job with the Edomites (traditionally the descendants of Esau) does not appear in rabbinic sources because of the rabbinic association of Edom with Rome.

[50] Ibid., 32–33.

[51] Job 1:1

[52] One may note the numerous instances in the NRSV of the footnote, "Meaning of Hebrew uncertain." See for instance Job 5:5; 6:6; 8:17, 19; 9:23; 11:6.

[53] See, for instance, the commentaries of Dhorme (*A Commentary on the Book of* Job) and Fohrer (*Das Buch Hiob*).

that the book of Job as we have it is a translation from an Aramaic original.[54] Such a theory tends to favor an exilic or post-exilic date. Dahood and Michel contest this argument and assert that the language and imagery of Job is best understood in the light of Northwest Semitic, specifically Ugaritic and Eblaite. This theory suggests that the book of Job has strong connections with cultures of the second and third millennium B.C.E. Although Michel does not propose such an ancient date for Job, he does find evidence of very ancient mythic and linguistic features in the book.[55]

In contrast to the poetic core of Job, the Hebrew of the prose frame is easy to read. It is also reminiscent in many ways of classical Hebrew, which has led some scholars to argue that the prose frame is derived from an ancient epic that predates the later composition of the poetic portions of the book.[56] Hurvitz, in contrast, argues convincingly on the basis of linguistic elements that while the *story* of Job may be ancient, the "final shaping of the extant Prose Tale [is] incompatible with a date prior to the Exile."[57]

[54] Tur-Sinai, xxx–xl; Dhorme, clxxv–clxxix. Tur-Sinai argues that the book was originally written in Aramaic by a Jew in the Babylonian exile. He also notes that Abraham ibn Ezra and other pre-modern commentators thought Job to be a translation from another language. Ibn Ezra writes in his commentary (II, 12): "It seems probable to me that it is a translated book and that is why, like all translated books, it is difficult to interpret" (cited in Tur-Sinai, 111).

[55] Michel includes in his assumptions: "[T]here is no real gap in time between Ugaritic and Hebrew." Likewise, "In spite of the tremendous difficulties and uncertainties, my methodological assumption is that Eblaite, Ugaritic and Phoenician-Punic are certainly of greater value for the understanding of Job than Aramaic, Arabic or postbiblical and rabbinic Hebrew" [Walter Michel, *Job in the Light of Northwest Semitic* (Rome: Biblical Institute Press, 1987) 1:3, 5]. Michel cites many of Dahood's articles on Job throughout his commentary. Though Michel does not discuss the date of Job, he obviously favors a pre-exilic one for at least the poetic sections of the book (17, 34).

[56] N. M. Sarna, "Epic Substratum in the Prose of Job," *Journal of Biblical Literature* 76 (1957) 13–25. Sarna argues for a number of "epic" features in the prose tale, including the use of repetition and the prominence of the number seven. He does not argue for a specific date for this "ancient Epic of Job" from which the present prose tale is "directly derived," but he associates it at length with Ugaritic epics (25). One would assume then that the ancient epic he perceives is much older than exilic texts. See U. Cassuto, *Knesset* 8 (1944) 142. Duhm argues that the prologue and epilogue were part of an independent *Volksbuch* from which the author of Job took his story [B. Duhm, *Das Buch Hiob* (Kurzer Handcommentar zum AT 16; Freiburg: J. C. B. Mohr, 1897)].

[57] Avi Hurvitz, "The Date of the Prose-Tale of Job Linguistically Reconsidered," *Harvard Theological Review* 67 (1974) 17–34. Hurvitz bases his argument on the presence of seven words or phrases in the prose tale that are not present in classical biblical Hebrew but are attested in late biblical Hebrew. The strongest example is the presence of הַשָּׂטָן in the prologue

Based on linguistic features alone then, scholars have not reached a consensus concerning the date of the book of Job. One might imagine that allusions to other biblical texts that are made within the book would result in a more reliable dating method. Unfortunately, the texts to which Job alludes often present their own dating problems.

The first intra-biblical connection between Job and other texts is found not in Job but in Ezekiel 14, where the prophet mentions Job along with Noah and Daniel/Danel as exemplars of righteousness.[58] Ezekiel's allusion to Job, of course, implies that his listeners must have been familiar with an ancient legend of the righteous Job, a story like that found in the prose frame of the book. Such a characterization of Job in Ezekiel, however, does not necessitate the existence of the *book* of Job as we have it.

Within the book of Job itself are allusions to other biblical texts. As has already been noted, the prose tale of Job makes a number of thematic and lexical connections between Job and the Israelite patriarchs in Genesis.[59] There seems to be a deliberate effort on the part of the author of the prose tale to depict Job as one of those patriarchs, though not specifically as an Israelite. Another strong connection to Genesis occurs in Job's first lament (chapter 3), where the poet has Job allude to the Priestly account of creation in Genesis 1.[60] The book of Job, then, has to be dated later than the Genesis

---

as a defined figure, "the Satan." Hurvitz acknowledges that there are many instances of classical Hebrew usage in the prose tale, but he considers these to be examples of "archaizing" language rather than "archaic" language (31). Hurvitz does not choose between an exilic or postexilic date for Job although he seems to lean towards the latter.

[58] Ezek 14:14, 20. Most commentators note this connection.

[59] Dhorme offers a helpful summary of the parallels between Job and the patriarchs (xx–xxi): Job's wealth of flocks and herds is comparable to that of the patriarchs (see Gen 26:13–14 and Job 1:3; Gen 30:29–30 and Job 1:10); the currency in Job is the קְשִׂיטָה (Job 42:11), just as in the time of Jacob (Gen 33:19; Josh 24:32); and the death of Job is described in the same terms as the deaths of Abraham and Isaac (Job 42:17; Gen 25:8, 35:29). Dhorme does not mention the following parallels: both Job (1:1) and Abraham (Gen 22:12) are described as men who fear God (יְרֵא אֱלֹהִים); Job is described as the "greatest of all the sons of the East" (1:3), while Jacob in his travels arrives in the land of the "sons of the East" (בְּנֵי קֶדֶם - Gen 29:1). Similarly, Davis has discussed the ways in which the histories of Jacob and Job are linked by the Joban poet, starting with the fact that both men are designated תָּם (Job 1:1; Gen 25:27) ["Job and Jacob," 100–14].

[60] For a list and discussion of the parallels between Gen 1 and Job 3, see Michael Fishbane, "Jeremiah IV 23–26 and Job III 3–13: A Recovered Use of the Creation Pattern," *VT* 21 (1971) 151–67. See also Habel, 104. See discussion below in chapter one.

Priestly creation account and the patriarchal narratives but still could be preexilic.

Psalm 8 appears to be the basis for Job's tirade in 7:17–21.[61] The Joban poet also alludes two times to the description of Wisdom in Proverbs 8.[62] Unfortunately, the connections with Psalm 8 and Proverbs 8 are of little help for dating Job, as the dates of the former texts are unknown.

The existence of fragments of a Job Targum at Qumran places the latest date for the book well before the first century B.C.E.[63] The connections with Genesis, Proverbs, and Psalms, however, do not help determine the earliest possible date for the book. Some scholars, therefore, turn to possible connections with other biblical texts, particularly prophetic texts that can be dated more easily. Most such connections are thematic or theological, making them less certain than direct echoes or quotations.[64]

One striking connection with a prophetic text does appear: the single use within the Joban dialogue of the tetragrammaton reveals a direct echo of Deutero-Isaiah: "The hand of YHWH has done this."[65] Of course, dependence here again can run either way, yet the use of the divine name in the poetic dialogue where it is otherwise nonexistent would suggest that the Joban poet is quoting a well-known phrase. The question remains whether the phrase is taken from Deutero-Isaiah or from a source common to both texts.

---

[61] While the psalmist asks, "What is humanity?" [מָה אֱנוֹשׁ] in the course of praising God, Job asks the same question in an ironic parody of the psalm. Most commentators note this connection between Psalm 8 and Job 7. See, for instance, Habel, 164-65; Rowley, 69; and Pope, 62.

[62] When Eliphaz asks Job at 15:7 whether he was "brought forth before the hills," he is echoing Proverbs 8:25. God's description of Behemoth (the "first of God's ways") in Job 40:19 is an allusion to Proverbs 8:22. While the dependency could run either way, I am inclined to think it more likely that the Joban poet has quoted a single passage from Proverbs rather than that the author of Proverbs 8 has combined two phrases from two different parts of the book of Job. See further discussion below in chapter two. Gordis notes the first parallel between Job 15 and Proverbs 8, but not the second one between Job 40 and Proverbs 8 (*The Book of God and Man*, 215).

[63] See Pope, xl.

[64] For lists of possible connections with other biblical texts, particularly prophetic texts, see Dhorme, clii–clxxii, and Terrien, "Job" (*IB*) 888–90. Both Dhorme and Terrien, for instance, connect Job 3 with Jer 20:14–18. While there are certainly strong similarities between the two passages, they can be attributed to the use of the same genre (the curse on the day of one's birth), not necessarily to direct dependence. While these scholars' arguments are suggestive, I do not find any of them conclusive.

[65] Job 12:9; Isa 41:20.

Gordis understands this verse as evidence that Job is dependent on the exilic prophet. He argues that the Joban poet expanded on Deutero-Isaiah's vision of national suffering (personified in the suffering servant) to speak of individual suffering.[66] In an important theological development, neither case of suffering is understood as a result of sin but as part of the "moral education" of the sufferer.[67] Gordis therefore dates Job later than Deutero-Isaiah, somewhere between 500 and 300 B.C.E.[68]

Given the many arguments over dating the book of Job, it would be foolhardy to offer here a seemingly conclusive answer to the problem. I am persuaded by linguistic studies like that of Hurvitz and theological ones like that of Gordis to place the composition of the book of Job no earlier than the Babylonian exile but it is altogether possible that the book is postexilic. The author of Job appears to be reacting to a profound tragedy. It is possible that the tragedy was one of national proportions as the poet appears to address an Israelite audience, an audience familiar with Israel's sacred texts. Gordis considers the book highly individualistic, reflecting a movement in postexilic Israelite religious thought.[69] I do not find his argument persuasive. Job is patterned after the Israelite patriarchs and is therefore able to represent the nation as a whole; as Davis argues, "Job's story, like that of the eponymous ancestors, is larger than life, large enough to encompass the experience of the whole people, as a people."[70]

Whether the tragedy to which the Joban poet responds is the Babylonian exile or some other event cannot be determined conclusively although I am sympathetic to dating the book to exilic or early postexilic times. Pope argues that Job could not have been written during the exile or immediately afterwards because the author exhibits no nationalist concerns; he even makes his hero a non-Israelite.[71] His argument fails to take into account the

---

[66] Gordis, *The Book of God and Man*, 144–45, 216.

[67] Ibid., 145.

[68] Ibid., 216. I am not persuaded by Gordis that there is a strong enough case to argue for direct dependence of Job on Deutero-Isaiah. The only direct connection between the two is the verse cited above, which could be a quotation of a source common to both poets. As Habel notes, Job as we see him in the final form of the book is no "suffering servant;" he does not go quietly as a lamb to the slaughter (Habel, 41–42). Nevertheless, the evidence suggests that there is some connection between Job and Deutero-Isaiah, which would make it unlikely that the former is preexilic.

[69] Gordis, *Book of God and Man*, 149.

[70] Davis, "Job and Jacob," 108.

[71] Pope, xxxv–xxxvi.

fact that wisdom writing in general tends to be more universalistic than other biblical writing; the book of Job is no exception.[72] Further, in comparison to other wisdom writing, the book of Job does indeed display some distinctly Israelite characteristics. The God revealed at the beginning and end of the book is YHWH, the God of Israel. It is this God who speaks to Job out of a storm, as he spoke to many of the prophets and to Israel at Sinai.[73] Job uses the quintessentially Israelite lament to make his case known.[74] Lastly, the poet uses the sacred scriptures of Israel throughout his work. While he does not write specifically of nationalist concerns as does Deutero-Isaiah, neither does the author of Job obscure all connections with his nation and history.

Why the Joban poet does not make these connections with Israelite sacred history more explicit is difficult to say. In order to explain the suffering he perceives in his people's current circumstances, the author of Job seems to be reaching back to a time before the establishment of the nation of Israel, before the Sinaitic covenant, to a time when God tested his faithful ones as he tests Job.[75] The important point to remember for this study is that he then bases his "answer" to the problem of undeserved suffering not on the *covenant* between God and Israel, but on the wisdom and care with which God establishes and provides for the whole *creation*. In other words, the vision of creation contained in the divine speeches offers an answer to undeserved suffering that the author of Job did not or could not otherwise find in the sacred history of Israel. The circumstances in which the Joban poet wrote must, therefore, have been grave enough to call into question the covenant relationship between God and Israel. Whether the circumstances were those of the Babylonian exile or some later event cannot be known. What is certain is that the author/redactor of Job has left to later generations a work that is both a profound meditation on undeserved suffering and a magnificent vision of creation, a work that continues to speak to people through the centuries.

---

[72] The book of Job is generally regarded as part of the wisdom corpus of Israel. See a discussion of the issues involved in such a designation in James Crenshaw, "Job, Book of," in *The Anchor Bible Dictionary* (ed. David Noel Freedman et al.; New York: Doubleday, 1992) 3:865–66. Gordis sees the choice of a non-Israelite hero as part of the "universalism of spirit which existed in Second Temple Judaism" (*Book of God and Man*, 213).

[73] See the list of such storm theophanies in Pope, 290: Exod 13:22; 19:16; Hab 3:5–6; Nah 1:3; Ezek 1:4; Zech 9:14.

[74] Claus Westermann sees the lament as the primary model for the structure of the book of Job [*The Structure of the Book of Job* (trans. Charles Muenchow; Philadelphia: Fortress, 1981)].

[75] See Gen 22 and the other connections with the Genesis patriarchs listed above.

We now turn to an examination of that work and of the vision of creation articulated therein.

CHAPTER 1

Creation Theology in Job 1–37

This study seeks to understand the theology of creation articulated in the divine speeches of Job 38–41 and to suggest what sort of "answer" the divine speeches offer to Job's dilemma. In order to understand the creation theology of the divine speeches, it is necessary first to survey the use of creation images in the rest of Job and so reveal the beliefs about creation to which the divine speeches are responding.[1]

This task is complicated by the fact that the book of Job is composed of different parts whose ideas are often in conflict with one another. The book is usually divided by scholars into two primary parts: 1) the prose frame (the prologue and epilogue); and 2) the poetic core of the book. The poetic core itself can be divided into separate parts: 2a) the poetic dialogue (chapters 3–27); 2b) the wisdom poem (chapter 28); 2c) Job's final defense (chapters 29–31); 2d) the speech of Elihu (chapters 32–37); and 2e) the divine speeches (chapters 38–41). Though linked thematically and lexically, each part of the book has its own distinct voice, its own genre, and its own concerns. Carol Newsom's recent book on Job delineates in great detail the distinct genres of the disparate parts of the book[2] and so serves as a useful dialogue partner

---

[1] By using words like "answer" and "respond," I do not wish to suggest a historical reconstruction of the composition of Job. The divine speeches may well have had an original setting quite distinct from the book in which they are now contained. Given, however, their present placement in the mouth of God and their climactic position in the narrative (after all the human speakers have had their say), the divine speeches must have been intended by the author/redactor of Job to offer an answer to Job's situation.

[2] Newsom, *Moral Imaginations*. Note that Westermann also addresses the issue of genre in Job in *The Structure of the Book of Job*. Westermann views the book as a more unified composition than does Newsom. Specifically, Westermann argues that the genre of the lament provides overall structure to the book. He calls the book "a dramatizing of the lament" (12).

in exploring the themes of creation and of humanity's place in creation in Job 1–37.

Prologue (Chapters 1–2)

The book of Job opens and closes with a prose narrative describing Job and his trials. The language and style of the narrative are simple and repetitive. Many commentators argue that this prose frame was derived from a well-known folktale that the author of the canonical book of Job used as the basis for his poetic reflections.[3] Job is a man from the land of Uz, a land whose location is unknown to modern readers and was perhaps unknown even to ancient readers.[4] Like the patriarchs in Genesis, Job is a man of great wealth and prestige, blessed with herds, flocks, servants, and children yet rooted in no specific time or nationality. One can easily imagine that the story was familiar to its original audience, yet if such a folktale did exist in ancient Israel, it is extant now only in the book of Job and in the brief mention of Job's name in Ezekiel 14.

The different parts of the book participate in other genres (the dialogue is a "disputation"), but the whole remains patterned by the lament, according to Westermann.

[3] See the discussion on the dating of Job in the introduction. For discussion of the folktale hypothesis, see Shalom Spiegel, "Noah, Daniel, and Job: Touching on Canaanite Relics in the Legends of the Jews," in *Louis Ginsberg Jubilee Volume* (New York: American Academy for Jewish Research, 1945) 305–56; and Albrecht Alt, "Zur Vorgeschichte des Buches Hiob" *ZAW* 55 (1937) 265–68. Duhm, among others, argues that the prologue and epilogue were part of an independent *Volksbuch* from which the author of Job took his story (Duhm, vii). Similarly, Ginsberg argues for the existence of a "book of Job the Patient" that contained not only the present prologue and epilogue but also chapters 27 and 28, as well as a now missing part that had the friends echo Job's wife and urge him to curse God (Ginsberg, 12–15). A later author then took the story and inverted the traditional roles of Job and his friends to make Job the "protestant" and his friends the "champions of orthodoxy" (ibid., 15). In contrast, Hurvitz, in "The Date of the Prose Tale of Job," argues that the prose tale is *not* an early tale to which the poetic section was added. To the contrary, the prose tale is an exilic or postexilic work, as is the rest of the book (Hurvitz, 33).

[4] The appendix to the LXX of Job places Uz on the borders of Edom and Arabia (42:17b). Apparently the LXX translators felt the need even in their time to specify the location of the mysterious land. There are two traditions about the location of the "land of Uz." One tradition, based on Lam 4:21 and Gen 36:28, identifies Uz with Edom. The other tradition, based on Gen 10:23 and 22:21, places Uz in the Hauran, connecting it with the Arameans. For an exhaustive discussion of the possible locations of Uz, see the commentaries of Dhorme, xxi–xxv, and Pope, 3–5.

Newsom argues that the term "folktale" is not useful as a description of the prose tale of Job because it is too general. Using the work of Hans-Peter Müller, Newsom designates the prologue and epilogue "a type of didactic tale . . . which also evokes certain aspects of the prophetic example story and of folktale style."[5] Giving the prose tale an intentionally sympathetic reading, Newsom describes its ethos as follows:

> [T]he most fundamental desire the prose tale elicits and offers to satisfy [is] the desire for a world that can be experienced as supremely coherent, a world of utterly unbreachable wholeness. As the story will go on to show, the experience of such a world is integrally linked to the practice of a certain kind of virtue.[6] (53)

Job exhibits such virtue in the prose tale. He is introduced in the first verse of the book as a man "blameless and upright" who "feared God and turned from evil." Job offers preemptive sacrifices just in case his children sinned and cursed God in their hearts. Like the Israelite patriarchs, Job acts as the family priest, offering sacrifices on behalf of those in his care (Job 1:5).[7] Even after his children die and his wealth is destroyed, he responds to his afflictions (at least initially) with praise.

The place of creation in such a "didactic tale" is extremely circumscribed. There is no place at first in the prose tale for anything that would threaten the coherence of its orderly world. Only domesticated animals (sheep, camels, oxen, and donkeys) find a place in the Joban world, and there is no initial

---

[5] Newsom, *Moral Imaginations*, 41. Hans-Peter Müller designates the prose frame a *weisheitliche Lehrerzählung* in his "Die weisheitliche Lehrerzählung im Alten Testament und seiner Umwelt," *Die Welt des Orients* 9 (1977) 77–98. Such "didactic tales," as Müller describes them, are "character-based stories in which the ethical quality of the main character is critical" (Newsom, *Moral Imaginations*, 40). Newsom accepts this genre classification but also considers the prose frame to participate in the genres of folktale and prophetic example story.

[6] Newsom initially reads the prose tale sympathetically rather than "against the grain" of its generic conventions. She later offers a reading that focuses on the "performative elements" of the story, an interpretation that takes into account many modern readers' horror at the injustices that afflict Job. In this reading (arguably anachronistic) Newsom speaks of the "violence" done to the character of Job even before the Satan afflicts him, a violence implicit in the "summing up" of Job by both the narrator and God, a violence in which the reader of Job is "complicit" (68–69). I find Newsom's first reading of the prose tale more insightful and more relevant to the interpretation of the book as a whole.

[7] See Gen 22:13; 31:54; 46:1.

hint of wild animals or beasts of prey.[8] As with the Israelite patriarchs (with whom Job is implicitly associated), domestic animals and children are a sign of God's blessing. As the Satan claims, a fence does seem to circumscribe Job, his family, and his possessions so that nothing harmful may enter. It is only after God allows the Satan to test Job that the wild forces of creation are allowed into Job's domain. Along with the Sabeans and the Chaldeans (human beings that are outside of Job's social world), the forces that destroy Job's world are a "fire of God" that falls "from the heavens" to consume Job's sheep and servants along with a "great wind coming from the wilderness" that causes the house in which Job's children are feasting to collapse on them (Job 1:16, 19). Aside from the domesticated animals enumerated as a sign of Job's wealth, these are the only elements of the natural world that are given a place in the prose tale, and it is noteworthy that these elements act as forces of destruction and chaos. The orderly world of the prose tale has no place for nondomesticated creation except as an instrument of testing and destruction. If God has indeed set a fence around Job and all that he has, then the natural world is outside that fence and is allowed to breach it only to test Job.

Creation then does not play a large role in the prologue at the beginning. The theme of procreation, however, appears early in the prologue and occupies a prominent place throughout it.[9] We are told early on that Job has seven sons and three daughters; as with his livestock, the enumeration of his children illustrates how much God has blessed him. The sons hold feasts by turn, each on "his day" [יוֹמוֹ]; and each one invites his brothers and sisters to join him (Job 1:4).

Janzen believes that these feasts are birthday celebrations as the word used to describe them is the same word [יוֹמוֹ] used to denote the day of Job's birth (in 3:1).[10] If so, then it is during a commemoration of the birth of Job's firstborn son–an event especially dear to the heart of a parent in the ancient Near East–that all of Job's children are suddenly killed. Notably, Job's response to this tragedy is itself couched in the language of birth: "Naked

---

[8] See Newsom, *Moral Imaginations*, 187–91, for a description of the moral world that Job occupies in chapter 29, where he reminisces about his former life. Newsom describes the boundaries of such a world, boundaries that exclude wilderness or wild animals. Such also is the world of the prologue.

[9] See Alter's discussion of the theme of procreation in the book of Job (99–103).

[10] Janzen, *Job*, 36.

I came from the womb of my mother, and naked I shall return there. YHWH
gave and YHWH has taken. May the name of YHWH be blessed" (Job 1:21).
    In the catastrophes that befall him, Job is stripped of all that belonged to
him: possessions, servants, and children. He essentially returns to the state of
a newborn. He is "naked" because he has lost all that "clothes" a person's life
with security and meaning–possessions and family.[11] His statement merges
the experiences of birth and death since returning "there" cannot literally
mean returning to the womb of his mother but rather to "the womb of Mother
Earth."[12] It is at once a poignant and strangely positive statement. By using
the metaphor of the mother's womb, Job places his experience of devastation
within the context of the ultimate life-affirming event, that of childbirth. As
Newsom states, "To unite this narrative structure [of leaving and returning]
with the emotionally charged image of the mother incorporates death (and
the losses likened to it) within a symbolics of security and protection."[13] To
"return to the womb" then is not necessarily a great evil. Though "naked" and
vulnerable as a newborn, Job still possesses a sense of security founded on
the one who gave him life and "clothed" him with possessions and children
in the first place: "YHWH gave and YHWH has taken. May the name of YHWH
be blessed." Acknowledgment of devastating loss can still lead–in Job's first
statement–to doxology. This will not hold true in his second response, which
remains reverent but includes no words of praise.[14]
    Images of procreation appear early in the book of Job and are used to
illustrate God's favor towards Job, as well as Job's piety in the face of
adversity. Procreation continues to be a recurring theme in the rest of the
book. A word here should be said about the second part of the prose frame, the
epilogue, which restores Job and the reader to the world of the prologue.[15] In
the epilogue we see Job again as a parent. He is restored to twice his former

---

[11] See Newsom, *Moral Imaginations*, 57–59 for an insightful discussion of Job's first
response, including the analogy of family and possessions to clothing.

[12] So Pope designates the referent of "there" (שָׁמָּה) in 1:21 (Pope, 16). He also cites
various ANE examples of "there" as euphemistic references to death. See Job 3:17.

[13] Newsom, *Moral Imaginations*, 58.

[14] The second response of Job in 2:10 can be read as ambivalent. His response is framed
in the form of a question rather than a statement. Also, the formula from 1:22 is changed
slightly: "In all this, Job did not sin" becomes "In all this, Job did not sin with his lips."
At the end of the prologue, Job indeed may be somewhat less "patient" than he was during
his first afflictions. Still, the Job of the poetic dialogue is vastly more angry and impatient
than the Job of the prologue.

[15] The epilogue will be discussed at more length in chapter three.

wealth, and he begets more children: as before, seven sons and three daughters (Job 42:13–15). As in the rest of the Bible, children here too are understood as a sign of blessing. In the prologue the mention of Job's children, coupled with his great wealth, support the claim that Job is "greater than all the people of the East" (1:3). Likewise, Job's restoration in the epilogue is evidenced in part by the fact that he has more children and that he lives to see his children and their descendants grow up: "Job lived after this one hundred and forty years and saw his children and his children's children, four generations. And Job died, old and full of days" (Job 42:16–17). The book ends as it began, on a note of fecundity, with the power of procreation alive and well. This is especially striking because in Job's first lament he will try to negate the power of procreation; in particular, he will try to negate the event of his own birth. Because of the many creation and procreation images in this first speech of Job, it warrants discussion apart from the rest of the poetic dialogue.

Job's First Lament (Chapter 3)

The poetic debate between Job and his friends begins with a speech by Job that employs images of creation and procreation and combines them into a powerful lament. The lament is an "un-creation account," calling on the forces of creation to undo Job's birth. Job curses both the day he was born and the night he was conceived: "That day—let it be darkness! Let God above not seek it. . . . /That night—deep darkness take it! Let it not rejoice among the days of the year" (Job 3:4, 6). In intention if not in effect, Job seeks here to reverse the act of creation itself. His language echoes the language of God in the Priestly creation account. Job's fiat, however, reverses God's first act of creation: "Let there be light!" [יְהִי אוֹר] (Gen 1:3). In contrast, Job curses the day of his birth with the words, "Let there be darkness!" [יְהִי חֹשֶׁךְ] (Job 3:4). As Fishbane and Habel have shown, Job's curses parallel the sequence of events described in the Priestly creation account. Job's curses begin, "Let there be darkness," and they end with an extended soliloquy on the "rest" he would find, not in Sabbath-keeping but in death (Job 3:13, 17, 26).[16] The intervening verses also follow the Genesis order of creation by using the

---

[16] The key verb in Job 3 for "rest" is נוח rather than שׁבת as in Gen 2:2–3. Nevertheless, it is striking that both creation accounts end with rest, one on the Sabbath, the other in death. Fishbane and Habel rightly surmise that the writer of Job was familiar with some form of the creation account of Gen 1. Fishbane's list of parallels between the two accounts is compelling.

same words and motifs found there: חשֶׁךְ (darkness) in Job 3:4a, 5a and Gen 1:2, 4; לילה (night), ימים (days), and שׁנה/שׁנים (year/years) in Job 3:6 and Gen 1:14; לויתן (Leviathan) in Job 3:8 and תנינם (the sea monsters) in Gen 1:21.[17] Job is in such agony that he wishes not just for his own demise but also for the destruction of the cosmos. In the process of cursing the day of his birth, Job articulates "an absolute and unrestrained death wish for himself and the entire creation." He seeks by his curses to unravel the "sevenfold knots and charms which bind the days of creation one to another."[18]

In the Priestly account, creation is largely a story of setting limits. God separates the light from the darkness; God separates the waters above the earth from the waters below the earth; God contains the waters so that dry land appears. Job in his lament seeks to abolish these limits. He calls on darkness to claim the day of his birth and likewise utter darkness to consume the night of his conception. Job abolishes the stars with which God marked the separation of day and night. Job further seeks to prohibit the night of his conception from being counted among the days of the year by banishing the light of sun and moon by which God separated both day from night and month from month (Job 3:6–9; Gen 1:14–16).

In the lament of chapter 3, Job the Patient suddenly has become Job the Impatient.[19] Instead of using his birth as a metaphor by which to impart meaning to his troubles, as he did in response to his first losses, Job now curses that event. He speaks first of darkness, gloom, and Leviathan, the cosmic and mythological forces that attack not only creation itself but also the dawn, the stars, and thereby the order of day and night. In his despair, Job seeks to return creation to primordial chaos, the same chaos that marks his current existence. Job then shifts his attention from the cosmic to the ordinary, rehearsing the scenarios that could have transpired at his birth:

[17] This list comes from Fishbane, "Jeremiah and Job," 154, and Habel, *The Book of Job*, 104.

[18] Fishbane, "Jeremiah and Job," 153–54. Fishbane claims that these verses in Job 3 "constitute their [the acts of creation] magical dissimilation and dissolution" and that the passage has a "magical *Sitz im Leben*" (155). He bases his claim not only on the parallels between Gen 1 and Job 3 listed above but also on a study of ANE magical incantations, which were often prefaced by cosmologies. I find his argument persuasive.

[19] See Ginsberg, "Job the Patient and Job the Impatient," for his theory of two distinct strata in the book of Job: a book of "Job the Patient" and a book of "Job the Impatient." See also footnote #3 above.

> Why did I not die from the womb?
>   Why did I not come from the womb and perish?
> Why were there knees to receive me
>   and breasts that I could suck?
> ....
> Or why was I not hidden like a stillbirth,
>   like infants that never see the light? (Job 3:11–12, 16)

Job wishes that he had been left to die at birth, like an infant abandoned to the elements. He turns the usually positive images of birth and motherhood into something negative; the knees that received him and the breasts that nourished him have become in Job's lament simply the means of prolonging his agony. He goes on to wish for something even more radical: that he had never seen light, that he had been a stillbirth or miscarriage expelled from the womb and hidden away in the earth. Job echoes this sentiment later in the dialogue, wishing to have been carried straight from the womb to the tomb (Job 10:19). Procreation (or at least *his* creation) is an affliction rather than a blessing in Job's estimation.

Job continues his lament by rhapsodizing about the grave and the refuge he would have found there from trouble. His life has become nothing but turmoil (רֹגֶז), as he says in the last word of his lament, and he wants only to find rest in death. Newsom argues that this last word of the chapter is key to understanding the whole lament: "*Rōgez* is to the order of lived experience as chaos is to cosmic order."[20] Job wants the day of his birth—and creation itself—to experience the same chaos he himself is experiencing. His lament inverts the usual conception of what constitutes good and evil so that death and darkness are desired over life and light.

In this last section of his lament, Job voices a bitter complaint: "Why is light given to one burdened with grief, and life to the bitter of spirit . . ./to a man whose way is hidden, whom God has fenced in [וַיָּסֶךְ אֱלוֹהַ בַּעֲדוֹ]?" (Job 3:20, 23). Newsom relates this complaint to the "inability of [a] person to plan and carry out purposive action. . . . What is lost is not simply the capacity to act but the meaningfulness of action."[21] Such is the condition of *rōgez* or chaos. The ordered world of the prose tale is nowhere to be found in Job's lament. It has reverted to chaos, and all purposive action Job might take in such a world is meaningless.

---

[20] Newsom, *Moral Imaginations*, 94.
[21] Ibid., 96.

Newsom is undoubtedly correct in her interpretation of Job's complaint. A person who is fenced in and whose way is hidden is one who is unable to act in any meaningful way. It is interesting to note, however, that Job's complaint also leads one back to another description of Job's place in the world: the description articulated in the prologue by the Satan. Thus, even as his lament negates the structured world of the prose tale, it echoes an account of that structure. The word Job uses in his complaint, "to fence in" [סוּךְ] (itself a relatively rare word), is similarly used in the prologue with the same preposition [בְעַד] but an alternate spelling.[22] The Satan asks God whether Job's piety is disinterested: "Is it for nothing that Job fears God? Have you not put a fence around him and around his house and around all that he owns [שַׂכְתָּ בַעֲדוֹ וּבְעַד בֵּיתוֹ וּבְעַד כָּל אֲשֶׁר לוֹ מִסָּבִיב]?" (Job 1:9–10).

These two occurrences of the verb שׂוּךְ/סוּךְ in the prologue and dialogue illustrate two differing views of creation and of the boundaries God places within that creation.[23] The Satan claims that God has put a protective fence around Job in order to guard Job and his household and all his possessions. Job is pious, in other words, only because creation is ordered in such a way that he is rewarded for his piety. Job in his lament, however, sees this boundary-making in another way. He too claims that God has placed a fence around him, but according to Job, this fence serves the purpose not of keeping the world out but of keeping Job in. The fence that once protected Job now has been drawn so tight that it threatens to suffocate him. Not only is he unable to engage in any purposive action (as Newsom argues), but now the fence that once restrained dangerous elements is used to deal with Job himself as one of those dangerous creatures. Job complains later in the dialogue:

Am I the Sea or the Dragon,
    that you place a guard over me?

[22] The word שׂוּךְ/סוּךְ is used only four times in the Bible to mean "to fence in," and three of these occurrences are in Job (1:10; 3:23; 38:8); the fourth occurrence is in Hos 2:8. It is used also with the meaning "to cover" in Exod 40:21, Ps 5:12, Ps 91:4, and Lam 3:43, 44. See also the related word סָכַךְ, "to weave together, to screen."

[23] The verb שׂוּךְ/סוּךְ is also used in the divine speech in 38:8, an occurrence that will be studied in the next chapter. Of course, discussing thematic links across the "boundary" between the prose and poetic sections of Job goes against the conclusions of Ginsberg ["Job the Patient and Job the Impatient"]. Although I am persuaded by his basic thesis of two strata in the book, I contend that in the combining of the two strata, the redactor/writer has introduced some thematic links between the prose and poetry sections of the book, including this theme of fencing in and the theme of procreation.

....
What is humanity, that you magnify them,
   that you pay attention to them,
that you visit them every morning,
   that you test them every moment?
Will you not turn your gaze away from me?
Will you not leave me alone until I swallow my spittle?
                                    (Job 7:12, 17–19)

As many commentators have noted, this passage parodies Psalm 8:4: "What is humanity that you are mindful of them, /the son of man that you take note of him?"[24] In Job's view of creation, God does not exalt human beings; instead, God places suffocating limits on them and then watches them like a hawk, waiting for them to make a mistake. God shows an unwarranted concern with very weak creatures, fencing them in as if they were cosmic forces of chaos.

This theme of fencing-in, of setting limits, is a link between the prologue and the poetic dialogue, and it has consequences for understanding the views of creation presented in each section. In the Satan's challenge we see an orderly world where those who obey God are granted protection against all that would harm them. The wild elements of creation have no place in such a world except as instruments of punishment or testing. It is a view of the world that one would expect in the prose tale: a world that is structured and coherent with built-in rewards for righteous behavior.

In Job's lament, the world is vastly different. It has become an oppressive place. God sets limits, but they are limits that suffocate human beings, fencing them in as if they were forces of chaos. In response, Job attempts to unleash the real forces of chaos to overturn the order built into creation: day and night, light and darkness, birth and death.[25] What order there was in Job's world has been overturned, and he likewise wants creation itself to be undone. The world Job once inhabited in the prose tale has descended into turmoil (rōgez) so that death has become the only escape.

---

[24] See Michael Fishbane, "The Book of Job and Inner-Biblical Discourse," in *The Voice from the Whirlwind: Interpreting the Book of Job* (ed. Leo G. Perdue and W. Clark Gilpin; Nashville: Abingdon Press, 1992) 86–98. Fishbane points out the stylistic and verbal features that connect Ps 8 and Job 7.

[25] Specifically, the forces Job seeks to unleash are those of darkness (חשׁך, צלמות), clouds (עננה), and "those able to rouse Leviathan"

The prose tale and Job's first speech paint different pictures of creation and of humanity's place in it. This is no surprise, given the two different genres employed. The didactic tale, of which the prose tale is an example, generally seeks to elicit righteous behavior by depicting the essential connection between such behavior and the blessing of God. The world of the prose tale is presented as an ordered, coherent place in which the person who pleases God can expect to be rewarded with material blessings. The role assigned to Job and to humanity in such a world is to serve as stewards of order and to remain pious even in the face of calamity ["YHWH gave and YHWH has taken. May the name of YHWH be blessed"]. The role of creation in this world is severely circumscribed.

The lament (or "the curse on the day of [one's] birth," as Newsom designates it) has a different purpose.[26] In Jer 20:14-18, the only other extant example of this genre, the curse on the day of one's birth is, in Zuckerman's words, "a lament-of-final-resort," whose function is "to portray a sufferer's distress in the most nihilistic terms possible for the purpose of attracting God's attention and thus leading to the rescue of the sufferer from affliction."[27] Humanity's place in this world of the lament is as the object of God's misplaced scrutiny, the recipient not of God's compassionate attention but of God's unwanted inspection.

Job's first lament opens an extended dialogue between him and his three companions, and it is interesting to note that the two views of the world articulated in the prose tale and the lament are both represented in that dialogue. The friends generally reiterate the Satan's description of God's ordering of creation while Job renounces it and expands on his own image of a God who oppresses the righteous.

---

[26] Newsom, *Moral Imaginations*, 93.

[27] Bruce Zuckerman, *Job the Silent: A Study in Historical Counterpoint* (New York: Oxford University Press, 1991) 125–26. While this description rings true for Jeremiah's lament, it is not a similarly accurate description of Job's lament (as Zuckerman readily acknowledges). Job does depict the world in nihilistic terms. He does so, however, not in hopes of rescue but because he actually does wish for death so that "he might find the one and only retreat where God would at last leave him alone with his integrity intact" (126).

Poetic Dialogue (Chapters 4–27)

The dialogue among Job and his friends consists of three cycles of speeches, structured in such a way that Job is given both the first and the last word. In each of the first two cycles, Job has a discussion first with Eliphaz, then with Bildad, and finally with Zophar. The dialogue breaks down in the third cycle of speeches, however, so that Bildad's speech is very short, Zophar speaks not at all, and Job seems to take their words into his own extended speech. Whether through textual corruption or authorial intent, the dialogue ends in confusion with no resolution to the issues debated.

According to Newsom, the poetic dialogue in Job does not reach resolution because it is an ancient Near Eastern "wisdom dialogue." Such compositions "seek neither to demonstrate the triumph of one voice over the other nor to argue their way to a resolution." The truths they set forth are "dialogic" rather than "monologic" in that they juxtapose two or more points of view that both require acknowledgment.[28] This genre, examples of which are extant in a few ANE texts, has four generic markers: 1) the form is that of a dialogue in which a single question is debated by two or more speakers with conflicting perspectives; 2) the dialogue explores the topic of inexplicable suffering or more generally, "the existence of a moral order in the universe"; 3) it uses an "exploratory stance" that is "interrogative" rather than "affirmative"; and 4) the dialogue exhibits a sophisticated style that suggests it was written by and for the intellectual elite of a society.[29]

These characteristics of the wisdom dialogue in Job stand in sharp contrast to the prose tale that opens the book, which offers a simple language and style, a more monologic stance, and the seemingly firm trust and piety of

[28] Newsom, *Moral Imaginations*, 85.

[29] Ibid., 79. Newsom builds on the work of Hans-Peter Müller and Karel van der Toorn in her discussion of the genre of the wisdom dialogue. Van der Toorn lists three primary texts that he considers examples of the genre, which he calls a "literary dialogue": the poetic section of Job (including the divine speeches), the *Babylonian Theodicy*, and the Egyptian text known as the *Dialogue of a Man with His Ba* ("The Ancient Near Eastern Literary Dialogue as a Vehicle of Critical Reflection," in *Dispute Poems and Dialogues in the Ancient and Medieval Near East: Forms and Types of Literary Debates in Semitic and Related Literatures* [ed. G. J. Reinink and H. L. J. Vanstiphout; Louvain: Uitgeverij Peeters, 1991] 59–75). Newsom limits the appellation of "wisdom dialogue" to Job 3–27 and adds two other texts to the corpus: the *Mesopotamian Dialogue of Pessimism* and the *Egyptian Complaints of Kha-Kheper-Re-Seneb*. She sees the strongest parallels between Job 3–27 and the *Babylonian Theodicy*, composed sometime between 1400 and 800 B.C.E.

its protagonist. The Job of the prose frame is acted upon by others (God and the Satan) and accepts his fate without question, while the Job of the poetic dialogue rages against the injustice he perceives and the (absent) God whom he blames for that injustice. The Job of the poetic dialogue develops his arguments over the course of the book. He moves steadily toward seeking justice rather than seeking the grave. He also moves from speaking only *about* God to speaking directly *to* God, thereby including the Almighty in the dialogue and setting up God's direct address to him in the divine speeches. Job's friends, though they advocate the practice of prayer, never address God directly.[30] Perhaps this situation lies behind God's chastisement of the friends in the epilogue, where God says that they did not "speak to me [אלי] rightly, as did my servant Job" (Job 42:7).[31] Neither Job's direct address to God, nor God's answer to the suffering Job, is paralleled in the other ANE examples of the wisdom dialogue. If the dialogue in Job does indeed participate in this genre, it has incorporated some significant changes.

Having spoken in general about the poetic dialogue, we turn now to exploring the creation images contained therein. While the opening lament of Job (with its "un-creation" of the natural world) contains the most radical use of creation images in the dialogue, the creatures and phenomena of creation continue to appear throughout the rest of chapters 4–27, although they are used in more conventional ways. Most commonly, the natural world is used to provide metaphors for the attitudes and actions of the characters in the drama: Job likens his friends to a wadi that dries up in the summer's heat; Bildad counters by comparing the wicked (and, by implication, Job) to papyrus that withers for lack of water; Eliphaz promises Job that once he repents, his offspring will then be as many as the grass of the earth; and so on.[32]

In Eliphaz's first speech, the natural world not only provides metaphors but also becomes a concrete means of blessing. Eliphaz promises Job that once he is reconciled with God, he will be at peace with the whole creation:

> At violence and hunger you will laugh;
>   and you will not fear the wild animals of the earth.

---

[30] Job starts to speak in the second person directly to God in 7:7. He continues to do so periodically in the rest of the dialogue.

[31] The more common translation is "They did not speak *about* me rightly, as did my servant Job." See further discussion of this verse below in chapter three.

[32] Job 6:15–17; 8:11–13; 5:25. For other metaphorical usages, see 4:8–11; 9:26; 14:11–12, 18–19; 15:32–33; 18:3, 16; 19:10; 24:5; 25:5; 29:19–23; 30:3–8.

For your covenant will be with the stones of the field,
and the wild beasts of the field will be at peace with you.

(Job 5:22–23)

The promise is not unlike those found in prophetic writings: visions of a
world where wild animals and humans live in peaceful coexistence.[33] In such
visions creation itself becomes one of the means by which the chosen people
are blessed. The harmony established between animals and humans at the
beginning of creation is re-established, and the desert blooms for the sake of
God's people.[34] Such harmony between humans and animals is, in the view
of Eliphaz, a reward for the righteous. A righteous Job will have no cause to
fear the wild animals. One might even say that in this speech of Eliphaz, the
protective fence of the Satan's worldview has been rebuilt around Job. If he
repents, Job will again be shielded from all that would harm him, including
the wild forces of the natural world.

If the natural world is a means of blessing, it can also be a means of
punishment, according to Job's friends. Zophar declares that the wicked will
be killed by poisonous snakes, that "the heavens will uncover their guilt, and
the earth will rise up against them" (Job 20:16, 27). In using such images,
Zophar echoes many other biblical texts, from the account of the poisonous
snakes that kill the complaining Israelites in the wilderness to the prophetic
warnings of barren land and wild animals that destroy the ungodly.[35] The

[33] See, for instance, Isa 11:6–9 and 65:25 as well as Hos 2:20, where covenant language
is explicit. See also Isa 35:1–10 and Ezek 34:25–28 for related promises that wild animals
will be banished from the land so that the people might live in peace. In both situations,
humans no longer need to live in fear of wild animals.

[34] Whether such promises reference a return to Eden is a matter of debate amongst scholars.
On the one hand, Volkmar Herntrich describes the imagery of Isa 11:6–9 as a return to paradise
[*Der Prophet Jesaja, Kapitel 1–12* (Göttingen: Vandenhoeck & Ruprecht, 1950) 213–15]].
Brevard Childs, on the other hand, argues, "The prophetic picture is not a return to an ideal
past, but the restoration of creation by a new act of God through the vehicle of a righteous
ruler" [*Isaiah: A Commentary* (The Old Testament Library; Louisville, Ky.: Westminster John
Knox, 2001) 104]. The reinterpretation of Isa 11:6–9 in 65:25, however, makes reference to
Gen 3 ("But the serpent, dust shall be his food!"), as Childs acknowledges (538). There is
then a good basis for describing such visions of a peaceable kingdom as a return to Eden.
As many scholars have noted, eschatological visions often allude to myths of origin.

[35] Num 21:4–9; Isa 15:6–9; 19:5–10; 34:9–17; etc. The description of Edom's desolation
in Isa 34 is in deliberate contrast to the promise of the wilderness blooming for the returning
exiles in chapter 35. See also Lev 26, where wild animals are instruments of both blessing
and curse. If the Israelites obey God, he will remove wild beasts from the land (v. 6). In

whole creation becomes in these texts an instrument of divine blessing or curse, a means by which God deals with humanity.

It is the relationship of God with humanity that is the primary concern of Job's three friends. They are particularly interested in God's punishment of the wicked. The friends do not speak much about God's work in the natural world, except as such work relates to humanity.[36] One recurring theme in the speeches of the friends, for instance, is the idea that the most glorious things in creation—the moon, the stars, and the heavens themselves—are unclean and untrustworthy in God's sight. Therefore, they ask Job, "Can a man be righteous before God [הַאֱנוֹשׁ מֵאֱלוֹהַ יִצְדָּק]?" (Job 4:17).[37] This statement about humanity's innate depravity comes out of a particular understanding of the structure of creation: just as the heavens and the beings that inhabit them (angels, moon, stars) are superior to human beings, so God is infinitely greater than both. One sees the same cosmic hierarchy in Psalm 8 although in the psalm humanity is only a "little lower" than the celestial beings (or God) and is given dominion over all creation (Ps 8:5–8). By contrast, the distance between humanity and God in the speeches of the three friends is incalculable. The heavens and the celestial beings are unclean in God's sight; how much more so are human beings who are perishable, who "drink iniquity like water" and who are "maggots" and "worms."[38] Human beings,

---

contrast, if they spurn God, wild animals will bereave them of their children and eat their livestock (v. 22).

[36] See, for instance, 4:10–11, where Eliphaz speaks of lions as a metaphor for the wicked and violent; and 11:7–10, where Zophar describes the "deep things" of God as higher than heaven and deeper than Sheol, such that no human can find them. Eliphaz does mention God's sending of rain on the earth (5:10), and Bildad discusses God's power briefly in 25:1–3: "On whom does his light not rise?" Nonetheless, there are no extended descriptions by the three friends of God's work in creation, unless one puts Job's speech of 26:5–14 into the mouth of Bildad, as many scholars do. See discussion of Job 26 below.

[37] See 4:12–21 for Eliphaz's full argument. See also 15:14–16 and 25:4–6 for similar arguments. Note that Ginsberg considers the passages in chapters 4 and 15 to be *Job's* words originally. According to Ginsberg, Job "the Impatient" claims in part that God has revealed the secret knowledge to him that no man can be righteous. Ginsberg's case is stronger for 15:14–16, as 15:13 could indicate a quotation. For the passage in chapter 4, however, Ginsberg has to postulate a "mechanical accident" and transpose the verses to the end of Job's speech in chapter 3 (Ginsberg, 18–23). He does not even address the similar passage in 25:4–6. For these reasons, while his argument is learned, I do not find it persuasive.

[38] Job 4:19–21; 15:16; 25:6. The first passage faults human beings because they live in "houses of clay," by which Eliphaz means humans are made of flesh. The other two passages likewise equate physical corruptibility with moral corruptibility.

in the speeches of the friends, deserve to be the objects not only of God's judgment but also of God's loathing. Although they draw on other biblical and ANE traditions, Eliphaz and Bildad end up with a view of creation that has no equivalent in other biblical texts.[39] The divine speeches, to be sure, emphasize the radical dissimilarity of God and humanity, but they do not denigrate creation in the process. To the contrary, they portray creation as a beautiful and awe-inspiring work of God.

Perhaps unsurprisingly, the three friends use the theme of procreation in much the same way as they use the theme of creation: to speak of God's favor or disfavor. Eliphaz says of the fool that "[h]is children are far from safety. They are crushed in the gate and there is no one to save." At the same time, he promises Job, "You will know that many will be your descendants, and your offspring will be like the grass of the earth." If the latter promise seems callous in light of the death of all Job's children, then Bildad's statement in the same cycle of speeches is simply cruel: "If your children sinned against him, then he delivered them into the hand of their iniquity."[40] Job himself articulates a similar belief in procreation as a blessing when he longs for the days "when the Almighty was with me, when my young ones were around me" (Job 29:5). In all these cases, as in the rest of the Bible and ANE literature, children are a sign of God's blessing and their loss a sign of God's disfavor.[41]

Though Job laments his own birth, he subscribes to this traditional view of procreation. He claims, however, that God has turned the system upside down, that God's favor rests upon the wrong sort of people. Rejecting Zophar's statement that the wicked will be punished, Job says, "Their descendants are established before them and their offspring in their sight." Not only that, but "his bull breeds without fail. His cow calves and does not miscarry. They send out their children like a flock, and their offspring skip about" (Job 21:8, 10-11).[42] The blessing of fecundity is granted both to the wicked man and

---

[39] See Newsom, *Moral Imaginations*, 139–43, for a learned exploration of the cultural sources of this topos. Newsom cites ANE texts about the "righteous sufferer" (*The Sumerian Man and His God, The Babylonian Theodicy, Ludlul*), as well as biblical Psalms and priestly holiness texts. She concludes that the Joban passages in question are a "sapiential development of an ancient Near Eastern religious topos, which makes novel use of concepts and imagery derived from both psalmic and purity discourses" (142–43).

[40] Job 5:4, 25; 8:4; see also 18:19; 20:10.

[41] For a succinct statement of this belief, see Ps 127:3–5.

[42] Job does appear to contradict this view later in 27:14, where he says that the children of the wicked will be destroyed. See discussion of Job 27 below.

to his livestock. It is a cruel contrast to Job's own situation, bereft of both children and wealth.

For Job, in contrast to his friends, creation itself provides not so much a means of blessing and punishment or even a lesson in human iniquity, as it does a testimony to God's overwhelming power. Job acknowledges at some length God's power over the cosmos and everything in it.[43] Such acknowledgment, however, does not lead Job to praise God. Instead, Job invokes God's power revealed in creation as the reason he cannot contend with God. In chapter 9 he echoes Eliphaz's earlier speech about the radical distinction between humanity and God: "Truly, I know that this is true: How can a man be justified with God [ומה יצדק אנוש עם אל]?" (Job 9:2). Scholars have noted that while Eliphaz uses the word יצדק in 4:17 in a religious sense ("be righteous"), Job's reiteration of his statement in 9:2 changes its context so that יצדק is used in a legal sense ("be acquitted").[44] Job says in the next verse, "If [a man] wanted to bring a lawsuit against him [לריב עמו], he would not answer him one in a thousand." The radical distinction between God and humanity as revealed in creation is not (for Job) proof of humanity's innate depravity; instead, it is the basis for his despair over getting a fair trial. God has all power and authority; how can a mere man hope to contend with the Almighty?

Job goes on in the same speech to illustrate God's immeasurable power over creation, invoking images of the divine warrior:

> He speaks to the sun and it does not rise,
>   he who seals up the stars;
> who alone stretched out the heavens,
>   who trod on the back of the Sea;
> the maker of the Bear and Orion,
>   the Pleiades and the chambers of the south. (Job 9:7–9)

Job describes a divine being who creates and destroys with equal ease. God "overturns mountains" and "shakes the earth from its place," but God also establishes the constellations and defeats the Sea. God has the power both to create and to negate creation, the latter something to which Job himself aspires

---

[43] Job 9:5–10; 12:7–10, 13–15; 26:5–14. Chapter 28 (also put in the mouth of Job) contains similar references to the natural world although there, the issue is not power but knowledge: God, rather than any entity in creation, knows where wisdom is found. See the discussion of Job 28 below.

[44] See Habel, *The Book of Job*, 189, and Newsom, *Moral Imaginations*, 143.

in his first speech. Yet Job is realistic enough to know his own limitations, and he laments those limitations: "For [God] is not a man, like me, so that I could answer him, so that we might come together to judgment" (Job 9:32). Job cannot undo creation; neither can he force God to enter into a law court with him. Innocent though he knows himself to be, Job cannot get a fair hearing in the face of such overwhelming force.

Though he does not echo the friends' statements about the innate corruptibility of human beings, Job does give credence to their belief that God has a certain contempt for humanity or at least for Job himself. At times in Job's speeches, God is depicted not just as the divine warrior but as the divine enemy afflicting Job unfairly: "If I washed myself with snow and cleansed my hands with lye, then you would plunge me into the pit, and my own clothes would abhor me. . . . /His anger tears and rages against me; he gnashes his teeth at me; my enemy sharpens his eyes against me" (Job 9:30–31; 16:9).[45] Job argues that the root of such contempt lies not in his own sinfulness but in God's despotic and arbitrary nature.

This depiction of God as a cruel and capricious deity bursts out periodically in Job's speeches. At other times, Job appeals to God instead as a just deity who has concern for his creation. In this, Job seeks the restoration of the world he has known and the restoration of his former relationship with God.[46] In the same speech in which he accuses God of plunging him into filth, Job makes a direct appeal to God, reiterating that he is part of God's handiwork, even at one point using a phrase found in the Yahwistic creation account: "Remember that you made me like clay, and to dust you will return me [ואל עפר תשיבני]" (Job 10:9).[47] He goes on to describe God's craftsmanship in forming his body:

> Did you not pour me out like milk,
>   and curdle me like cheese?
> With skin and flesh you clothed me,
>   and with bones and sinews you knit me together.
>   (Job 10:10–11)[48]

---

[45] See Lam 3:1–20 for similar images of God as the divine enemy.

[46] See S. Wagner, "'Schopfung' im Buche Hiob," *Die Zeichen der Zeit* 34 (1980) 96

[47] The second stich echoes Gen 3:19: "For you are dust [עפר] and to dust you will return [ואל עפר תשוב]."

[48] See Job 10:3, 8 and 14:15 for references to God's creation of Job.

This account of his creation does not move Job to praise God (as does the writer of Psalm 139, in a similar passage) but rather to echo his first speech: "Why did you bring me forth from the womb? Oh that I had died, that no eye had seen me, that I were as if I had not been, borne from the womb to the grave" (Job 10:18–19).[49] Nevertheless, Job acknowledges that God, the maker of the heavens and the earth, is also the creator of Job himself, with a relationship to him as intimate as that of a weaver or potter to his handiwork. Even in his despair then, Job appeals to God's sense of responsibility for his creation.

There is a significant problem with such an appeal, however: to the extent that an artist rejects his or her handiwork as flawed, it may become as much an object of loathing as one of care. Newsom speaks of this ambiguous relationship between an artist and his or her work: "The psychology of creation is inherently ambivalent. That which I make is an object over against me but also in some sense a part of me. I may take pride in it, love it, be pleased with it. But insofar as it is, or as I perceive it to be, defective or inadequate, I may despise it, loathe it."[50] Newsom argues that this ambiguous view of the creator/creation relationship is at the heart of the divine loathing for humanity that appears in the speeches of Job, Eliphaz, and Bildad. Humans share certain characteristics with God (because they are created in God's image) and therefore receive special attention from God that is not accorded to other, non-human creatures. Such attention may be a very positive thing; however, insofar as flawed humanity is not like God, it may become the object of divine loathing.

Job protests vehemently against such divine scrutiny of humanity: "If I sin, you watch me, and you do not acquit me of my iniquity. . . . /Are not my days few? Cease! Let me be, that I might cheer up a little" (Job 10:14, 20). It is the same complaint Job first voiced in chapter 3 and that he repeats a number of times thereafter.[51] In the first example of direct address to God in the dialogue, Job complains to his Creator:

---

[49] See Ps 139:13 for the image of God "knitting/weaving" [סכך] an infant in the womb.

[50] Newsom, *Moral Imaginations*, 146. Regardless of whether one accepts Newsom's characterization as a general psychological phenomenon, it offers a plausible explanation of the divine loathing described in Job. The divine speeches, of course, do not validate this characterization of the divine/human relationship. Though humanity plays little part in God's vision of creation, it is certainly not depicted as an object of loathing.

[51] See Job 3:23; 7:12–21; 9:13–19; 10:14–22; 13:27; 14:1–6; 19:6–11; 30:18–23.

Remember that my life is mere breath
....
While your eyes are upon me, I shall cease to be
....
Am I the Sea or the Dragon, that you place a guard over me?
....
What is humanity, that you magnify them,
    that you pay attention to them,
that you visit them every morning,
    that you test them every moment?
Will you not turn your gaze away from me?
    Will you not leave me alone until I swallow my spittle?
              (Job 7:7a, 8b, 12, 17–19)

God is inordinately concerned with human beings, according to Job—or at least inordinately concerned with Job himself. In this passage and again in 9:13–14, Job contrasts himself with chaos monsters and wonders why God is disturbed by such a feeble creature as he.[52] Human mortality indeed is one of the primary grounds for Job's argument that God should leave him alone, that humanity is an inappropriate object of God's scrutiny. For his friends, in contrast, the physical corruptibility of human beings is evidence of their moral corruptibility and thereby one of the chief justifications for God's loathing of humanity.[53] Despite these differences, all participants in the dialogue believe that humanity is one of the principal objects of God's attention and the most important of God's creatures.

Job continues to focus on humanity even in those passages where he speaks of the rest of the natural world. In a speech that seems to anticipate the divine speeches, Job tells his friends:

But ask the beasts and they will teach you,
    the birds of the heavens and they will tell you.
Or speak to the earth and it will teach you,
    and the fish of the sea will tell you.
Who among these does not know
    that the hand of YHWH has done this?
In his hand is the life of every living creature
    and the breath of all human flesh. (Job 12:7–10)

---

[52] There are less explicit comparisons of Job with Behemoth and Leviathan in 6:12 and 15:7.

[53] See Job 4:17–21 and 14:1–3.

It is noteworthy that the name YHWH is used here, the only place in the dialogue in which the covenant name of God appears.[54] In contrast, the tetragrammaton appears numerous times in the prologue and epilogue and a few times in the divine speeches. This use of the divine name within the dialogue appears in a phrase (כי יד יהוה עשתה זאת) that also appears in Isaiah 41:20, in both cases referring to people *knowing* (ידע) this truth.[55] The prophet speaks of YHWH's saving acts on behalf of Israel. Job, as to be expected, instead uses the prophet's words to accuse God, not to praise God.

In this passage Job again acknowledges God's overwhelming power, directing attention to the "classroom" of creation for his evidence. The animals, the birds, the earth, and the fish all will be the teachers of humanity, but the lesson will not be what Job's friends expect. The things that "the hand of YHWH has done" are these: "The tents of robbers are at peace, and the dwelling places of those who provoke God" (Job 12:6).[56] God does not punish such people, Job contends; instead, God humiliates those who establish and lead human society: kings, judges, priests, and elders. For Job, even God's provision of rain on the earth is evidence of God's capricious nature: "When he holds back the waters, they dry up; when he sends them out, they overturn the earth" (Job 12:15).[57] There is little recognition in Job's speeches of a providential Creator who cares for his creation, a motif that runs through the divine speeches. Instead, God's work in the natural world is portrayed as a mirror image of God's dealings with humanity: God creates and destroys at will with no clear justification for his actions.

Job continues to speak of God's acts in creation at the end of the dialogue. As the dialogue begins to break down, Bildad (in an abbreviated speech) echoes Eliphaz in asking how a mortal can be righteous before God. Job answers with images that would not be out of place in the divine speeches:

[54] The tetragrammaton is used also in some Hebrew manuscripts at 28:28 (the end of the wisdom poem) although the Leningrad Codex (thus BHS) has instead אדני.

[55] See Robert Gordis, *The Book of God and Man*, 144–45 and 216, for a discussion of the thematic and lexical links between Job and Deutero-Isaiah. Gordis uses Job 12:9 as evidence for his argument that Job is dependent on Deutero-Isaiah. The present argument does not require such dependency; the author of Job may be quoting Deutero-Isaiah, or both authors may simply be using a common liturgical phrase. See discussion of the date of Job above in the introduction.

[56] The word בטחות is parallel to אהלים. For בטחות as "dwelling places," see Gordis, *The Book of Job*, 137.

[57] The dealings of God with human authorities are discussed in 12:17–21.

He binds the waters in his clouds

....

He has drawn a circle on the face of the waters,
   as the boundary between light and darkness

....

By his power he stilled the Sea,
   and by his understanding he smote Rahab.   (Job 26:8, 10, 12)

Many scholars have seen the attribution of this passage to Job as a corruption of the text, and they choose instead to credit these words to Bildad, whose speech in the previous chapter is unusually short.[58] Likewise, it is argued that Job's "fate of the wicked" speeches in 24:18–25 and 27:7–23 should be attributed to Zophar, who is given no voice at all in the third round of speeches. Indeed, in these last chapters of the dialogue, Job unexpectedly espouses the traditionally pious belief that the wicked will be punished, a belief that he has repeatedly refuted.

While the theory of textual corruption explains these incongruities in Job's speech, there are problems with such an approach. No textual evidence supports the view that Job's speeches were originally part of the speeches of Bildad and Zophar. As Newsom states, the attempt to attribute the apparent difficulties to textual corruption "is simply a desperate gesture in response to an interpretive embarrassment."[59] Additionally, the proposed rearrangement of the dialogue is not a minor matter; it involves transposing significant portions of the text.[60] Even were one willing to rearrange the text in such a radical manner, one is still left with textual problems: Job's reply to Bildad now itself is unusually short, and he offers no reply at all to the repositioned speech of Zophar.[61] It would be odd that, at the very end of the dialogue, Job is the one silenced and Zophar is given the last word.

---

[58] Pope, xx, 180–81; Dhorme, xlvii–li, 368–76. These scholars come to this conclusion not only because Bildad's speech in the previous chapter is short, but also because it begins on the same theme as this passage (26:5–14): God's power displayed in creation.

[59] Newsom, *Moral Imaginations*, 161.

[60] See, for instance, Pope's rearrangement, where Job's reply to Eliphaz consists of verses from chapter 24 in the following order: 24:1–3, 9, 21, 4–8, 10–14b, 15, 14c, 16–17. Pope's rearrangement of the rest of the text is just as convoluted: Job's reply to Bildad consists of 27:1; 26:1–4; 27:2–7; and Zophar's final speech (missing in the final form of the book) consists of 27:8–23; 24:18–20, 22–25 (Pope, 174–75, 187–89).

[61] Job's original reply to Bildad, according to Pope, is only nine verses long, a little more than half the length of Bildad's speech. All Job's other speeches in the dialogue are at least as long, if not longer, than those of his friends. As for an answer to Zophar, neither

Less destructive to the received text, and therefore more persuasive, are the theories of scholars like Janzen. Rejecting the theory of textual corruption, Janzen holds open the possibility that the problematic passages are indeed part of Job's speech, but that they are to be understood as lengthy quotations of what Job knows Bildad and Zophar will say. Job, tired of arguing, finishes his friends' arguments for them, effectively silencing them.[62] I find this theory persuasive because it negates the need for a significant re-shuffling of the text and offers a plausible explanation for the form of the text as we now have it.

Newsom takes a similar approach, arguing that Job's reiteration of his friends' ideas forces "those who listen to him into a painful cognitive dissonance, a loss of mastery, that is an echo, however faint, of what Job has experienced of the world."[63] The same cognitive dissonance is apparent in the oath Job swears by "the life of God who has taken away my right, and Shaddai, who has made my spirit bitter" (Job 27:2). Usually one swears by something or someone that is trustworthy and true, but Job swears by the very deity who oppresses him. By the dialogue's end, Job is in a state of cognitive and emotional turmoil, and his speech reflects that turmoil.

Interpretations like those of Janzen and Newsom are persuasive for the problem of the "fate of the wicked" speeches Job gives in chapters 24 and 27. These speeches contradict earlier things Job said and do indeed seem to echo the sentiments of his friends.[64] Such resolutions of interpretive problems are unnecessary, however, in the case of Job's speech in chapter 26, where he describes God's action in creation. This view is not incongruous with

---

the wisdom poem of chapter 28 nor Job's final defense in chapters 29–31 can easily be understood as such a reply.

[62] Janzen, *Job*, 172–74. He holds that the same is true for 27:13–23, which sounds much like Zophar's last speech in chapter 20: the wicked will receive punishment. See also Gordis, *The Book of God and Man*, chapter 13, "The Use of Quotations in Job," 169–89.

[63] Newsom, *Moral Imaginations*, 167.

[64] See Job 20–21, where Zophar argues that the wicked will be punished and Job there rejects that argument. Other ANE "wisdom dialogues" do not end in such confusion. It is worthwhile to note, however, how the *Babylonian Theodicy* ends: the friend of the sufferer espouses ideas that the sufferer himself spoke earlier in the dialogue. Their dialogue, in other words, leads to some acknowledgment of one side by the other. Though ironic or deliberately disconcerting in tone, Job's "fate of the wicked" speech at the end of the dialogue could participate in the same generic convention. I am reading the translation of the *Babylonian Theodicy* found in Benjamin R. Foster's *Before the Muses: An Anthology of Akkadian Literature* (Bethesda, Md.: CDL Press, 1993) 806–14.

Job's previous speech in chapter 9, in which he acknowledges God's power over creation and over the forces of chaos like Sea and Rahab (invoking the divine warrior myth).[65] In both instances, Job acknowledges God's power without compromising his argument that God is unjust. Indeed, Job cannot hope to win his case against God precisely because God is the all-powerful creator (and not merely a human being). Those who would attribute 26:5–14 to Bildad do not take into account that it is Job—not Bildad or any of his other friends—who earlier in the dialogue described at length God's power as it is revealed in creation. It is therefore not inconsistent with his arguments that he would continue to do so at the end of the dialogue.

In these ways, the wisdom dialogue of Job makes use of both creation and procreation images. God's power over creation, humanity's place in that creation, and the blessing or curse of procreation are themes that run like a thread throughout the speeches of Job and his three companions. Though they use similar language and images in many instances, the four participants in the debate are unable to come to any resolution, and the dialogue ends in confusion, with silence on one side and cognitive dissonance on the other. The wisdom poem that immediately follows the dialogue seems to comment on this lack of resolution and on the futility of human attempts to find answers to perplexing questions like that of undeserved suffering.

The Wisdom Poem (Chapter 28)

The wisdom poem, while formally a part of the poetic dialogue, is of a different genre altogether; it is an example of the "speculative wisdom poem," whose subject matter is "the accessibility or inaccessibility of transcendent wisdom to human beings."[66] The poem is considered by many scholars to be a redactor's addition to the book of Job.[67] Other scholars argue that because of its verbal and thematic affinities with the rest of Job, the poem must have

---

[65] See Job 9:8, 13, and 26:12. Note that both passages (chapters 9 and 26) mention Rahab and that the chaos monster is named in the book only in these two passages (which both are part of Job's speeches and not those of his friends).

[66] Newsom, *Moral Imaginations*, 173. Other examples of speculative wisdom poems are Proverbs 8, Sirach 1 and 24, and Baruch 3:9–4:4. Claus Westermann (*The Structure of the Book of Job*, 135–38) classifies chapter 28 as a "pure wisdom speech" that expands upon the proverb found in verses 12, 20, and 23.

[67] See Pope, xx; Driver and Gray, 232–34; Perdue, *Wisdom in Revolt*, 84.

been composed by the same author. It functions, however, as a commentary on what has come before it, "the poet's personal reflection on the debate thus far."[68]

Inserted into the poetic dialogue between two distinct speeches of Job, the wisdom poem is a self-contained unit and has little connection to what immediately surrounds it. It could be understood as one of Job's speeches, but such a reading presents difficulties. The poem is not an answer to any of the friends; they are not acknowledged in it as they are in many of Job's other speeches. It is not introduced with the formula, "Job answered," as are all his other speeches.[69] More to the point, the wisdom poem is distinct in language, subject matter, and tone from the poetic dialogue. The wisdom poem does not reflect Job's state of mind as revealed in his other speeches; its tone is calm and reasoned, not despairing or angry. The poem does not contain any discussion of righteousness, wickedness, or justice, as does the rest of the dialogue. Its subject matter is the inaccessibility of wisdom, which cannot be found on earth nor acquired with the greatest treasure. Only God knows where wisdom is found; human beings can find it only through piety: "The fear of the Lord is wisdom, and turning from evil is discernment" (Job 28:28).

While such observations seem to support the argument that the wisdom poem is a later addition to the book, it need not be understood as such. The poem exhibits connections with the divine speeches, the prologue, and (to a lesser extent) the poetic dialogue. It is the most extended description of creation in the book outside of the divine speeches and contains strong verbal and thematic links with those speeches. The wild animals play a part in the search for wisdom, as do certain mythological entities (Death, the Sea, the Deep), all of which appear also in the divine speeches. The wisdom poem refers to God's creative power in establishing the world and uses two unusual

---

[68] Habel, 392. Dhorme similarly argues that the author of the poetic dialogue wrote both chapter 28 and the divine speeches but at a later time when he felt a "new inspiration," allowing himself "to be transported by an afflatus which raises him to heights which the discussion between Job and his friends could not reach" (xcvi–xcvii). Tur-Sinai also considers chapter 28 an original part of the poem, but he argues that it has been displaced. He places the poem in the mouth of God at the conclusion of the divine speeches. It is "the conclusion of the book and God's final answer to Job's doubts" (395).

[69] See Job 3:2; 6:1; 9:1; etc. Of course, the lack of this formula in 28:1 could simply mean the speech is a continuation of chapter 27. The tone and language are so changed in chapter 28, however, that it is hard to reconcile it with Job's speech in chapter 27. Also, note that chapter 29 begins with the formula, "Job again took up his speech," perhaps implying that chapter 28 is not Job's speech.

phrases found elsewhere only in the divine speeches: ודרך לחזיז קלות ("a way for the thunderbolt"), and בני שחץ ("sons of pride").[70] That these phrases appear in the Bible only in Job 28 and in the divine speeches points to mutual authorship of the texts or at least to a borrowing of one from the other.

The poem of Job 28 also uses key words that are prominent in the divine speeches: *way* [דרך], *path* [(ה)נתיב], *place* [מקום], *discernment* [בינה], and *wisdom* [חכמה].[71] Whether the author of the wisdom poem was the author of the divine speeches or a later redactor, there is ample evidence of a deliberate effort to connect these disparate parts of the book thematically and lexically. Likewise, the last verse of the poem connects it back to the prologue of the book. The description of wisdom's source in 28:28 corresponds to the description of Job in 1:1, where he is described as a man who "feared God and turned from evil" (וירא אלהים וסר מרע). Again, in 28:28 the source of wisdom is described: "Truly, the fear of the Lord (יראת אדני) is wisdom, and turning from evil (וסור מרע) is understanding." Thus, Job (at least in the prologue) is to be understood as the epitome of wisdom.

Habel sees connections between the wisdom poem and the poetic dialogue. He argues that the exploits of the miner in 28:1–11 are reflective of the mighty acts of God described in the dialogue: overturning mountains, bringing hidden things to light, and establishing limits.[72] The stronger connection between these two parts of the book is the placement of the wisdom poem. Set immediately after the poetic dialogue, the wisdom poem acts as a commentary on that dialogue, as many scholars have noted.[73] Job and his friends have been trying to use human wisdom to answer Job's dilemma. The poem asserts that authentic, transcendent wisdom is inaccessible to unaided human beings, animals, and cosmic entities alike. Only God knows wisdom, and only the pious person can hope to acquire it.

It is this last assertion that differentiates the wisdom poem from the divine speeches. Humanity plays an impressive role in the wisdom poem: overturning mountains, finding hidden things, putting an end to darkness.

[70] Job 28:26 and 38:25; 28:8 and 41:26.

[71] דרך - Job 28:23, 26; 38:19, 24–25; 40:19; (ה)נתיב - 28:7; 41:24; מקום - 28:1, 6, 12, 20, 23; 38:12, 19; בינה - 28:12, 20, 28; 38:4, 36; 39:17, 26; חכמה - 28:12, 18, 20, 28; 38:36–37, 39:17.

[72] Job 28:3, 9, 11; cf. 9:5; 11:6-7; 12:22; 14:5 (Habel, 392). These lexical connections are not as exact as those between the wisdom poem and the divine speeches and prologue.

[73] So Habel, 392; Newsom, *Moral Imaginations*, 174; Westermann, *Structure of the Book of Job*, 137.

Humanity plays virtually no role in the divine speeches; instead, creation is held up for admiration. Indeed, the divine speeches highlight the impotence and ignorance of humanity. Likewise, the piety that the wisdom poem recommends does not enter the divine speeches. Even the very pious Job cannot hope to know what God knows or to do what God does in creation. While there are strong connections between the two parts of the book, then, they do not offer the same answer to Job's dilemma. The wisdom poem —addressed as much to the reader of Job as it is to the participants in the poetic dialogue—argues that such a dialogue is futile, that what is needed is right attitude and action, to "fear the Lord" and "depart from evil" (Job 28:28).[74] Interestingly, with this final statement on the place of piety in human life, the wisdom poem serves as a link to what immediately follows it, Job's final defense of his own piety.

Job's Final Speech (Chapters 29–31)

After the poetic dialogue and the wisdom poem of chapter 28, Job offers a final speech that sets out his case and challenges God to answer him. Job begins by reviewing his life before God afflicted him. He notes that he occupied a place of importance in the social order. He was revered by his associates and blessed with children and wealth. Job then contrasts those memories with his current existence: those who were formerly his inferiors are now mocking him. Lastly, Job ends his defense (and all his speeches) with a long oath, protesting his innocence and calling on God to answer him.[75]

Though still a part of the poetic dialogue, Job's final speech is set apart from that dialogue by the wisdom poem; and it is appropriate that it is set apart because it differs markedly from the dialogue. There is no acknowledgment of his friends in Job's final speech; he does not refer to their arguments, as he often does in his previous responses to them. This final speech is also much longer than any of Job's previous speeches. As Newsom notes, the

[74] Some scholars consider this verse an addition to the original wisdom poem (see Pope, 206). If such is the case, then the conclusion of the wisdom poem is more radical: wisdom is completely inaccessible to human beings; only God knows it.

[75] One might fruitfully compare Job 29–31 with the last speech of the sufferer in the *Babylonian Theodicy*. The sufferer there, after a dialogue with a friend, offers a final defense in which he lists his pious behavior and indirectly calls on the gods to have mercy on him. See *Before the Muses*, 806-14.

language and tone of the speech are different from that of the dialogue; its style is simple and direct with no parody, irony, or hostility toward those who listen.[76] In this speech Job constructs a vision of the world and his place in it that is unlike anything else in the book.

The genre of Job's final speech is difficult to classify as it seems to participate in a number of different genres: lament, judicial appeal, legal testimony.[77] It is probably closest to lament, but instead of ending with a cry for help (as do other laments), Job's speech ends with an oath of innocence. Newsom thus designates it a "testimony," though not in the legal sense. It is "the giving of an account of events, of one's experience, or of oneself."[78]

As in the poetic dialogue, creation and procreation images continue to appear in Job's final defense. Job remembers with fondness the days "when the Almighty was with me, when my young were around me." As usual, children are understood as a sign of God's blessing. Even nature itself joined in blessing Job, as the rocks poured out streams of oil for his sake (Job 29:5–6). Job deserved such blessing because he helped the poor and the afflicted. The people of the land, both great and small, looked to him:

> They waited for me like rain,
>   and they opened wide their mouths for the spring rain.
> I laughed (אֶשְׂחַק) at them, that they did not believe
> ....
>   I chose their way and sat at the head.
> I dwelt as a king with his troop,
>   as one who comforts mourners. (Job 29:23–24a, 25)

Before his troubles, Job possessed a position of authority, and his counsel was sought eagerly by old and young alike. In contrast, Job now sees those same people mock (שָׂחַק) him (Job 30:1).[79] The word שָׂחַק indicates the attitude of a superior to an inferior. It is used a number of times in the divine speeches, where creatures of the animal kingdom "laugh" at the weapons and machinations of human beings. In this speech, the word שָׂחַק highlights the disparity between Job's previous existence and his present state. His position

---

[76] See Newsom, *Moral Imaginations*, 183–85, for a discussion of other distinguishing features that set Job's final speech apart from the rest of the book.

[77] See Habel, 404–5; Westermann, *Structure of the Book of Job*, 38–42; and Zuckerman, 107.

[78] Newsom, *Moral Imaginations*, 185.

[79] See the discussion in the appendix on 39:7.

vis-à-vis his inferiors has changed; they now mock the one who once helped them. Job has no doubt who has caused this change: the God who "has thrown me into the mire" (Job 30:19).

Job's self-description here draws on various elements of the natural world. He compares himself to the spring rain, necessary for life; he also asserts that he controlled the unrighteous as he would wild animals, shattering their "fangs" [מתלעות] to make them drop their "prey" [טרף] (Job 29:17).[80] He thought that he would die in his "nest" [קן], not as an outcast, and that he would "prolong [his] days like the phoenix." Job likens himself to a strong and vigorous tree: "My roots [שרש] open to water and dew resting on my branches [קצירי]" (Job 29:18-19).[81] In describing his former existence, Job relies on images from creation and mythology that represent life and vigor: the spring rain, the phoenix, a strong tree. When he turns to contemplating his current state, however, Job uses images from the natural world that connote sorrow and affliction. His happiness has passed away like a cloud, and he has "become like dust and ashes (עפר ואפר)" (Job 30:19).[82] He is abandoned by all and has become a "brother to jackals and a companion to ostriches" (Job 30:29).[83] Like these wild animals, he wanders in desolate places and utters mournful cries.

---

[80] The word מתלעות could also mean "jawbone." It is a rare word but apparently connected with wild animals as it is used in Joel 1:6 and Ps 58:7 in reference to lions. The word טרף, "prey," most often refers to the food of wild animals.

[81] The translation "phoenix" for חול in verse 18 is contested. Everywhere else in the Bible, חול means "sand." Multiplying one's days like sand certainly makes sense. The reference to "my nest" (קן) in 18a, however, would suggest that "phoenix" is also a legitimate translation. Gordis follows M. Dahood in arguing for the translation "phoenix" (*The Book of Job*, 321-22), citing the Talmud (*B. Sanh.* 108b) and *Midrash Genesis Rabba* (chapter 18). W. F. Albright translates the Ugaritic *ḥl* as "phoenix" in the Keret Epic ["Baal Zephon," in *Festschrift für Alfred Bertholet* (ed. Walter Baumgartner; Tübingen: J. C. B. Mohr, 1950) 1-14]. Pope, however, finds fault with Albright's translation of the Ugaritic and argues for the translation "sand" here in Job (214–16). To make the verse more cohesive, Pope amends קני to, זקני "my old age." I have chosen "phoenix" as the translation to avoid the problem of needing to emend קני. Whether Job refers to a phoenix or to sand, he is utilizing features of the natural world to describe himself in this passage.

[82] The phrase עפר ואפר plays an important part in Job's response to the divine speeches. See discussion in the appendix on 42:6.

[83] See Micah 1:8 for the same pairing of animals. Both the jackal and the ostrich were noted for living in desolate areas and for producing equally desolate sounds.

Job's defense closes with a long oath in which he denies any wrongdoing and calls on God to answer him. In a striking image, Job uses the theme of procreation to speak of the way in which he treated his slaves:

> If I rejected the cause (מִשְׁפַּט) of my male or female slaves
>   when they brought a dispute (בְּרִבָם) against me,
> then what should I do when God arises?
> When he calls to account, what should I answer him?
> Did not the one who made me in the womb make them;
> Did not the same one form us in the womb?
>   (Job 31:13–15)

Because Job and his slaves were created by the same God, Job could not reject their just complaints. The words מִשְׁפָּט and רִיב are taken from the language of litigation and are crucial to Job's own statement of his dispute with God. They are used a number of times in the dialogue, most often in Job's speeches. Job complains that there is no justice (מִשְׁפָּט), that God has taken away his rightful claim (מִשְׁפָּט).[84] He wishes to contend (רִיב) with God but knows that God is too powerful for him. He wonders why the Almighty attacks him and on what basis he disputes (רִיב) with him.[85] In his final speech Job claims that he dealt justly with his servants when they brought a dispute against him. Given the tone of his earlier speeches, and his use of רִיב and מִשְׁפָּט, the implication is that God should follow Job's example by dealing justly with Job's complaint.

Although Job considers God unjust, it is God who is the basis for Job's just treatment of his slaves. He dealt with his slaves fairly because in the most basic sense, he and they came from the same source; that is, the same God created them both. A common source-a common creation, one might say-becomes the basis for just human relationships.[86] It is ironic then that

---

[84] Job 19:7; 27:2. The word מִשְׁפָּט is used twenty-four times in the book of Job, twenty-three times in the poetic dialogue and once in the divine speeches. Of the uses in the poetic dialogue, over half occur in Job's speeches or in quotations of Job's speeches. Most of the rest are in Elihu's speech. For an extended discussion of the use of מִשְׁפָּט in the dialogue and in the divine speeches, see chapter three below.

[85] Job 9:3; 23:6; 10:2. The root רִיב occurs ten times in the book of Job, once in the divine speeches and the other nine times in Job's speeches.

[86] See G. Fohrer, *Studien zum Buche Hiob* (1956–1979) (Berlin: Walter de Gruyter, 1983) 88. Fohrer, too, emphasizes that equality before God in this passage is the basis for equality under the law. For similar passages about creation as the basis for human justice, see Prov 14:31; 17:5; 22:2; 29:13.

the creator God does not deal with *his* servant as that servant dealt with his own servants.

Job's final speech makes use of other creation and procreation images. Job has "from [his] mother's womb" dealt kindly with the orphan and the widow. He has worshiped neither sun nor moon. His land has not cried out against him.[87] Had the land reason to do so, he protests, it then should have produced thorns and weeds instead of grain.

The world Job describes in his final speech is the one that he occupied in the prose prologue. This world is ordered, hierarchical, and structured around domestic life. Newsom describes this social world (familiar from biblical and other ANE literature) as a "village patriarchy" grounded in kinship and patronage structures, in which older male heads of households possess ultimate authority. These village patriarchs are the ones who judge at the city gate and protect those at the margins of the society, the orphan and the widow.[88] Job describes himself as chief among these elders.

In this social world as in the prologue, the wild elements of creation have no real place. Wild animals are used as metaphors for those outside the boundaries of this ordered world: those who are unrighteous, those whose fathers Job would not have put with his sheepdogs, those who scavenge like animals in the rocks and gullies of the wilderness (Job 29:17; 30:1–8). Job had no dealings with such people in his former life, except to save the poor from them. In his current state, however, his world has been invaded by just those wild elements; he is made to ride on the wind and is tossed about by a storm. He is afflicted so much, in fact, that he himself becomes kin to jackal and ostrich, denizens of desolation (Job 30:22, 29).

The contrast with his former state could not be greater. His self-description in chapter 29 is unapologetically grandiose; his worth to his companions was as great as that of life-giving rain, his place among them like that of a king. In his current state, he has been displaced, removed from the center of his social world, and made to dwell with the wild animals, those outside the boundaries of that world. In all this Job's final speech hints at what is to come in the divine speeches, where the focus shifts to the vast cosmos

[87] Job 31:18, 26, 38. In verse 26, "light" (אוֹר) is interpreted to mean "sun." In vss. 38–39, the land would have cried out against Job had he treated its occupants badly, not paying them for its yield and/or causing their deaths.

[88] Newsom, *Moral Imaginations*, 187–91, describes this social world at great length.

outside the boundaries of Job's social world and where the wild animals assume center stage.

As in the previous chapters of the book, the theme of procreation continues to be a motif in Job's final speech, but it is used in a radically new way. While a continuing sign of God's blessing, it is also the foundation for a surprising egalitarianism. Job acknowledges that he and his slaves were formed in the womb by the same God (Job 31:15). Such a claim is striking, given his soliloquy on the preeminent place he occupied in his social world. One is reminded of Job's first lament, where he places "the small and the great" together. There, however, the common denominator was death, not birth (Job 3:19).[89] This use of the theme of procreation will surface again in the divine speeches, where Job's origin is equated even more radically with that of another of God's creatures, this time not another human being but the mythological beast Behemoth.[90]

Elihu's Speech (Chapters 32–37)

Before the long and detailed description of creation that comprises the divine speeches, a fourth friend appears and offers his arguments concerning Job's situation. This speaker, Elihu, is not mentioned either before or after his speech and does not appear with the other three friends in the epilogue. Job does not respond in any way to his arguments. Additionally, the divine speeches follow most naturally not Elihu's speech but rather Job's final defense, where Job calls on God to answer him. For these reasons and others, most modern scholars consider the Elihu speech a later addition to the book of Job.[91]

---

[89] In Job 3, the grave is the great equalizer and the place of rest, where the slave is free of his master.

[90] See in the appendix the discussion on 40:15–19.

[91] See Pope, xxvii–xxviii, and Gordis, *The Book of Job*, 546–53, for a discussion of the textual issues. Note that Gordis does not agree with the historical-critical consensus that the Elihu speech is a later addition to the book of Job, asserting instead that the author of the Elihu speech is the author of the rest of the book. The Elihu speech, argues Gordis, contains the author's mature insights, which he inserted at a later time into the book. Pope disagrees, seeing little value in the Elihu speeches: "It is hard to see how some critics can regard them so highly" (lxxix). See also David Noel Freedman, "The Elihu Speeches in the Book of Job," *HTR* 61 (1968) 51–59. Freedman hypothesizes that the author of the Elihu speech was also the author of the divine speeches. Dissatisfied with the result of the Elihu speech, the author abandoned it and used some of the material from it to write the divine speeches.

Whether a part of the original text of Job or not, Elihu's speech (like the rest of the book) contains an abundance of creation images, primarily in its last section, 36:24–37:24. Elihu, more than the other three friends, speaks of the majesty and power of God that is revealed in creation. Newsom argues that the writer of the Elihu speech makes use of a genre in the last section of the discourse (Job 36:24–37:13) that was unavailable to the earlier writer of the rest of Job: that of the "sapiential nature hymn," the only other example of which is found in Sirach 42:15–43:33.[92] While itself not a theodicy, Elihu's hymn nonetheless represents an attempt to address the issue of injustice raised by Job. Like the divine speeches, it does so by pointing to creation; and further like the divine speeches, its purpose is to change Job's perspective, to offer him "an encounter with the divine that displaces him from the center of value and judgment."[93] Nevertheless, the hymn is not "directly imitative" of the divine speeches, as is the very end of Elihu's speech (Job 37:14–20).[94] It differs from the divine speeches in its human speaker and in its "comments upon the purposiveness of the divine acts in nature."[95]

Elihu's speech, by describing God's work in creation, echoes some of Job's statements while foreshadowing the content of the divine speeches.[96] The writer of Elihu's speech obviously was familiar with the divine speeches; but because his speech is placed prior to the divine speeches, the writer cannot allow Elihu to allude directly to them. Nonetheless, there are many parallels between the two sets of speeches. For instance, Elihu goes into great detail about the power God has over meteorological forces: "God thunders wonderfully with his voice. He does great things that we do not know. For he says to the snow, 'Fall on the earth.' . . ./By the breath of God ice is formed. The wide waters are frozen fast" (Job 37:5, 10).[97] Such language would not

---

[92] Newsom, *Moral Imaginations*, 220–30. Newsom defines the "sapiential nature hymn" as a detailed description of creation that combines the characteristics of a hymn of praise and a sapiential teaching.

[93] Ibid., 228, 231.

[94] Ibid., 221

[95] Ibid., 230. Newsom cites 36:31 and 37:12–13 as examples of this commentary on the idea of divine purpose in nature. I am not completely persuaded by Newsom's characterization of Elihu's speech. Do two extant examples constitute a "genre," or could Ben Sira simply be imitating Job? Newsom is certainly correct, however, in finding the inspiration for the end of Elihu's speech in the divine speeches.

[96] See Job 9:5–10; 12:7–10, 13–15; 26:5–14, where Job describes the power of God in creation.

[97] See also 38:22, 29–30, 38.

be out of place in the divine speeches, which describe at length God's power over storms, rain, wind, snow, and ice. Likewise, the words מעונות (dens) and ארב (lair), which Elihu uses to speak about the wild animals (Job 37:8), appear only one other time in the book, in the divine speeches (Job 38:40). There, God describes young lions. The word הוד ("majesty") is used twice in the divine speeches and only once outside of them: in Elihu's speech to describe God (Job 37:22).[98] These thematic and lexical connections between Elihu's speech and the divine speeches point to a borrowing of one from the other, and there is little question which is the later text.[99]

This borrowing from the divine speeches continues in the very last section of the Elihu speech. Elihu asks Job a series of questions that echo God's questions and follow two basic forms: "Do you know x that only God knows?" and "Can you do x that only God can do?" Elihu's recital of God's power seeks to expose Job's weakness and ignorance: "Hear this, O Job. Stand and consider the wondrous things of God" (Job 37:14–18). It is not a new sentiment; the three friends have already compared Job's knowledge and power unfavorably with God's (Job 11:7–10; 15:7; 25:1–3). In its use of rhetorical questions and in its detailed description of creation, however, Elihu's argument is more closely tied to the divine speeches than to the speeches of the friends.

There are then many parallels between Elihu's speech and the divine speeches, all of which point to a deliberate borrowing by the former from the latter. Nonetheless, one must also note significant differences between the two texts. Perhaps the most obvious difference is the distinct lack in Elihu's speech of any sustained reference to the animal world. While the divine speeches speak in great detail about various animals, Elihu's speech only mentions animals as foils to human beings: "One does not say, 'Where is God my Maker . . . /who teaches us[100] more than the beasts of the earth and makes us wiser than the birds of the air?'" (Job 35:11). Elihu later mentions

---

[98] The word הוד is used in the divine speeches to describe the war horse (39:20) and when God challenges Job to clothe himself with "majesty" (40:10).

[99] Freedman is an exception to the majority opinion that the author of the Elihu speech borrowed from the divine speeches. Freedman, as noted above, argues that the dependency runs the other way, that the author of the Elihu speech used it as the basis for his later composition of the divine speeches.

[100] מלפנו is a contraction of the participle מאלפנו, (in the Piel, "to teach"), as evidenced by the Targum, which preserves the א and by the parallelism of the next verb, יחכמנו ("to make wise").

animals again but only to say that they (like human beings) hide in their dens when God causes it to rain (Job 37:8).

Much of Elihu's speech concerns human beings, who rarely are mentioned in the divine speeches. This silence about humanity in the divine speeches may account for the impulse of the Elihu writer to add to them. Even in the section of Elihu's speech that most resembles the divine speeches (Job 36:24 –37:24), humanity still plays a prominent role. Human beings are the primary (perhaps the only) observers of God's work. God sends abundant rain on human beings, governs the peoples, and provides food for them (Job 36:24–31). While it is true that in Elihu's speech humanity remains under God's control and must live humbly, nevertheless humanity (according to Elihu) also is one of the primary objects of God's attention and the most important of his creatures. In this respect Elihu's view of creation has more in common with the views set forth in the prologue and poetic dialogue of Job than with the vision articulated in the divine speeches.

Elihu's speech and the divine speeches differ in one other important way. For all his attention to humanity, Elihu ends his speech with a statement about God's inaccessibility to human beings: "The Almighty, we cannot find him." That statement is then challenged two verses later by the appearance of God to Job: "YHWH answered Job from the whirlwind" (Job 37:23; 38:1). The divine speeches, while radically non-anthropocentric, *are* addressed to an *anthropos*. After being spoken *about* by the three friends and Elihu, and spoken *to* only by Job, God finally enters the dialogue.

"What Is Humanity?"

Before discussing the divine speeches, it will be fruitful to explore what the first thirty-seven chapters of the book of Job have to say about the place of humanity in creation. The book of Job can be read as a sustained meditation on the question Job asks (in a parody of the psalmist), מה אנוש, "What is humanity?"[101] When Job poses this question, he is not necessarily seeking an answer. He simply wants God to leave him alone, to stop hounding him and waiting for him to sin. Nevertheless, it is useful for understanding the book of Job to take Job's question seriously and to seek the answers to it offered throughout the rest of the book.

---

[101] Job 7:17; Ps 8:4.

What is humanity? Most often in the book of Job, that question can be answered by considering the question, "Who is Job?" In the prologue, Job is "blameless and just, fearing God and turning from evil." He is one abundantly blessed by God, one in whom God takes delight. He is even, one might say, the pinnacle of God's creation, the one being to whom God calls special attention in his conversation with the Satan: "Have you taken note of my servant Job? There is no one like him on earth" (Job 1:1, 8; 2:3). Humanity, then, in the prologue, is at least potentially (in the person of the exceptionally pious Job) a part of creation in which God takes great pride and delight. Human beings are objects of God's attention and capable of pleasing God by being "blameless and upright, fearing God and turning from evil." They are also participants in maintaining the order God has established in creation by mirroring that order in their social world. Job acts as a priest for his children and a judge and protector for the poor and the oppressed.[102]

The Satan answers the question, "What is humanity?" by asking a question of his own: "Does Job fear God for nothing? Have you not set a fence around him and around his house and around all that he has?" (Job 1:9–10). In the Satan's view, human beings are God's favored creatures. The Satan challenges this favored status by claiming that humanity is self-serving. Human beings are pious only because piety ensures protection from all that would harm them. The Satan, in other words, denies the existence of disinterested piety.

The friends, for the most part, reiterate the Satan's view about the place of humanity in creation; that is, that God accords the righteous man the highest place of honor in the world. Over and over, they affirm the belief that God protects the righteous and punishes the wicked although in order to maintain this belief, they must accuse Job himself of wickedness.[103] Yet even as they accuse Job, the friends hold out the promise that the righteous (including a repentant Job) ultimately will find favor with God. One of the manifestations of such favor will be a new relationship for Job with the rest of creation.

> At violence and hunger you will laugh;
>   and you will not fear the wild animals of the earth.
> For your covenant will be with the stones of the field,

---

[102] The latter roles are not articulated in the prologue but in Job's self-description in chapter 29. The social world described is the same for both parts of the book.

[103] The friends are relatively gentle with Job at the beginning of the dialogue, but by the end, they are accusing Job of all sorts of wickedness. See particularly Eliphaz's speech in chapter 22.

and the wild beasts of the field will be at peace with you.
(Job 5:22–23)

In this view, creation itself becomes a means of blessing for humanity and God's fence is rebuilt around the repentant sinner to protect him from the wild forces of the natural world. More accurately, the fence is no longer necessary because the wild animals are at peace with humanity.

Because Job consistently protests his innocence, the friends change their approach at times to talk about the inherent corruption of creation and humanity. As noted above, Eliphaz echoes Job's question but offers a different answer:

> What is humanity [מה אנוש] that it can be pure,
>   that one born of woman can be righteous?
> He does not trust even his holy ones,
>   and the heavens are not pure in his eyes.
> How much less one who is abominable and corrupt,
>   a man who drinks iniquity like water. (Job 15:14–16)[104]

In this view, creation itself is corrupt in God's sight; even the most righteous human being cannot measure up to God's standards. Therefore all human beings, including Job, deserve punishment. To question the Creator about undeserved suffering is absurd because there is no such thing as undeserved suffering. Human beings cannot be righteous or pure because they are human beings. God is righteous because God is God.[105]

The Job of the dialogue does not believe in the protective fence of the Satan's and the friends' worldviews. In his first lament, Job claims that God has indeed "fenced" him in; he has done so, though, not to protect Job but to oppress him (Job 3:23). Job wishes only for death so that he might rest, but God will not leave him alone.[106] Job believes God overestimates Job's significance; he is merely a human being, not a threat to God's sovereign rule: "Is my strength the strength of rocks? Is my flesh bronze?" (Job 6:12). Job appeals to God on the basis of the fact that Job is only human, that he is mortal. God is inordinately and inappropriately concerned with humanity, and particularly with Job.

---

[104] See also 4:17–19 and 25:4–6.

[105] Such is the characterization of the friends' theology by Wagner, 95.

[106] For passages about God's unwarranted concern with human beings, see Job 7:12–19; 9:18; 10:14; 13:20–27; 14:1–6; 19:8, 22.

At the same time, Job reminds God that human beings are God's creatures, that God made them and therefore should have a certain beneficent concern for them: "Remember that you made me like clay, and you will return me to dust" (Job 10:9). Job describes the proper concern that God should show toward humanity:

> If a man dies, will he live again?
> All the days of my service I would wait, until my release
>   comes.
> You would call, and I would answer you.
> You would long for the work of your hands.
> Though now you number my steps,
>   you would not keep watch over my sins.
> My transgression would be sealed up in a bag,
>   and you would cover over my iniquity. (Job 14:14–17)

It is not then that God should leave humanity alone but that God should understand humanity's relative weakness and have compassion upon "the work of [God's] hands" (Job 14:15).

Given Job's emphasis on his own weakness and mortality, it is striking that the friends see a different attitude in Job, and they accuse him of being prideful: "Are you the first man born? Were you brought forth before the hills? Do you listen in to the council of God? And do you limit wisdom to yourself?" (Job 15:7–8). While Job has disavowed any parallel between himself and chaos monsters, the friends perceive in him an attitude that assumes a position of preeminence in God's creation. They therefore accuse him of unwarranted pride. Such a view does indeed arise a few times in Job's own speeches. Despite his emphasis on humanity's weakness and mortality, Job also displays what seems a certain *hubris*, calling God to account, demanding a fair trial from the Almighty. This *hubris* is apparent both in his first lament, where Job tries to annul his own birth by cursing creation itself, and in his final speech, where he not only calls himself a "king," but also equates himself with the spring rain – eagerly sought after, necessary for life.[107]

Such is the view set forth in the prologue and poetic dialogue of Job's place (and thereby also humanity's place) in the world. On the one hand, the Satan and the friends believe that God protects human beings (at least those who are righteous) and bestows on them one of the highest places in

---

[107] Job 3; 29:19–25.

creation.[108] On the other hand, Job contends that God is inordinately concerned with human beings, oppressing them with a scrutiny that should be reserved only for chaos monsters. On the one hand, Job contends that he was once a man among men; on the other hand, he reminds God that he is only human, made of clay, a mortal being.

Whether humanity is considered clean or unclean, favored or oppressed, the place of humanity vis-à-vis the rest of God's creation remains basically the same. That is, humanity is considered by all participants in the dialogue to be the chief object of God's attention and the most important of God's creatures. Even Elihu's vision, which affirms humanity's dependence on God and emphasizes humanity's lack of power and wisdom in relation to God, nevertheless also grants humanity an exalted place in the natural world as one of the chief objects of God's attention, thereby echoing the views of the Satan, Job, and the three friends. Humanity, in Elihu's speech, is the main observer of God's handiwork and the primary beneficiary of God's creative acts. The divine speeches, coming after the speeches of all the human participants, call their visions of creation (and of humanity's place in creation) into question.

---

[108] As has already been noted, the friends also at points subscribe to the view that all of creation, and particularly humanity, is corrupt and unclean.

CHAPTER 2

Creation Theology in the Divine Speeches

The majority of the book of Job is taken up with the poetic dialogue between Job and his four companions, culminating in Job's final defense. Throughout the dialogue, Job at times turns from his human discussion partners and speaks to God directly, calling on the Almighty to answer him, to let him know why he is being oppressed. Job's friends, for their part, never address God directly. Job's direct address to God anticipates and sets the stage for the eventual address of God to him.[1] Accordingly, at the end of the book, after all the human participants have had their say, God speaks.

The speech of God is divided into two parts (38:1–40:2 and 40:6–41:26), separated by a brief, ambiguous answer from Job (40:3–5). The first speech of God is a series of questions to Job concerning the vast expanse of creation: questions about the founding of the world and the origin of the Sea, as well as about the nature of such things as meteorological forces, the constellations, and wild animals. God's second speech describes two mythological beings: Behemoth and Leviathan.[2] The questions in both divine speeches follow similar lines of argument: "Who are you to question God?"; "Do you know

---

[1] See Job 10:2, where Job challenges God, "make known to me (הודיעני) why you contend with me," and 13:23, where he says, "my sin and my transgression make known to me (הדיעני)." God answers him in 38:3 and 40:7: "I will question you, and *you* make known to *me* (הודיעני)." Job has tried to call God to account. Now the tables are turned, and it is Job who must give an accounting if he can.

[2] By using the term "mythological," I do not mean to imply that the author and the original audience of the divine speeches thought Behemoth and Leviathan to be fictitious. I am simply differentiating between the wild animals of the first divine speech and these two creatures who are more than mere animals. Both Behemoth and Leviathan have powers greatly exceeding those of the other animals and both seem to be primordial. Using the term "mythological" also serves to remind readers of the fact that Leviathan, in particular, has a prominent place in

x that God knows?"; and "Are you able to do, or have you done, what God has done?"

It is difficult to assign a genre to the divine speeches. They participate in a number of different genres. Given their attention to myriad entities in creation, they are certainly related to ancient Near Eastern wisdom writings like the Egyptian *onomastica*, encyclopedic lists of plants, minerals, birds, animals, etc.[3] Gerhard von Rad argues that the first divine speech, in particular, is derived both from the Egyptian *onomasticon* and the Egyptian polemical satire, the latter literary form itself derived from catechetical instructions designed to teach young men the geography of neighboring countries.[4] The divine speeches share some elements with ANE creation myths, particularly in their descriptions of the limits set on the Sea.[5] The speeches may also be

---

ANE myths. See the appendix on Job 40:15 and 40:25 for more detailed arguments supporting the designation of Behemoth and Leviathan as "mythological" creatures.

[3] Such *onomastica* seem to have been well known in the ancient Near East. Solomon's wisdom is said to have consisted at least in part of his knowledge of such encyclopedic lists: "He would speak about trees, from the cedar which is in the Lebanon to the hyssop which grows in the wall. He would speak about the animals and the birds and the reptiles and the fish" (1 Kgs 5:13). Thanks to Professor James Kugel for this observation. For a discussion of similar "noun lists" in ancient Mesopotamia, see R. B. Y. Scott, *The Way of Wisdom in the Old Testament* (New York: Macmillan, 1971) 36.

[4] Gerhard von Rad, "Job XXXVIII and Ancient Egyptian Wisdom," in *The Problem of the Hexateuch and Other Essays* (New York: McGraw-Hill, 1966) 281–91. The "catechetical" influence on the divine speeches is evident in their interrogative form. Von Rad also traces the influences of *onomastica* on hymns of praise such as Psalm 148. For a discussion of the later life of encyclopedic lists in apocalyptic literature, see Michael E. Stone, "Lists of Revealed Things in the Apocalyptic Literature," in *Magnalia Dei: The Mighty Acts of God* (ed. F. M. Cross, W. E. Lemke, and P. D. Miller; New York: Doubleday, 1976) 414–51. Stone acknowledges the strong influence of Wisdom writings like Job 28 and 38 on the "lists of revealed things" in apocalyptic literature but sees in these lists also "catalogues of actual subjects of speculative investigation, study, and perhaps even of the contents of ecstatic experiences of the apocalyptic authors" (436). Michael V. Fox disputes von Rad's hypothesis that Job 38–39 was based on lists derived from observational sciences ["Egyptian Onomastica and Biblical Wisdom," *VT* 36 (1986) 302–10].

[5] See *Enuma Elish*, tablet IV, lines 135–40, where Marduk splits Tiamat's dead body in two to create the world, making a boundary for the waters and posting guards so they will not cross the boundary. Likewise, God makes bars and doors for the Sea in the divine speeches. The Sea is not the chaos monster in the divine speeches, however, that it is in ANE myths. It is not a defeated enemy, but a willful child. A stronger connection with ANE creation myths is found in Job 26:12–13, which uses the divine warrior myth (God/the gods defeating the Sea/sea dragon in order to establish creation) to speak of God's defeat of the Sea and its cohorts. See Pope, 185–86, for specific thematic and lexical connections

compared to other theophanies in the Hebrew Bible.[6] Westermann, for his part, argues that the divine speeches participate in two different genres: the "disputation speech" (which answers Job's summons to God to enter into a lawsuit) and the "salvation oracle" (*Heilsorakel*) found typically in a lament after the sufferer has articulated his deep distress.[7]

Newsom answers the question of the genre of the divine speeches by pairing them with Job's final defense in chapters 29–31 and designating the whole "a disputation between a person and his God."[8] That designation, while descriptive, does not allude to a specific genre. There are examples in ancient Near Eastern literature of a righteous sufferer's appeal to a deity, but only in the book of Job does the deity reply directly to the sufferer in detail and at length.[9] All of these genres (*onomasticon*, creation myth, theophany, lawsuit, lament, and the appeal of a righteous sufferer) contribute elements to

---

between Job 26, *Enuma Elish*, and the Baal cycle from Ugarit. See the appendix on 40:25 for more on the divine warrior myth.

[6] See Ezek 1:4, where the theophany to the prophet is accompanied by a "whirlwind" (סְעָרָה), as in Job 38:1 and 40:6. The striking difference between the theophany in Ezekiel and that of the divine speeches is that the former offers a detailed description of God's appearance, while the latter contains nothing of the sort. No narrative description precedes God's speech in Job as it does in Ezekiel. The divine speeches in Job describe creation rather than the Creator.

[7] Westermann, *Structure of the Book of Job*, 105–23. Westermann sees the lament as the overarching structure of the book. Another major theme that appears, though, is the lawsuit between Job and God. In the divine speeches, these two genres are joined (105–6).

[8] Newsom, *Moral Imaginations*, 238. Newsom argues that Job's final defense and the divine speeches are meant to be juxtaposed, and that the Elihu speech is a later addition that interrupts this dialogue. Job's rhetorical challenge in 31:35–37 sets up the divine speeches; Job then responds to God in 40:1–5 and 42:1–6 with words and gestures that echo his own final speech. He is silent and places his hand on his mouth (40:4–5), just as others used to do in his presence (29:9–10). He also refers to himself as "dust and ashes" both in 30:19 and 42:6 (Newsom, 238–39). I agree with Newsom and all the other scholars who consider the Elihu speech a later addition and who place the divine speeches right after Job's final speech. I do not, however, consider the divine speeches to be as closely and exclusively tied to Job's final speech as Newsom does; she argues that God's speeches and Job's "stand over against each other somewhat like the facing panels in a diptych" (239). I would argue that the divine speeches address every part of the book, including the prologue and the wisdom dialogue as well as Job's final speech.

[9] Newsom notes that Marduk's response to the sufferer in *Ludlul* is mediated by messengers who appear in the sufferer's dream. In the "Dialogue of a Man with His God," the deity answers the sufferer, but the answer is nothing like the divine speeches in content or length (ibid., 238).

the divine speeches, but the speeches do not participate fully in any of them. The divine speeches are, as befits their speaker, wonderfully unique.

Coming as they do at the end of the book, after all the human participants have had their say, the divine speeches would logically be expected to offer the final answer to the problem of Job, an answer not found in any of the preceding sections of the book.[10] The primary difficulty with this understanding of the book, of course, is that the divine speeches do not directly address Job's situation: the problem of the suffering of the righteous. Instead, they offer Job a God's-eye view of creation in all its complexity. Indeed, if the speeches of Job and his companions are marked by a number of references to creation, the speeches of God are filled with nothing but creation images. God uses the creation images, however, to a different effect. Whereas Job tries to "uncreate" creation, seen from a highly personal perspective, in his first speech (Job 3), God portrays the initial act of creation in all its splendor and holds up the nonhuman world in all its power and beauty. While Job and his companions use creation images largely to talk about human beings, the divine speeches remain virtually silent concerning humanity. Even the motif of procreation, which appears with some frequency in the dialogue, is used in startling new ways in the divine speeches to speak of entities not normally associated with conception and birth.[11]

This chapter will explore the creation theology of the divine speeches, comparing and contrasting it with creation theologies found in earlier chapters of Job and in other texts from the Hebrew Bible. This exploration will be organized around three themes: the establishment of creation, procreation,

---

[10] Newsom concedes that this view of the divine speeches is plausible, given that their speaker is God, whom she curiously calls "that great authority figure" (ibid., 18). She argues, however, that the epilogue disrupts this notion that the whole book has been a kind of "progressive education of the moral sensibility" because the epilogue returns the reader to the world of the prologue and "seems morally at odds with the perspective implied in the divine speeches" (ibid., 20–21).

[11] It is possible, of course, that the Joban poet is alluding to ANE myths that describe the process of creation in terms of conception and birth rather than in terms of being made and formed. Such myths are largely lost to us, except for references in texts like *Enuma Elish* that speak of the gods being born. Note, however, that even in that text, the physical world (as distinct from the gods) is formed out of Tiamat's corpse rather than born of her living body (*ANET*, 61–62, 67). See the section on Job 38:28–30 in the appendix for other possible Egyptian references to such procreation myths. In any case, no other biblical text refers to the creation of the Sea, rain, etc., in terms of conception and birth.

and the place of humanity in creation. All three themes play a major role in the book of Job.

The Establishment of Creation

As noted already, the poetic dialogue of the book of Job begins with an extended lament by Job in chapter 3, a lament that calls for the destruction of the day he was born and the night he was conceived. The lament is radically nihilistic, calling on forces of darkness, chaos, and death to negate light, life, conception, birth, and ultimately creation itself. This poem, notes Robert Alter, is "a powerful, evocative, authentic expression of man's essential, virtually ineluctable egotism." Its movement is inward, toward darkness, death, and the grave: "The external world—dawn and sunlight and starry night—exists in these lines only to be canceled."[12] In the egocentrism of despair, Job closes in upon himself and wills creation, too, to collapse into darkness and chaos. This death wish is the first and most radical use of creation images in the poetic dialogue.

Later, Job acknowledges God as the all-powerful Creator, but he claims that God uses his power in a capricious manner:

> How can a man be justified before God
> Who removes mountains, but they do not know it;
>   when he overturns them in his anger;
> Who shakes (המרגיז) the earth from its place
>   and its pillars shudder;
> Who speaks to the sun so that it does not rise,
>   and seals up the stars.
> Who alone stretched out the heavens
>   and trod on the waves of the Sea? (Job 9:2b, 5–8)

God's actions in creation are matched by God's capricious dealings with human beings, according to Job. God overturns judges, princes, and rulers; God destroys the wicked and the righteous alike (Job 9:22; 12:17–21). One might say Job's image of God is as the divine warrior run amok. God overturns not only forces of chaos like the Sea, but also things created to provide structure in the world: mountains, pillars of the earth, sun, stars, and even human authority figures. Job's own world has descended into turmoil

---

[12] Alter, 96.

or chaos (רגז), and he attempts to inflict that chaos on creation itself; first by
cursing creation, then by ascribing chaotic tendencies to God.[13]

Job's challenge to God's order cannot go unanswered. In the divine
speeches, the creation is, as it were, re-created. More accurately, God reaffirms
the order already established in creation from the beginning, an order Job had
tried to negate. God describes his actions in creation, when he first laid the
foundation of the earth; and the morning stars, far from being darkened (as
Job tries to do in 3:9), sang together for joy. God created limits for the Sea:
"Thus far you shall come and no further," shutting it in with bars and doors
(Job 38:11). God commanded the morning and taught the dawn its place.
God created a way for the rain and thunder and continues to provide for the
wild animals that inhabit his creation. God also provides for Behemoth and
Leviathan, creatures that are part of the chaos that God holds in check.

Alter notes that the structure of the first divine speech is "implicitly
narrative":[14] God describes first how he created the world, then how he
established within it the complex interplay of meteorological forces, and
finally how he looks after the dazzling array of wild animals that inhabit the
world. The second divine speech heightens and focuses this description of
creation by concentrating on two of creation's most fearsome creatures. The
movement of Job's first lament is answered by that of the divine speeches.
While the former poem describes a "withdrawal inward and turning out of
lights," the latter "progresses through a grand sweeping movement that carries
us over the length and breadth of the created world."[15]

The "implicit narrative" of the divine speeches recreates what Job negated
in his first lament. According to Newsom, one of the primary resources the
friends offer to Job for resisting chaos or רגז is to construe his experience in
terms of a narrative structure. Job counters by using images "that suggest
the radical nonnarratability of human existence in general and his own in
particular."[16] The friends' arguments do not succeed in moving Job out of
his state of desolation.

---

[13] Note the use of the root רגז in 9:6 and its prominence as the last word in Job 3. Job
later uses the word רגז as a description of the general lot of humanity in 14:1: "A man, born
of woman, few of days and full of turmoil (רגז)." See the discussion of this word above in
chapter one.

[14] Alter, 94.

[15] Ibid., 97. Alter considers the first divine speech, in particular, to be a direct answer to
Job's death-wish in chapter 3.

[16] Newsom, *Moral Imaginations*, 96–97.

Combining Newsom's understanding of the friends' speeches with Alter's characterization of the divine speeches yields a fruitful reading of the latter. The friends are unable to provide a narrative structure that makes sense of Job's situation; God provides that structure. That is, the divine speeches offer a more fundamental response to Job's sense of chaos than do the speeches of his friends. The divine speeches do this in two ways: 1) they describe to Job the most basic, essential narrative of God's establishment and ordering of creation; and 2) they show him the vast expanse of creation that exists outside of himself and his own self-involved despair.

The narrative of creation begins, appropriately enough, with God's founding of the world, described in terms of the construction of a building. Its "bases" (אדניה) are sunk and its cornerstone laid by God (Job 38:6). It is striking that the poet uses the word אדן, which appears repeatedly in the Exodus and Numbers accounts of the building of the tabernacle. In fact, the word אדן appears dozens of times in the Bible, yet only here and in Cant 5:15 does it describe something *other* than the construction of the tabernacle. The Joban poet thus plays upon the association between temple building and world building prevalent in the Bible and other ancient Near Eastern texts.[17] The divine speeches, however, make no mention of an actual temple; instead, the cosmos itself becomes the temple, the arena in which God's power and glory are revealed, and in which God himself is made manifest. Job acknowledges as much in his final response to the divine speeches: "I had heard of you by the hearing of the ear, but now my own eyes have seen you" (Job 42:5).[18] Job has not seen God's overt appearance here, though; instead, God is revealed in the forces and creatures of the cosmos God has created.

The narrative of creation continues with a description of the birth of the Sea. Job has already evoked the image of the divine warrior trampling the back of the Sea (Job 9:8). The divine speeches, in contrast, portray God not as the divine warrior but as a cosmic midwife, attending the birth of the Sea and wrapping it in swaddling bands. God establishes limits for the Sea, "Thus far you shall come and no further. Here shall your proud waves be fixed" (Job 38:11). Contrary to Job's assertions in chapter 9, God here does not act arbitrarily or with violence against his creation. God instead

---

[17] For an extended description of the connection between cosmogony and temple building in biblical and other ANE texts, see Levenson, 66–99. See Brown, *Character in Crisis*, 92–93, for a discussion of this passage in the divine speeches.

[18] See below (chapter three) for a more extended discussion of Job's final response to the divine speeches.

establishes order in creation, starting with limits for the Sea and continuing by commanding the morning and causing Dawn to "know (ידעתה) its place (מקמו)" (Job 38:12–15).[19] Job had stated, "[God] speaks to the sun so that it does not rise" (Job 9:7), and here, the divine speeches correct that assertion. God does not interrupt the rhythm of sunrise and sunset but establishes that rhythm from the very beginning of creation. Dawn acts as God's agent, every morning shaking the wicked out of the earth like so much dust out of a rug (Job 38:13).[20]

It is helpful here to remember another earlier speech by Job, in which he argued that God did not pay heed to the prayers of the oppressed and worse, that God allowed the wicked free sway in the darkness of night:

> In the darkness (בחשך) [the wicked person] digs through houses;
> by day he shuts himself up.
> He does not know the light (אור).
> For morning (בקר) is to him the same as deep darkness (צלמות).
> For he is acquainted with the terrors of deep darkness
> (צלמות). (Job 24:16–17)

Images of light and darkness dominate this passage. Job asserts that חשך and צלמות are friends to the thief and the adulterer, that the wicked do not know the light (אור) because they shut themselves off from it, hiding by day. The divine speeches take up these images to make a different claim: that the wicked cannot escape morning (בקר) or Dawn. It catches them and exposes their deeds so that they stand as those shamed (Job 38:14). Light (אור) is withheld from the wicked, then, as a punishment, not because they hide from it. God does preserve the moral order and has built into the cosmos a means for dealing with the wicked.

Images of light and darkness also dominated Job's lament in chapter 3 where he wished for חשך and צלמות to obliterate the day of his birth. He wanted the stars of its dawn to be darkened (יחשכו) so that it would look for light (אור) but find none (Job 3:5, 9). God responds to Job's lament:

---

[19] Contrast Job 9:5–6, where Job accuses God of overturning "the mountains and they do not know (ידעו)," and of shaking "the earth from its place (מקומה)." This passage in the divine speech seems to be responding to Job's accusations in chapter 9, using the same words Job uses

[20] Here, for the first time, the divine speeches exhibit a concern with the human moral order.

Have the gates of Death (מות) been revealed to you?
Have you seen the gates of deep darkness (צלמות)
Which is the way to the dwelling place of light (אור)
And where is the place of darkness (חשך)
That you may take it to its territory and know the paths
to its home? (Job 38:17, 19)[21]

Job has wished for death (מות) a number of times and has wished darkness
(צלמות) to obliterate light (אור). Now God challenges him simply to find these
elements of creation. Job does not even know where they dwell, much less
can he summon them to do what he commands.[22] Job's curse is negated.

God not only establishes creation; God also preserves and sustains it. God
sends rain on the wilderness where no person lives "to satisfy the desolate
and wasteland (שאה ומשאה) and to cause the parched land to sprout grass"
(Job 38:27). The phrase שאה ומשאה, signifying total desolation, is used only
three times in the Bible: in this verse, in Job 30:3, and in Zeph 1:15, where
the prophet is speaking of the terrible day of YHWH. In Job 30:3 the phrase is
used by Job to describe the habitat of those despised by society, those whom
Job in his former days accounted less than dogs. These disreputable people
are described in terms usually reserved for wild animals. They "wander" or
"gnaw at" (הערקים) the desolate ground (שאה ומשאה); they live in holes and
among rocks; they "bray" (ינהקו) like donkeys.[23] Connecting this passage
with the divine speeches, the use of שאה ומשאה in both passages implies
that God provides life-giving rain even to those places and people Job had
despised. Newsom aptly contrasts these two views of the desolate land: Job
had considered it "godforsaken," a thing to be feared, a place of punishment.
God, on the other hand, characterizes it as "human-forsaken," a wilderness
where no person lives, and a thing of beauty.[24] God "satisfies" even such a
desolate place, providing rain so that it sprouts grass, bringing forth life in
a land that humanity has rejected as worthless.[25]

---

[21] See also 38:24, where אור is best translated "lightning."

[22] The only thing Job can "darken" (מחשיך) is "counsel," something of which God
accuses him at the very beginning of the divine speeches (38:2).

[23] Job 30:3, 6–7. Cf. Job 6:5, where נהק is used of the wild ass.

[24] Newsom, *Moral Imaginations*, 240.

[25] God brings forth "grass" (דשא) in the desolate land (38:27). One could read here an
allusion to Gen 1:11–12, where this relatively uncommon root is used three times to describe
the moment of creation when the dry land first produces vegetation. The sprouting of vegetation
in the desolate land of Job can be read as a repetition of that initial act of creation.

God's providence is evident in his care for the wild animals as well. The divine catalog of animals is introduced by reference to their search for sustenance:

> Have you hunted prey for the lioness?
> Have you filled the appetite of the young lions,
> When they crouch in dens,
>   when they lie in a thicket as a lair?
> Who provides for the raven his food
>   when his young ones cry to God for help,
>   and wander about for lack of food? (Job 38:39–41)

Though cast in the form of questions, the implication here is clear: it is God who provides for the lion and the raven.[26] It is God, in the subsequent verses, who sets the wild ass free and gives the horse strength. It is God who causes the hawk and the eagle to soar. It is God who made Behemoth and Leviathan, and only God who can control them.[27]

God says of Leviathan (the last and the greatest of the creatures in the divine speeches) that its eyes are like the "eyelids of the dawn" (עַפְעַפֵּי־שָׁחַר) (Job 41:10). Only one other verse in the Hebrew Bible includes this phrase: Job's wish in his first lament that the night of his conception would not see the "eyelids of the dawn" (Job 3:9). Job also calls on those who "rouse (עֹרֵר) Leviathan" to curse the night of his conception. God says no one is so fierce as to dare to rouse (עוּר) Leviathan.[28] God challenges the audacity of Job's wished "un-creation" by showing him the awe-inspiring majesty of creation and the untamable power of the creatures that inhabit it. Job cannot darken

---

[26] For similar motifs of animals looking to God for sustenance, see Joel 1:20; Ps 104:21, 27–28; 145:15–16; and 147:9, which speaks specifically of the raven and its young.

[27] Job 39:5, 19; 40:15, 19; 41:2–3. For the translation of 41:2–3 that asserts God's mastery of Leviathan, see the appendix.

[28] Job 3:8; 41:2. See Pope, 30, for a discussion of the parallel expression in 3:8a. Pope relates the idea of day/sea-cursers to similar images drawn from ANE myths like the Ugaritic Baal cycle, where the god Koshar pronounces incantations over Baal's weapons so that they might be more effective in fighting Yamm. Cf. Tur-Sinai, 56–58, who reads 3:8b as "the heroes that Leviathan awoke." Tur-Sinai argues that the reference here instead is to a myth in which Leviathan calls on dead "king-heroes" to awaken and help him fight God. While such a reading is possible, the parallel expression in 41:2 would seem to argue for the translation given here. Tur-Sinai overcomes this objection by making God, rather than Leviathan, the object of the verb עוּר in 41:2 (567). In both verses, the reference seems to be to an ANE myth. See Rowold, who also considers 41:2 to be an answer to 3:8. [Henry Rowold, "הוּא! מִי הוּא? לִי : Leviathan and Job in Job 41:2–3," *JBL* 105 (1986) 104–9].

the "eyelids of the dawn"; neither can he hope to control Leviathan, whose eyes are as bright as the "eyelids of the dawn."

The questions God asks Job are designed to put Job in his place, to make him understand that not he, but God, is in control of creation. Job has already acknowledged as much, however, in the dialogue.[29] Perhaps more importantly, God's questions also show Job the order God has built into creation and the care with which God provides for it. Job had tried metaphorically to annihilate creation, and here, in a direct response to that attempt, God uses some of Job's own words and phrases to show that he cannot negate creation. God has established creation and continues to provide for it. In the divine speeches, Job's "un-creation" is abrogated.

There are a number of verbal and thematic connections between the divine speeches and earlier passages in the book of Job. Alter sees the strongest connections between the first divine speech and Job's lament in chapter 3.[30] Newsom, in contrast, understands the divine speeches to be a direct response to Job's final speech in chapters 29–31.[31] These approaches need not be isolated: the divine speeches in fact address *both* speeches by Job, but they also respond to the book of Job as a whole, including speeches by characters other than Job. One particular lexical connection, for instance, links the prologue, Job's first lament, and the divine speeches.

The word in question is the relatively rare term שׂוּךְ/סוּךְ, with the meaning "to fence in." As we have already noted, this term appears first in the prologue and again in Job's first lament. In the prologue the Satan claims that God has put a protective "fence" around Job and all that he possesses (Job 1:10).[32] Then, in Job's first lament, he claims that God has "fenced" him in so that he cannot see or act meaningfully (Job 3:23). Finally, God himself uses the term, saying that he "shut in" (סוּךְ) the Sea with doors when it came gushing out of the womb (Job 38:8).

These three occurrences of the word שׂוּךְ/סוּךְ illustrate three different understandings of creation and of the order God places within creation.

[29] Job 9:1–24; 12:7–25; 26:5–14

[30] "These first thirty-seven verses of God's response to Job constitute a brilliantly pointed reversal, in structure, image, and theme, of that initial poem of Job's" (Alter, 96). Alter compares the divine speeches with other parts of the book of Job, as well, but spends most of his time connecting chapters 3 and 38, an admittedly very strong connection.

[31] "[T]he speech by Job and the speech by God stand over against each other somewhat like the facing panels in a diptych" (Newsom, *Moral Imaginations*, 239).

[32] See discussion of שׂוּךְ/סוּךְ and its first two uses in Job above in chapter one.

The Satan claims that the world is ordered in such a way that those who are righteous are protected from anything dangerous. In fact, the Satan argues that people are righteous precisely because of this promised protection. "Does Job fear God for nothing?" asks the Satan, a key question in this book full of questions (Job 1:9). There can be no such thing as disinterested piety, according to the Satan, because the world is ordered in such a way that piety is always rewarded with protection and prosperity. The friends' understanding of creation has affinities with this view; hence, their need to find some fault in Job in order to explain his suffering. Job, in contrast, finds in his first lament no perceptible order in the world, certainly nothing like the protective fence that the Satan describes. Creation for Job has descended into chaos. The fence that he describes in his lament is not a protective one, but a restrictive one. Job argues that God is inordinately concerned with him and fences him in. Any order Job perceives in creation is a capricious and cruel one, where the righteous are oppressed and the wicked allowed free rein.

Such are the two views of creation expressed by the first two uses of the word שׂוּךְ/סוּךְ. The third and final occurrence of the word is put in the mouth of God, and this last occurrence calls into question the two previous views. God, too, speaks about limits and fences, but God shifts the object and the scope of the term. From the divine perspective, God is not concerned with setting boundaries (protective or restrictive) around Job or any other human being; instead, God speaks of "shutting in" the Sea with bars and doors. There is a tension in that act, and it is crucial for understanding the view of creation presented here to understand that tension. As Janzen observes, God limits the Sea and Leviathan, but he also gives them a place in the created order.

> All systematic attempts to read existence . . . according to a principle of justice involving strict recompense or retribution break themselves against the fact that the sea is given a place in the cosmos. All attempts to exegete the Book of Job in such a way as to arrive at the conclusion that God there is indifferent to matters of justice overlook the fact that the place of the sea in the cosmos is delimited by divine decree. (235)

Boundaries are set; the forces of chaos are not allowed free course over the world. These boundaries, however, do not exclude all things wild and dangerous.[33] The Sea, understood mythically as a force of chaos, is given a place in creation, but it is also given limits: "Thus far you shall come, and no further." Leviathan, too, is given a place in creation, but he is subject to God. Even the Satan, while given a place in the heavenly court, must work within the limits God imposes—he may afflict Job but he may not take his life (Job 1:12; 2:6).[34]

In the divine speeches God does not answer Job's questions about why he is in such dire straits. God does, though, answer Job's accusations about God's rule of creation. God's creation is neither what the Satan imagines it to be nor what Job believes it to be. God's creation is an ordered world under God's rule. Nevertheless, in that creation God makes a place for wild forces that are indifferent towards, and therefore dangerous to, human beings. As Fretheim notes,

> [I]mages of wildness and strangeness are present, including the wild seas, wild animals, wild weather (rain, hail, ice, snow, lightning), the uncertainties of the night, and Behemoth and Leviathan. . . . For all the world's order and coherence, it doesn't run like a machine; a certain randomness, ambiguity, unpredictability, and play characterize its complex life. (239)[35]

---

[33] Alter expresses a similar view of the use of שׁוּך/סוּך in the divine speeches. He identifies the word with תְּסֻכֵּנִי. ("You sheltered me/wove me in my mother's belly"), in Ps 139:13, and writes, "[T]he word carries after it a long train of associations having to do with protection and nurture, so that the negative sense of the verb in Chapter 3 is in a way combined with the positive sense in which the frame-story uses it. What results is a virtual oxymoron, expressing a paradoxical feeling that God's creation involves a necessary holding in check of destructive forces and a sustaining of those same forces because they are also forces of life" (Alter, 100). While I think the verb used in Ps 139 is the related סֹכַך ("to weave together, to screen"), Alter's conclusions about the use of שׁוּך/סוּך in Job are certainly correct. Newsom has a similar interpretation of the birth of the Sea: "Here the chaotic waters of the sea are represented not only as the object of divine limitation but also of divine care" (Newsom, *Moral Imaginations*, 244).

[34] The Satan figure in Job is not, of course, the full-fledged demonic character that he becomes in later writings. He is something of a prosecuting attorney, part of God's heavenly court and so part of God's ordering of the world. He is not, therefore, a force of chaos like the Sea or Leviathan. Nonetheless, the effect of his actions on Job is to plunge the latter's world into chaos.

[35] Fretheim offers an insightful discussion about the divine speeches, and makes a strong case for the fact that "the speeches do in fact speak to Job in his suffering and about his suffering" (234).

It is noteworthy that God seems to take delight precisely in those forces and beings not under human control: the Sea, the snow and rain, the wild animals, Behemoth and Leviathan. They have a beauty in the divine speeches that is intrinsically tied to their wildness—yet they are still subject to God. In this view of creation, the world is not a "safe" place for human beings, but it is an ordered place. Again, the chaos into which Job sought to plunge the world in his first lament is negated and God's ordering of the cosmos is reaffirmed.

Procreation

Job rhetorically "un-creates" the world in his first lament as a means of negating his own existence. His is such extreme distress that he wishes not just for death but that he had never been born in the first place. Job's lament in chapter 3, then, is both an attack on creation and an attack on the power of procreation. As we have seen already, this motif of procreation comes up again and again in the book of Job, both in the prologue and in the dialogue.[36] It is not surprising, then, that the motif of procreation also permeates the divine speeches. It appears particularly in the first of those speeches, where fecundity is ascribed not just to the wild animals but also to entities not usually associated with conception and birth.[37]

Procreation language appears first in the divine speeches in the startling image of the birth of the Sea:

> Who fenced in the Sea with doors
>   when it came gushing out of the womb,
> When I made a cloud its clothing
>   and thick darkness its swaddling clothes? (Job 38:8–9)

Usually understood in biblical and other ancient Near Eastern texts as a primordial force of chaos, the Sea here is instead a boisterous infant.[38] The myth of the divine warrior defeating the Sea (or the sea monster) had been

---

[36] See the extended discussion of the motif of procreation in chapter one.

[37] Alter sees the metaphorical use of procreation images in the first divine speech as a deliberate shaping device of the poet, clear evidence that "the poem in Chapter 38 was purposefully articulated as a grand reversal of the poem in Chapter 3" (Alter, 99). He discusses the theme of procreation in the divine speeches at length, 99–104.

[38] See the discussion of a possible allusion to an alternate myth of creation in the appendix on 38:28–30.

evoked by Job in a few of his earlier speeches.[39] If this myth plays a part in the divine speeches, however, it is far in the background. God here is not a divine warrior violently suppressing the chaos monster Sea. Instead, God acts as a cosmic midwife, attending the birth of the Sea, wrapping it in clouds as swaddling bands.[40] The Sea is not the enemy in the divine speeches as it is in earlier parts of Job; rather, it is a life force, gushing out of the primordial womb. The image is immensely positive: God as midwife tenderly attending the birth of the Sea, full of life and vigor. The boundaries God puts on the Sea are envisioned as swaddling bands, protecting the infant from hurting itself or others.

The divine speeches move from cosmology to meteorology, and God uses birth imagery more conventionally in a challenge to Job:

> Which is the way to the dwelling place of light,
>   and where is the place of darkness?
> You know, for you were born then,
>   and the number of your days is great! (Job 38:19–21)[41]

This challenge of God's relies partly, of course, on the commonplace notion that wisdom comes with age, as Bildad asserted earlier in the book (Job 8:8–10).[42] The challenge also implies a comparison between Job and God that will become more explicit in chapter 40, where God challenges Job to acquire divine attributes.

The use of procreation imagery continues in the divine speeches with something that sounds like a riddle. God asks Job:

> Does the rain have a father,
>   or who begot the drops of dew?
> From whose womb has the ice come forth?
>   and who bore the hoarfrost of heaven? (Job 38:28–29)

---

[39] Job 7:12; 9:8, 13; 26:12–13

[40] Note the use of עָנָן/עֲנָנָה ("clouds") in 3:5 and 38:9. Job wants clouds and darkness to act as a sort of anti-life-force, to claim the day of his birth. God, by contrast, uses clouds to contain and nurture the essential life-force of the Sea at its birth.

[41] In an earlier speech, Eliphaz had sarcastically called Job the "firstborn of humanity" (Job 15:7). Such a designation of Job by Eliphaz and God, whether sarcastic or not, portrays him as a type of Urmensch. Thanks to Prof. Jon D. Levenson for this observation. See Ezek 28:11–19 for a parallel Urmensch image used of the king of Tyre.

[42] Elihu refers to this belief, but then refutes it in 32:6–9. Though he is "young," he will speak more wisdom than the older friends of Job.

Again, the use of procreation images in these verses is startling. While rain and dew may connote fecundity, ice and frost are sterile, frozen entities not usually associated with begetting and birth. Though most of the questions of the divine speeches evoke the answer, "God has done all these things," these verses do not elicit that response. It makes little sense to say that God is the "father" of the rain or the "mother" of the ice, though God is, of course, the creator and the source of both.[43] Alter sees here a sort of riddle: "[N]o one is the father of the rain, but the rain is the father of life."[44] In other words, God is alluding in these verses to the generative power of water in the arid Near Eastern climate. Such an interpretation fits nicely with the verses immediately preceding these: God sends rain on the wilderness and causes the desolate land to sprout vegetation. This meteorological section of the divine speeches is brimming with allusions to water: snow, hail, rain, dew, ice, rain clouds, "the water bottles of heaven." Particularly in an arid land, water is the essential source of life. It is appropriate, then, that water imagery should be joined with procreation imagery in these verses; both affirm the ongoing, self-renewing power of life.[45]

The divine speeches move from the subject of meteorology to that of zoology at the end of chapter 38, and the motif of procreation continues to appear. In this zoological section of the divine speeches, however, the use of procreation images ceases to be metaphorical and becomes quite literal:

[43] Gregory Vall (" 'From Whose Womb Did the Ice Come Forth': Procreation Images in Job 38:28–29," *CBQ* 57 (1995) 504–13) argues that the answer sought by these questions is, "No, the rain does not have a father. God is the source of the rain." The point of these verses, according to Vall, is to distance Israel's God from the nature deities of the ancient Near East. Though Vall could be correct, Alter's interpretation (see below) seems to me more pertinent to the context of the divine speeches.

[44] Alter, 101. Alter offers an insightful analysis of these poetic lines and the ones following. The movement is from father to mother, from fluid to solid. "The tension of opposites that is at the heart of God's vision of the world is strongly felt here: fluid and stone-hard solid, white-frozen surface and watery depths."

[45] See Michael Welker, *Creation and Reality* (trans. John F. Hoffmeyer; Minneapolis: Augsburg Fortress, 1999) 6–20. Welker offers a reading of Gen 1 that emphasizes the participation of creatures in creation. The created world, in Welker's interpretation, is not simply acted upon by God, but itself *participates* in the act of creation. The stars, sun, and moon separate day from night and provide structure to time (Gen 1:14); the earth brings forth vegetation (1:11–12); the waters and the earth produce creatures (1:20, 24); the creatures reproduce themselves (1:22). The divine speeches paint the same picture of creation, especially with their emphasis on procreation; both meteorological forces and animals continue the ongoing act of creation, fructifying the earth and bearing offspring.

Who gives to the raven its food,
  when its young cry to God
  and wander around for lack of food?
Do you know the time the mountain goats give birth?
  Have you observed the calving of the hinds?
Do you count the months they fulfill?
  Do you know the time of their delivery?
They crouch, bringing forth their young,
  delivering their offspring.
Their young grow strong. They grow up in the open field
  They go forth and do not return to them. (Job 38:41–39:4)

God provides for both the raven and its young. This picture of the raven is mirrored at the end of the zoological section by a similar description of the eagle, who lives on cliffs and feeds its young on the blood of the slain (Job 39:27–30). These descriptions of birds of prey form the frame for the rest of the zoological section, and the mention of the birds' offspring in both instances emphasizes the importance of procreation in the whole section.

God knows the reproductive cycle of the mountain goat and the deer. God paints a picture for Job of the latter, describing both gestation and the moment of birth. Alter connects verse 2, "Do you count the months they fulfill?" (תספר ירחים תמלאנה) with the related phrase in 3:6, "Let it not come into the number of months" (במספר ירחים אל־יבא). Again, the divine speeches answer Job's maledictions in chapter 3. Job had wished that the night of his conception be obliterated from the calendar. God shows Job instead "how time becomes a medium of fruition under the watchful gaze of the divine maker of natural order."[46] Job's concern was with his own conception and birth; God speaks instead of the gestation and birth of the deer. Job tried to eliminate a day and a night from the calendar; God shows him that the cycle of day and night cannot be stopped and that life itself continues in ways beyond Job's imagination.

At the risk of using an argument from silence, I want to suggest something more about these procreation images in the first divine speech. Given the picture of Job in the prologue, one can assume that Job in his former life was never all that interested in the birth of wild animals. The Job of the prologue would have been far more concerned with the fecundity of his domestic animals. The life cycle of the mountain goat and deer were outside the boundaries of his world and of his attention. When trouble came, Job's

---

[46] Alter, 103.

world became even smaller, in a sense. He withdrew into his own suffering and wished the world to disappear into darkness. In the divine speeches God expands Job's vision of the cosmos by drawing his attention both to cosmic events like the "birth" of the Sea and to everyday events, which are nevertheless still outside the purview of human existence, like the birth of mountain goats.

It must be noted that not all the animals in the divine catalog are ideal parents. The ostrich is portrayed as a careless parent. She leaves her eggs on the ground, to be warmed in the dust, forgetting that they might get crushed. She is, in this respect, "the comic-book anti-type to Job's own anxious style of parenting," exemplified by his "preemptive sacrifices" for his children in the prologue.[47] The ostrich is a careless parent because God has made her forget "wisdom" (חכמה) and has given her no part in "understanding" (בינה) (Job 39:17).[48] Nevertheless, her young survive through God's providence and she is given other remarkable attributes. When she "wings up on high," she laughs scornfully at the horse and its rider (Job 39:18).

[47] Ellen F. Davis, *Getting Involved with God: Rediscovering the Old Testament* (Cambridge, Mass.: Cowley, 2001) 137–38. This issue of Job as parent will be discussed more fully in the next chapter.

[48] Both words (חכמה and בינה) are used extensively in biblical wisdom literature. The word חכמה, in particular, has already played a significant part in the preceding chapters of the book of Job. Eliphaz proclaims that human beings have a short, miserable existence, then die devoid of wisdom, while Zophar wishes that God would show Job wisdom. Job himself doubts the common adage that wisdom is with the aged and affirms that wisdom (חכמה) and understanding (תבונה) are found with God. Job and his friends mock each other's claims to wisdom (Job 4:21; 11:6; 12:2, 12–13; 13:5; 15:8; 26:3). The whole of chapter 28, of course, is taken up with the search for wisdom, which proves fruitless until the last verse: "The fear of the Lord, that is wisdom (חכמה), and to turn from evil is understanding (בינה)" (Job 28:28). Finally, Elihu expresses disdain at the older participants' lack of wisdom and pompously declares that he will teach it to them (Job 32:7, 13; 33:33).

    Wisdom and understanding in the divine speeches are gifts of God, as is everything else in creation. The participants in the poetic dialogue would agree with such a statement. The beings to whom God gives wisdom, however, are unexpected. Contrary to the well-known adage in 28:28, there is no mention in the divine speeches of human beings, whether God-fearing or not, acquiring wisdom. To the contrary, God mocks Job's attempts at wisdom and understanding (Job 38:2, 4; 39:26). Instead, God sets wisdom and understanding in the firmament, and numbers the clouds with wisdom (Job 38:36–37). God makes the hawk soar but withholds both wisdom and understanding from the ostrich (Job 38:17, 26). Wisdom and understanding, usually associated in biblical wisdom literature with God and with pious human beings, become in the divine speeches attributes which God instills not in human beings, but in creation itself.

The theme of procreation permeates the first divine speech, appearing in its discussions of cosmology, meteorology, and zoology. In contrast, the second divine speech does not include many references to procreation. This is to be expected, as Behemoth and Leviathan (unique, mythological figures that they are) do not bear or raise young, as do normal animals. Nevertheless, it is worth noting that part of the description of Behemoth has to do with its procreative powers:

> Behold now, his strength in his loins,
> and his power in the muscles of his belly.
> He stiffens his tail like a cedar.
> The sinews of his thighs are knit together. (Job 40:16–17)[49]

Though Behemoth is a singular creature, formed by God at the beginning of time, it seems that he at least potentially has the power to beget young, like the animals described in the first divine speech.

The use of the motif of procreation in the divine speeches continues its use in the preceding chapters of Job. Its use in the divine speeches, however, contrasts sharply with its function in the prologue and poetic dialogue. In the prologue fecundity is used as evidence of blessing in Job's life. In the dialogue it serves much the same purpose, though Job asserts that God blesses the wicked, not the righteous, with the gift of children. In the divine speeches, by contrast, the language of procreation is used to speak not of God's blessing or punishment of *human beings*, but of the ongoing, inexorable life-force instilled in *creation*. The Sea comes gushing out of the womb; the rain fructifies even the barren wilderness. The wild animals, even the foolish ostrich, bear and care for their young. These wild animals and their offspring, unlike their domestic cousins, are of no use to human beings. Their offspring will not increase humanity's wealth. Indeed, they raise their young sometimes at the expense of human beings, as the eagle's offspring drink the blood of slain warriors (Job 39:30).[50] Procreation, according to the divine speeches,

---

[49] Many commentators, including Pope and Habel, attribute sexual connotations to verse 17, which is variously translated, "It makes its tail stiff like a cedar" (NRSV); "His tail arches like a cedar" (Pope); "When erect his tail is like a cedar" (Habel). The sexual allusion seems probable and adds to the presence of the procreation theme in the second divine speech.

[50] The "slain" (חללים) refer always in the Bible to human beings, usually those killed in battle. Given the previous reference to battle in the description of the war horse, such is surely the interpretation here.

does not have to do simply with blessing humanity. It is more fundamental and more universal than Job or his friends imagine.

The use of procreation images in the divine speeches also has much to do with God's answer to Job's challenge concerning the fact of his own birth. In his first lament Job wishes not just that he were dead, but that he had never been given life in the first place. It is a serious challenge to One in whose hand is the life and breath of every living being (Job 12:10). God answers that challenge in the divine speeches by reasserting the power of fecundity in his descriptions of the Sea, the rain, and the wild animals. Even the mythological beast Behemoth is described in terms of its capacity to reproduce. God does not let Job's challenge go unanswered. Job cannot annihilate creation. Neither can he stop the powerful, life-affirming force of procreation. "Reproduction and nurturing are the very essence of a constantly self-renewing creation as the poet imagines it."[51] God not only establishes creation; God also ensures, through the powerful force of procreation, that life will continue.

What Is Humanity?

The question, "What is humanity?" (מה אנוש), asked by both Job and Eliphaz, was a useful one to ask in exploring the views of creation contained in the first 37 chapters of Job.[52] Though that particular question does not appear in the divine speeches, God addresses to Job a number of related questions. God first asks Job: "Who is this (מי זה) that darkens counsel with words lacking knowledge?" (Job 38:2). It is at once a question of identity and an implied statement designed to put Job in his place. The later questions are similar: Where were you when x was created/occurred? Are you able to do x? Who has done all these things? On the most obvious level, the questions highlight the vast difference between God and Job: Who does Job think he is to challenge or question God? On another level, the questions could be read as asking Job to consider his own position vis-à-vis God and God's creation: Who does Job think he is in relation to the rest of the creation? In other words, "What is humanity?"

The divine speeches may not at first appear to answer this question. Humanity has almost no place in God's description of creation. Human beings appear only as creatures peripheral to the world God describes. They

[51] Alter, 103.
[52] See Job 7:17; 15:14 and discussion above in chapter one.

are largely absent from the divine speeches, except for their occasional appearance as objects of scorn or judgment.[53] Indeed, it is noteworthy that the word אֱנוֹשׁ ("man/humanity") does not appear in the divine speeches, while the related words אִישׁ and אָדָם are used only once each, in Job 38:26, where God describes sending rain on the wilderness, which is devoid of human beings.[54] Likewise, the word גֶּבֶר ("man") is used by God only twice: "Gird up your loins like a man. I will question you and you declare to me" (Job 38:3; 40:7).[55] In contrast, all four words are used numerous times in the rest of the book of Job.[56] The human interlocutors are greatly concerned with humanity although they disagree as to what is essential about human nature. The three companions emphasize humanity's innate depravity, evidenced by human mortality, while Job appeals to God to leave him alone precisely because he is mortal.[57]

Given the primary importance accorded to humanity by all the human participants in the dialogue, it is all the more striking that human beings have little or no place in the portrait of creation contained in the divine speeches.[58] God describes the establishment of the earth and the meteorological forces, and one expects that humanity has little part in such events. When the

---

[53] Dawn shakes "the wicked" out of the earth; the wild ass mocks the tumult of the city; the ostrich is faster than the horse and its rider; the eagle drinks up the blood of "the slain"; God challenges Job to abase "the proud"; traders and merchants have no hope of capturing Leviathan (Job 38:13; 39:7, 18, 30; 40:11–13, 30).

[54] The word אִישׁ also appears in 41:9, where it refers to the scales of Leviathan, clinging one to another.

[55] Alter connects these verses with 3:3 and considers the use of גֶּבֶר in all three instances further evidence that chapter 38 is a direct response to chapter 3: "It is as though God were implying: you called yourself man, géver, now gird up your loins like a man and see if you can face the truth" (97).

[56] Job 3:3, 23; 4:13, 17; 5:7, 17; 7:1, 17; 9:32; 10:5; 11:2, 12; 14:1, 10, 12; 15:14; 17:4; 25:4, 6. This is by no means an exhaustive list. All four words appear often throughout the book of Job, except in the divine speeches.

[57] See the discussion in chapter one.

[58] James Crenshaw is one of a handful of scholars who discusses this point at some length. He notes the "virtual silence about humankind" in the divine speeches and argues that the speeches constitute a "radical criticism of the anthropocentric presupposition of ancient sages" ["When Form and Content Clash: The Theology of Job 38:1–40:5," in *Creation in the Biblical Traditions* (ed. Richard J. Clifford and John J. Collins; Washington, D.C.: Catholic Biblical Association, 1992) 80]. Crenshaw notes that most scholars tend to concentrate more on the "radical challenge" that the rest of the book poses to the traditional understanding of retributive justice.

Almighty moves on to describing the creatures of the earth, however, one would expect some mention of humanity. After all, in a similar list of creatures in Psalm 104, human beings are listed right between cattle and trees and again between lions and sea creatures (Ps 104:14–15, 23). The divine speeches, in contrast, do not include human beings in the catalog of earth's creatures.

The divine speeches underscore the relative insignificance of human beings by pointedly implying that humanity is not the center of creation:

> Who has made a trench for the flood,
>   and a way for the thunderbolt;
> To make it rain on an uninhabited land
>   (land-with-no-man ארץ־לא־איש)
> The wilderness where no person lives
>   (wilderness-with-no-person-in-it מדבר־לא־אדם בו)
>   (Job 38:25–26)

The passage emphasizes that the elements are not meant to be servants of humanity; God sends the rain to make the desolate land sprout grass, to bring forth life even in the wilderness where no human being lives. This pronouncement stands in contrast to Elihu's statement that God provides rain abundantly *to human beings* (Job 36:28). While the two statements are not necessarily in conflict, the one in the divine speeches could be understood to "correct" the other, to make it more accurate. Yes, God provides rain to human beings, but God also provides rain to a land unused and unusable by human beings, a land Job has already rejected as worthless and God-forsaken.[59]

The divine speeches are radically nonanthropocentric. They reinforce this theme by using words and images from earlier chapters of the book to compare Job with creation itself. For instance, Job has used the metaphor of rain (מטר) to speak of his importance among people; God counters that he sends rain (להמטיר) "on a land where there is no man, the wilderness in which no person lives" (Job 29:23; 38:26). Likewise, God describes the גאון ("pride") of the waves of the sea and the הוד ("glory") of the horse; he later challenges Job to clothe himself with גאון and הוד (Job 38:11; 39:20; 40:10).[60]

The most persistent comparison between Job and the other creatures of creation has to do with the recurrent use of the word שחק ("to smile, to mock,

---

[59] See Job 30:3 and 38:27. See also the discussion in the appendix on 38:24–27.

[60] Brown lists other parallels between Job and the animals of creation: "Job finds himself mysteriously mirrored in creation and creation mysteriously mirrored in himself. Yahweh has turned Job's declaration of independence into one of interdependence" (Brown, *Character in Crisis*, 107). See 104–5 for parallels between Job and Behemoth.

to laugh"). The word first appears when Eliphaz promises Job that God will restore him and he will "laugh at devastation and famine"; and more, that he will not fear "the wild animals of the earth" (Job 5:22). Job then uses the word שׂחק twice in his final speech. First he recalls how in former days he "smiled" or "laughed" at his neighbors, the same ones who waited for his word as eagerly as they awaited rain, those among whom he sat as "king." The verb here seems to imply both beneficence and superiority. A few verses later, he contrasts that memory with his current situation, where the outcasts of society now "laugh" at him; the connotation being one of mockery (Job 29:23–25; 30:1). The tables are turned, and Job is now the object of mocking laughter.

The divine speeches use the word שׂחק six times. Contrary to Eliphaz's promise, however, it is not Job who "laughs." In fact, it is not human beings at all (whether elders or outcasts) who laugh. Instead, it is the wild animals of Eliphaz's vision who "laugh" scornfully at humanity and at humanity's inventions. As the wild ass roams across the open country, it laughs at the tumult of the city, that quintessential human habitation. God has "set it free" from any human restraint so it "does not hear the shouts of the taskmaster" (תשׁאות נוגשׂ לא ישׁמע: Job 39:5, 7). The latter phrase echoes Job's earlier statement that prisoners in the grave "do not hear the voice of the taskmaster" (לא שׁמעו קול נגשׂ: Job 3:18).[61] The use of שׂחק continues with the description of the ostrich, which "laughs" at the horse and its rider. The war horse itself "laughs" at fear in the midst of battle. And Leviathan, that fiercest of all creatures, "laughs" at feeble human weapons that bounce off its impenetrable skin.[62] In each instance, the word denotes the attitude of a superior to an inferior. In his own representation of his situation, Job perceives that he has traded positions with the outcasts of society and become the object of their scorn. In the case of the divine speeches, the animals are the ones in the position of superiority over against the human beings who try to control them. At the least, it can be said that these creatures are not in any way subject to humanity. God emphasizes this point by challenging Job to "laugh" at or

---

[61] These two verses are the only ones in Job where the word נגשׂ is used. Freedom is found not in death, according to the divine speeches, but in the living, wild creatures of the earth and in creation itself.

[62] Job 39:7, 18, 22; 41:21. The word שׂחק is used also in 40:20, where the wild beasts "play" or "laugh" in the wilderness.

"play" with (שׂחק) Leviathan as he would a bird, an incomprehensible act given the awesome power of the sea monster (Job 40:29).[63]

All these wild creatures know what Job has not understood: humanity is only one part of creation and perhaps not even the most important part. Human beings do not control the wild animals and cannot use them for their own purposes. None of the animals listed (with the exception of the war horse) are of any use to humanity; and, as Davis says, the war horse is the exception that proves the rule.[64] Even in the case of the war horse, human beings can use its innate fierceness for their purposes, but they cannot master it. The horse delights mightily in human conflict and facilitates the killing of human beings by other human beings. In a more explicit example, the wild donkey and the wild ox, unlike their domestic counterparts, are of no use whatsoever to humanity. The wild donkey does not "hear the shouts of the taskmaster," and the wild ox will certainly not serve humanity by plowing or bringing in the harvest. In the same vein, in a satirical set of questions, God lists ways in which Job might make use of Leviathan: Will Leviathan submit to being Job's servant? Will Job play with him or leash him for his children? Will traders or merchants divide him up like a fish? (Job 39:7, 9–12; 40:28–30). All the ways in which human beings make use of animals—as beasts of burden, as pets, as food—are ludicrous when applied to that fiercest of creatures, Leviathan. The divine speeches assert repeatedly that humanity does not have dominion over the wild animals and cannot make use of them. Indeed, humanity is often the object of their scorn (שׂחק).

William Brown shows how the vision of creation portrayed in the divine speeches contrasts sharply with a common motif found in ancient Near Eastern royal inscriptions.[65] In the latter wild animals are appropriated as symbols of the king's power and/or portrayed as enemies to be hunted. "[T]he

---

[63] The poet appears to be echoing Ps 104:26, where God "plays" or "sports" with Leviathan (Leviathan is named in only five biblical passages, including these two). Both verses use שׂחק in the Piel, with the prepositional phrase בּ (in contrast, every other occurrence of the verb in Job uses the prepositions ל, אל, or על). Because of the use of the prepositional phrase בּ and the context, the translation "sport with" or "play with" is preferable to "laugh" in Job 40:29 and Ps 104:26. For the possibility that Psalm 104 is the "intentional foil" for the divine speeches, see Carol Newsom, "The Book of Job: Introduction, Commentary, and Reflections," *The New Interpreter's Bible* (12 vols.; Nashville: Abingdon, 1996) 4:596–97.

[64] Davis, *Getting Involved*, 137

[65] Brown, *Ethos of the Cosmos*, 350–60. In this work, Brown builds on and adds nuance to the work of Keel in *Jahwes Entgegnung an Ijob*. Keel uses iconography rather than inscriptions in his study.

predators of chaos," notes Brown, "were turned into instruments of human hegemony, conscripted into the arsenal of royal propaganda."[66] By contrast, in the divine speeches the wild animals serve no human purpose and are celebrated as "icons of freedom and dignity."[67]

YHWH's second speech continues to compare Job with creation in the form of the two creatures Behemoth and Leviathan.[68] The first statement about Behemoth is this: "Look at Behemoth, which I made with you" (הנה־נא בהמות אשר־עשׂיתי עמך) (Job 40:15).[69] Though it is not completely clear what is meant by the comparison between Job and Behemoth, the statement implies at least one clear affinity between the two: the same Creator made them both. In the dialogue, Job twice espoused an egalitarianism among human beings, based both on their common mortality and on their common Creator. In his initial lament Job wished that he were in the grave, where slaves are free from their masters, where king and slave dwell together (Job 3:19). Likewise, in his last speech Job affirmed that he and his slaves were made by the same Creator and therefore he had to treat them justly (Job 31:15).[70]

The divine speech espouses an egalitarianism more radical than either of the above instances. Job had put himself on the same level as other human beings; God puts Job on the same level as one of the nonhuman creatures. Not only is Job incapable of controlling or using Behemoth; he may in fact have no greater importance than the wild beast in the sight of the God who made them both!

God's further description of Behemoth and Leviathan continues the comparison between Job and these two mythological beasts, and Job comes out of that comparison looking inferior. Job had asked of God in the dialogue, "Is my strength the strength of stones (אבנים)? Is my flesh bronze (נחושׁ)?" He wants God to acknowledge his human frailty so that God will leave him alone. In the divine speeches, God does, in fact, highlight Job's lack of power and knowledge, but the Almighty may be adding insult to injury when he

---

[66] Brown, *Ethos of the Cosmos*, 360.

[67] Ibid., 366.

[68] Note Brown's list of parallels between Job and the creatures of the divine speeches (Ibid., 373).

[69] The prepositional phrase עמך could, of course, be translated many different ways, "at the same time as you"; "along with you"; "in the same way as you." Whatever the translation, the verse implies some sort of affinity or similarity between Job and Behemoth.

[70] See Fohrer, *Studien zum Buche Hiob*, 87–88. Fohrer discusses this connection between creation faith and justice towards one's fellow human beings.

says that it is Behemoth's bones that are of bronze (נחושה) and Leviathan's heart like stone (אבן).[71]

Eliphaz sarcastically had asked Job whether he was the "firstborn" of humanity: "Are you the first (ראישׁון) man born? Were you brought forth before the hills (לפני גבעות חוללת)?" (Job 15:7). In a similar phrase, God affirms that it is Behemoth—not Job—who is the "first of God's ways (ראשׁית דרכי־אל)" (Job 40:19).[72] Eliphaz's statement indicates a temporal priority. God's could be taken as either temporal or qualitative.[73] In either case, Job is given the subordinate position as compared to Behemoth. The two statements, however, are connected not only in their use of the related words ראישׁון and ראשׁית but also in their echoes of the self-description offered by Woman Wisdom in Proverbs 8. With just a change in the pronominal suffix from second to first person, Eliphaz's question of Job is a direct quotation of Proverbs 8:25, where Woman Wisdom proclaims, "I was brought forth before the hills (לפני גבעות חוללתי)." Again, when God proclaims that Behemoth is the "first of God's ways," he is echoing the beginning of Wisdom's speech in Proverbs 8:22: "YHWH created me the first of his ways (ראשׁית דרכו)."[74] Both Job and Behemoth, then, are compared subtly to Woman Wisdom. The comparison of Behemoth with Wisdom is favorable; he is the "first of God's ways" just as she is. Job, though, is found wanting.

---

[71] Job 6:12; 40:18; 41:16.

[72] Ellen Davis translates this phrase, "the best thing I ever did," a colloquial translation that aptly captures the tone of God's speech. God is proud of Behemoth (Davis, *Getting Involved*, 138).

[73] Gammie argues that this phrase in 40:19 (ראשׁית דרכי־אל) is related to the phrase קצות דרכו in 26:14, and should be interpreted as meaning that Behemoth is the "prime object lesson" for Job in understanding God's glory (222). Such a reading is possible, but it is more likely that the reference is to a temporal priority, to be compared to Proverbs 8:22, where Wisdom is ראשׁית דרכו, in a context which appears to be temporal.

[74] Neither of these phrases occurs elsewhere in the Bible, which makes it probable that the poet of Job is quoting from Proverbs or vice versa . The dependency could run either way. As it is very difficult to ascribe a date either to Job or to Proverbs 1–9 [see Michael V. Fox, *Proverbs 1–9* (The Anchor Bible; London: Doubleday, 2000) 48–49], a strong case cannot be made either way. I favor the priority of Proverbs simply because the two phrases occur in the same passage there, whereas they are spoken by different characters in Job. It makes more sense to imagine the poet of Job quoting in a couple of instances from one passage he knows, rather than the author of Proverbs 8 combining two phrases from two disparate parts of the book of Job. Perhaps the phrases are best taken as evidence that Proverbs 8 and the book of Job are from about the same period in Israelite history. The issue of the dating of Job is taken up in the introduction.

Imposing as Behemoth is, the final, climactic place in the list of wild animals is given to Leviathan, that legendary sea monster.[75] Leviathan, in the last and longest description in the divine speeches, is portrayed as the most powerful, most formidable of all the animals. Though bearing some resemblance to the crocodile with its close-fitting scales and fearsome teeth, Leviathan also breathes fire, something no mere earthly animal can do (Job 41:6–13). His strength and invincibility surpass even that of Behemoth. The latter is described in terms of bronze and iron, while Leviathan "regards iron as straw and bronze as rotten wood" (Job 40:18; 41:19). Leviathan inspires fear in all who encounter him; no one "on earth" [literally, "on dust"] is his master. Only God is his master; only God can silence him (Job 41:1–4, 25).[76] The question God asks about Leviathan, מִי הוּא ("Who is he?"), recalls the first question he asks of Job, מִי זֶה ("Who is this?"). According to the book of Job and (in the case of Leviathan) ANE myth, both Job and Leviathan have challenged God, and according to the divine speeches, both belong to God: "Under the whole heaven, he is mine (לִי הוּא)!"[77]

God asks Job whether he can capture Leviathan as one would capture a fish, whether he can make use of it in any way. The suggestion of course is ludicrous, as even the gods are afraid of the sea monster. God challenges Job to "laugh" at or "play" (שׂחק) with Leviathan.[78] Again, the suggestion is absurd. Leviathan is not a pet, and he himself "laughs at" or "scorns" (שׂחק) all human weapons, which bounce off him like so much chaff (Job 41:21). God further asks Job whether Leviathan would be willing to "make a covenant" with him, to be "taken as a servant forever." Again, the question

---

[75] See the discussion of Leviathan's place in biblical and ANE texts in the appendix on 40:25.

[76] Though the translation of Job 41:1–4 is a matter of scholarly debate, I believe the passage refers to God's mastery of Leviathan. See the discussion of these verses in the appendix. Cf. Fretheim's statement: "[I]t is not helpful to suggest that these creatures [Behemoth and Leviathan] are fully within divine control; God has set creational limits (e.g., 38:8–11), but within those limits there is no sense of divine micromanagement" (Fretheim, *God and the World,* 235). While I do not think that the divine speeches portray God as a "micromanager," I argue that the passage in question (Job 41:1–4) does emphasize God's power over Leviathan. The phrase "on dust" [עַל־עָפָר] in verse 25 is, of course, best translated "on earth." Given the association of "dust" with mortality in Job, however, the allusion is probably also to those who are mortal. Again, only God, not mortals, is the master of Leviathan.

[77] Such is the interpretation of Rowold, "מִי הוּא? לִי הוּא!," 106–7.

[78] Job 40:25–41:1; 40:29. Cf. Ps 104:26, where God himself "plays" (שׂחק) with Leviathan. See discussion below.

stands in contrast to Eliphaz's earlier vision, in which Job's "covenant" will
be with the stones of the field and with "the wild animals of the field [who]
will be at peace" with him (Job 40:28; 5:23).[79] To the contrary, says God,
that fiercest of creatures, Leviathan, will not serve Job and will not make a
covenant with him. Neither, one may assume, will the other wild animals
be at peace with him.

Leviathan's abode is יָם ("the Sea") and תהום ("the Deep"). When it moves
through the waters, it makes them foam and boil, gilding the Deep with foam
(Job 41:23–24).[80] Leviathan's home is as fearsome as the sea monster himself.
God has already pointed out Job's inability to gain access to these entities:
"Have you come to the springs of Sea (יָם), or have you walked around in the
depth of the Deep (תהום)?" (Job 38:16). Job's answer is negative; Leviathan,
by contrast, makes the Deep boil. These verses about Leviathan's habitat are
the last and best example of a recurring theme in the divine speeches. God
repeatedly draws Job's attention to the inaccessibility of certain habitats to
human beings. Job cannot find the gates of death, the dwelling place of light
and darkness, the storehouses of snow and hail. The wild ass roams the salty
wastes and mountains, inhospitable places for human beings, while it scorns
the human habitat of the city. The eagle's home is on the cliff, out of reach
of humankind. Behemoth's home is the swamp, and he is not afraid even
when a river rushes against him.[81] Finally, Leviathan inhabits the Sea and
the Deep, places of terror for humanity.

The world of the prose prologue had no place for the forces of creation,
except as instruments of destruction. Job's world was destroyed by "fire from
heaven" and "a great wind from the wilderness" (Job 1:16, 19). Before these
events, the ordered world of the prose tale did indeed seem to be surrounded
by a protective fence that kept out all things wild and dangerous. This is the
world described in Job's final speech, a place where he himself occupied the
central position, surrounded by concentric circles of society: first his children
and domestic household, then the people of civic society (the elders and nobles
at the city gate), and lastly, the poor and needy to whom Job owed protection

---

[79] *Covenant* (ברית), while an important word in Israelite theology, is found only three
times in Job: in these two passages and in 31:1, where Job "makes a covenant" with his
eyes not to look on a virgin.

[80] The word תהום, of course, resonates with other creation accounts in the Bible: Gen
1, Prov 8, Ps 104. The term refers to a primordial entity. That Leviathan has such an effect
on it indicates his mythological nature.

[81] Job 38:17, 19, 22; 39:6–7, 28; 40:21–23

and benevolence.[82] The boundaries of this ordered world are blown apart in
the divine speeches. Job is made to see how narrow his vision was. He is
given a view of the cosmos that includes places and beings he never imagined
in his former life. Before, the wilderness and the wild animals that inhabit it
were to Job "the Other against which human culture defined itself."[83] In the
divine speeches, that which was alien to Job is described in great detail, with
attention to its beauty. In the social world of the prologue, Job occupied the
central position. In the divine speeches Job is de-centered; he is vouchsafed a
vision of spaces and creatures terrifying and inaccessible to human beings, yet
possessing beauty and a place in the order that God creates within the cosmos.
As Levenson asserts, in the divine speeches "there is a kind of reclamation
of the violent 'other' as part of the unfathomable creation of the inscrutable
Deity."[84] The Sea and the Deep are outside the boundaries of human life, as
is the terrifying sea monster they house; nevertheless, all three are given a
place in God's ordered world and are essential to that order.

The last verse of the divine speeches draws one more distinction between
the world as God created it and how Job imagined that world—one more
distinction, in particular, between Job and Leviathan. In his final speech, Job
had described himself as preeminent among his contemporaries.

> I chose their way and sat as a chief
> I dwelt as a king (כמלך) among his troops,
> as one who comforts mourners. (Job 29:25)

Of all the other creatures, human and nonhuman, in the book of Job, only
Leviathan is likewise labeled a מלך: "He surveys all who are lofty (גבה)./ He
is king (מלך) over all proud beings (בני־שחץ)" (Job 41:26). The latter phrase

[82] See the insightful description of this structured world in Newsom, *Moral Imaginations*,
187–90. She is describing the social world of Job's final speech, but the same social structure
is evident in the prose prologue and epilogue.

[83] Ibid., 245. Newsom notes that the ancient attitude toward wild animals bears a striking
resemblance to modern attitudes concerning things like anthrax or the cancer cell. That is, wild
animals were not something to be protected or appreciated. They were instead the "terrifying
biological other" to be feared and destroyed if possible (284). See also Keel, 61–125, who
likewise characterizes the ANE attitude towards wild animals as one that views them as a
threat to order and civilization, at times even as demonic figures. While there are biblical
passages that support this view (Isa 13:19–21; Jer 50:39; etc.), numerous other biblical
passages celebrate wild animals as part of God's good creation (Gen 1:24–25; Ps 96; 98;
104; 148). Certainly the divine speeches are one of the primary examples of the latter.

[84] Professor Jon D. Levenson (private communication).

(בני־שחץ) was used earlier in the book to refer to lions.[85] Likewise, God has
already challenged Job to clothe himself with "loftiness" (גבה: Job 40:10).
The "lofty" and the "children of pride" could, then, be interpreted to include
not only animals but also human beings. Job had established himself as a
ruler over other human beings, but God does not give credence to such a
claim. Instead, it is Leviathan whom God designates as "king" over *all* proud
beings. Job is again compared with Leviathan and found wanting.[86]

   The divine speeches are not the first instance in the book of a comparison
between Job and chaos monsters. As noted already, Job himself in the dialogue
has drawn such a comparison: "Am I the Sea or the Dragon (תנין), that you
place a guard over me?"[87] Job is convinced in the dialogue that God is treating
him as if he were a force of chaos. Job points out that he is a mere mortal man,
not a chaos monster. God should therefore stop scrutinizing him and instead
should have mercy on him, a fragile human being. In the divine speeches,
God in essence agrees with Job's assessment. Job is not a chaos monster; he
is not equal in power to either Behemoth or Leviathan. But God calls into
question Job's characterization of God's ordering of the cosmos. The divine
speeches contend that God is not inordinately concerned with Job, watching

---

[85] The phrase בני־שחץ occurs in Job 28:8, in parallel with *lion*. It could, therefore, refer
specifically to wild animals.

[86] This conclusion runs contrary to the argument of John G. Gammie, who asserts that
"the Leviathan in the Leviathan pericope was intended, in part at least, as a figure of Job"
(Gammie, 225). I agree with this assertion. Gammie goes on to argue, however, that what
comes forth from Leviathan's mouth (fire and light) are intended as symbols of Job's own
verbal defenses, and that the passage affirms those very protests. Rather than understanding
the figures of Behemoth and Leviathan as "exemplars of the divine defeat of prideful man,"
Gammie argues that they "celebrate . . . Job's triumph" (226). I do not find his argument
persuasive, as the comparisons between the chaos monsters and Job seem to me to point
out the great distance between them, rather than any kind of parity. Also, how does one
reconcile an affirmation of Job's arguments in the Leviathan pericope with God's assertion
that Job has "darkened counsel with words lacking knowledge" (38:2) and with Job's own
admission that he has "spoken what [he] do[es] not understand" (42:3)?

[87] Job 7:12. See also Job 9:13–14. Granted, Leviathan is not mentioned by Job in these
passages, but the Sea, Rahab, and the Dragon (תנין) are all associated with Leviathan in
biblical and ANE literature. See Isa 27:1 and Day, 1–7. Gammie sees another comparison
between Job and Leviathan in 3:8: "Job likens himself at birth to Leviathan: 'Let those who
curse the day curse it,/ those midwives who laid bare Leviathan'" (Gammie, 224). Gammie's
translation requires not just an emendation of the verb, but an unattested myth about the
"birth" of Leviathan. Of course, such an interpretation is not impossible, given the parallel
"birth" of the Sea in the divine speeches. If Gammie is correct, the comparison Job draws
between himself and chaos monsters is strengthened.

his every step. Job is simply not that important in the grand scheme of things. He is not a king; he is not a chaos monster. Job is a creature among other creatures in God's creation. Such is the answer of the divine speeches to the question, "What is humanity?" Human beings are merely one sort of creature among many in God's creation. In the vision vouchsafed to Job of creation, human beings play a very minor role. The divine speeches, in other words, are radically nonanthropocentric. They celebrate creation in all its wildness and beauty and pay particular attention to the nonhuman creatures in that creation. The splendor of the cosmos is displayed and the climax of that vision is not humanity, but the sea monster Leviathan, who is "king over all proud beings."

Humanity has very little significance in the divine speeches, particularly as compared with the rest of the book of Job. There is, however, one section of the divine speeches where the description of creation is interrupted for a brief time to speak about the human moral order. A discussion of the divine speeches would not be complete without touching on this particular section (Job 40:7–14). Just prior to this point, Job has responded to the first divine speech by affirming that he cannot answer God. He has neither God's knowledge nor God's power over creation. God begins his second speech, then, by challenging Job to take on divine attributes:

> Will you indeed annul my justice (מִשְׁפָּטִי)?
>   Will you condemn me so that you may be justified?
> Do you have an arm like God's,
>   and can you thunder with a voice like his?
> Adorn yourself with pride and exaltation.
>   Clothe yourself with splendor and majesty. (Job 40:8–10)

This is the only passage in the divine speeches to mention מִשְׁפָּט, a word crucial to the arguments contained in the rest of the book.[88] This passage appears to take up the human interlocutors' concerns with justice and righteousness, and uses them to challenge Job to administer justice in the

---

[88] What the divine speeches mean by מִשְׁפָּט, and how that understanding may answer Job's concerns from the dialogue will be the subject of the last chapter of this book. Scholnick asserts, for example, that מִשְׁפָּט has two different meanings: one having to do with judging and the other with ruling ("The Meaning of *Mishpat*," 521–22).

world. God tells him to abase the proud and to hide the wicked in the dust. Then God will "praise" Job for his powerful right hand (Job 40:11–14).

Brenner argues that this passage is not ironic but a "straightforward, although partial, admittance of divine failure." That is, God admits that he has "little or no control over evil."[89] Such an admission, however, would be incongruous with the overwhelming display of divine power in the divine speeches. Immediately after this passage, God describes the immense power of Behemoth and Leviathan while also emphasizing his mastery over them. A more likely interpretation of this passage, then, is offered by Habel, who connects it with the ongoing contrast in the divine speeches between Job's limited human vision and God's ordering of the cosmos. Job wants the world to be run according to "a rigid law of moral retribution." God shows Job another way:

> [T]he world is not run according to the moral principle Job and his friends had espoused. Chaos and evil are part of the world; God's role as Ruler is not to annihilate them, but to keep them in check in accordance with the primordial wisdom principle which governs his cosmic design. Rule according to the wisdom principle leads to balance and freedom; rule according to the principle of retributive justice leads to imbalance and rigidity.[90]

If a place is given in the world to the Sea and Leviathan, those cosmic forces of chaos, then space is also reserved for the possibility of human wickedness. Such is the freedom God establishes in creation. One must remember, however, that God places limits on the Sea and has control over Leviathan. God must, then, also limit human wickedness, as demonstrated earlier in the divine speeches by his establishment of the Dawn, which shakes the wicked out of the earth like dust out of a rug (Job 38:12–15). The potential for human pride and wickedness is somehow part of the cosmos, but it does not annul God's ordering of that cosmos. Indeed, the human longing for justice (so prominent in Job's own speeches) may itself be understood as part of the ordering of the cosmos, even if that longing is often disappointed.[91]

This passage speaks more about humanity than any other passage in God's response to Job. Here, as in the rest of the divine speeches, however,

---

[89] Brenner, "God's Answer," 133.

[90] Habel, 564.

[91] Thanks to Prof. Ellen Davis for this suggestion (private communication).

humanity is primarily represented by the "proud" and the "wicked." The one human being who is the recipient of God's vision cannot know or control God's creation; neither can he take on the attributes of God. This passage, while it briefly speaks of humanity's place in creation, continues the pointed contrast between Job's limited human vision of the world and God's vision, knowledge, and rule of the same.

The Divine Speeches and Other Biblical Creation Accounts

The divine speeches view creation and humanity's place in it in a markedly different way than do Job and the other human characters in the book. The creation theology of the divine speeches also stands in marked contrast to the creation theologies articulated in many other passages in the Hebrew Bible. While an exhaustive survey of biblical creation accounts is not within the scope of this book, exploring the contrasts with a few of those accounts will help to clarify the creation theology contained in the divine speeches.[92]

The two creation stories in Genesis 1–3 must, of course, be included in any survey of creation theologies in the Hebrew Bible, as they are the most well-known creation accounts therein. The Priestly creation story in Genesis 1, as we have already seen, probably served as a foil for Job's "uncreation" account in chapter 3.[93] Job seeks by his curses to undo the order and boundaries God placed in creation at the beginning. Job also seeks to undo the power of procreation exemplified in God's command to "be fruitful and multiply; fill the earth and subdue it" (Gen 1:28).[94]

---

[92] I have chosen for discussion a few of the most well-known creation accounts in the Hebrew Bible. There are, of course, many other passages in the Bible that could be called "creation accounts," but the ones I've chosen are representative of the whole. For a book-length discussion of many biblical creation accounts, see Terence Fretheim's *God and World in the Old Testament: A Relational Theology of Creation*.

[93] See Fishbane, "Jeremiah and Job," 153–54, and Habel, 104. Also see discussion above in chapter one.

[94] Westermann argues that this blessing of fertility is the first and primary blessing of humankind, and is one that humankind shares in common with the animals. The Priestly account of the establishment of procreation stands in contrast to the ANE divinization of fertility which gave rise to a variety of fertility cults. "It is the Creator who dispenses this power . . . . This blessing which was given at creation will in the course of history become the cultic blessing" (Claus Westermann, *Creation* [trans. John J. Scullion; Philadelphia: Fortress, 1974] 55).

The divine speeches, with their reestablishment of creation, also reestablish the order God placed within creation as described in the Priestly account. God gives limits to the Sea so that it cannot overwhelm the land. God assigns a place to light and darkness. God establishes the rhythm of sunrise. God also populates the earth and sea with animals. God affirms the power of procreation, describing many of the animals in terms of their fecundity. In these respects, the divine speeches echo the Priestly creation account of Genesis 1.

In regard to the place of humanity in creation, however, the divine speeches differ sharply from the Genesis account. The Priestly creation account clearly considers humanity the crown of creation. God's fashioning of humanity is the culmination of his creation of all the animals, and it is only humanity that is created in the image of God (Gen 1:26–27). God expressly gives humanity dominion over all the other creatures, and tells them to "fill the earth and subdue it" (Gen 1:28). It is only after humanity is fashioned that God pronounces creation not just "good" (טוב) but "very good" (טוב מאד) (Gen 1:26–28, 31).[95]

The Yahwistic creation account in Genesis 2 and 3 is more ambivalent than the Priestly account about humanity's creation. The Yahwistic account moves immediately from the story of Adam and Eve's formation—itself humbler than the account in the Priestly narrative—to the story of their disobedience. Nevertheless, in this creation account, too, humanity is the focus of the story. YHWH forms Adam first of all the creatures. All the other animals are then created apparently for the express purpose of finding a companion for the first man, and he is given the power to name them (Gen 2:7, 18–20).[96] Although nothing is said in this creation story of humankind

---

[95] God pronounces creation "good" in Gen 1:4, 10, 12, 18, 21, and 25. For a more detailed exploration of the role of humanity in Gen 1, see Welker, *Creation and Reality*: "The Priestly creation accounts describe *the whole creation*, not only and not firstly human being [*sic*], as itself active, separating, ruling, and imparting rhythm, as itself producing and giving life" (11, emphasis his). Welker admits that humanity's role is depicted as particularly significant in this regard but rightly points out that other beings of the natural world also participate in the act of creation. Nonetheless, the contrast with the divine speeches is still acute; humanity in the speeches plays virtually *no* role (and certainly no significant role) in the ongoing process of creation, as opposed to the rain, the Dawn, the animals, etc.

[96] Fretheim sees a deliberate echo of this story in the divine speeches, as the animals are paraded before Job so that he might see them (Fretheim, *God and the World*, 237). I find his argument persuasive, especially given the other links with the Genesis creation accounts already noted.

being made in God's image, human beings are given the responsibility to care for God's garden and seem to act as God's closest companions. After they disobey YHWH, they are exiled from the garden for becoming too much like God, knowing good and evil (Gen 2:15; 3:3–9, 22–23).

In contrast to the Genesis creation stories, the divine speeches in the book of Job portray humanity as neither the crown of creation nor its master. Human beings in the divine speeches have no control over the wild animals or the other forces of nature. Humanity does not occupy a place of preeminence in the natural world. Not only are humans *unable* to "subdue" the earth, but they are not even told to do so. There is no evidence of the idea of the *imago Dei* in the divine speeches, nor are human beings in any danger of threatening God by becoming too much like him. To the contrary, the divine speeches emphasize the vast gulf between God's power and knowledge and that of human beings.

Another creation account, Psalm 8, largely reiterates Genesis's view of humanity's place. Westermann considers the psalm an "echo" of the Priestly account of the creation of humankind. Both passages speak of humanity's dominion in royal language, and "those subject to this dominion are in the first place the animals."[97] Psalm 8 praises God for the creation of humanity. According to the psalmist, God created humanity only a little lower than God himself (or "the gods"/"the heavenly beings"). God gave humanity dominion over the works of his hands and put "all things under their feet," including "the beasts (בהמות) of the field" and that which "passes through the paths of the sea" (Ps 8:6, 8–9).[98] In the divine speeches the poet of Job emphatically denies the claims of the psalmist, asserting again and again that humanity does not control the wild animals. In particular, humanity has no hope of controlling the greatest of the beasts, Behemoth (בהמות), or a certain creature that "passes through the sea," namely, Leviathan. In this emphasis on humanity's dominion over creation, Psalm 8 echoes Genesis 1, and both creation accounts stand in sharp contrast to the divine speeches.

One of the longest and most detailed biblical descriptions of creation is found in Psalm 104. This psalm bears a strong resemblance to the divine speeches in its description of God's establishment of creation and in its

[97] Westermann, *Creation*, 51.

[98] The author of Job has already demonstrated knowledge of Psalm 8 in an earlier passage from one of Job's speeches (Job 7:17), in which he offers a parody of Psalm 8:5. See the discussion of these verses in chapter one.

mention of Leviathan.[99] The psalmist, like the poet of Job, begins with an account of the foundation of the earth and the limiting of the Sea and then reviews the animal kingdom, listing many of the same animals that populate the divine speeches: the wild ass (פרא), the wild goats (יעלים), the young lion (כפיר), and, of course, Leviathan.[100] The psalmist pays particular attention to God's provision of food for his creatures, a theme also prevalent in the divine speeches.[101] Finally, the psalmist includes mention of the wicked in his account of creation, as does the Joban poet.[102]

The description of Leviathan further connects the divine speeches with Psalm 104. Leviathan is named in only five passages in the Bible, including Job 3, the divine speeches, and Psalm 104. It is striking that both of the latter passages speak of "playing/sporting" with Leviathan (שחק בו).[103] In the divine speeches God challenges Job to play with Leviathan as he would with a bird. In the psalm God himself forms Leviathan to play with it.[104] Both poets agree that Leviathan is no human plaything or pet; it is only God who can "sport" with the sea monster.

There are clearly many parallels between Psalm 104 and the divine speeches. One of the primary differences between the two texts, however, is the generally favorable view of humanity found in the psalm.[105] While

---

[99] See Newsom, " Job," 596–97, for the suggestion that Ps 104 is the intentional foil for the divine speeches: "The genre upon which the disputation in Job 38–41 primarily draws is the hymn of God the creator, especially as it is represented in Psalm 104" (596).

[100] The sets of comparison include Job 39:5/Ps 104:11; Job 39:1/ Ps 104:18; Job 38:39/ Ps 104:21; Job 40:25/ Ps 104:26.

[101] Ps 104:27–28; Job 38:39–41; 39:40; 40:20. Newsom notes that the motif of lions seeking food from God is found only in Ps 104 and Job 38 ("Job," 597).

[102] Ps 104:35; Job 38:12–15; 39:10–14.

[103] Ps 104:26; Job 40:29. As noted above, the context of these verses and the use of the prepositional phrase בו make the translation "play with" preferable to "laugh" in these instances.

[104] The phrase can also be translated, "sport in it," i.e. God formed Leviathan to play in the sea. I find the translation of God playing with Leviathan more likely, as "the sea" is removed from the prepositional phrase בו by almost two full verses. Leviathan, rather than the sea, is therefore more likely to be the antecedent of the pronoun.

[105] Hans-Jürgen Hermisson ["Observations on the Creation Theology in Wisdom," in *Creation in the Old Testament* (ed. Bernhard W. Anderson; Philadelphia: Fortress, 1984) 118–34] designates Ps 104 a wisdom psalm and asserts that it "corresponds indeed with the often noted 'anthropocentric' character of wisdom." It is not completely anthropocentric, however. Its vision is of a world that "does not only exist for the sake of man, but in which everything has a meaning," a world beautiful in its order (124).

the divine speeches mention humanity only peripherally and always as "the wicked" or objects of scorn, the psalmist includes humanity in his list of beings God has created and emphasizes God's care for humanity. God provides food from the earth, wine to gladden the human heart, oil to make human faces shine, and bread to strengthen the human heart. The rhythm of night and day is established at least in part to aid human beings in their daily cycle of work (Ps 104:14–15, 23). The psalmist does not speak of humanity's dominion over the wild animals, as does the writer of Psalm 8, and he does include in his portrait of creation the "sinners" and the "wicked" (Ps 104:35). Nevertheless, as Newsom argues, the vision of Psalm 104 is "a vision of the world as a harmonious place in which the spheres of the human and the animal coexist as complementary creations of God."[106] Such is certainly not the view of the divine speeches. The view in Psalm 104 of humanity's relationship to creation has more in common with Eliphaz's vision of a "peaceable kingdom" (Job 5:22–23) than it does with the vision of the divine speeches, where creation is not necessarily a safe or friendly place for human beings.

One more example of biblical creation theology, this time from the prophets, may suffice to clarify the unique vision of the divine speeches. Isaiah 35 contains a prophecy of the exiles' return to Zion. At that time, the prophet proclaims, the wilderness (מדבר) and the desert will become fertile. Water will flow where water never before flowed, and the desert will bloom. A highway will be established through this suddenly hospitable land, and the people of God will walk on it back to Zion. On this highway they will not be in any danger from wild animals because none will be allowed on it (Isa 35:1–10). Eliphaz, as we have seen already, prophesies a similar future for Job if only he will repent and acknowledge his sin (Job 5:22–23). In the visions of both Isaiah and Eliphaz, the righteous, those God favors, will be rewarded for their righteousness at least in part by a harmonious relationship with the rest of creation. Such visions of a "peaceable kingdom" are found in a number of other prophetic texts.[107]

As already noted, the divine speeches make no such promise of a future harmonious relationship between humanity and the wild animals. To the contrary, humanity is the object of the animals' scorn and even (in one case)

---

[106] Newsom, *Moral Imaginations*, 245.

[107] See Isa 11, 35, 65; Ezek 34; Hos 2.

the source of food for their young.[108] Additionally, in stark contrast to Isaiah
35, the divine speeches portray a God who indeed sends rain on the wilderness,
but not for the sake of returning exiles. Rather, God sends rain specifically
on the land where no person lives, "the wilderness (מדבר) with no person in
it" (Job 36:26).[109] The desert blooms in Isaiah for the sake of the redeemed
walking to Zion. In the divine speeches, God specifically sends rain on a
land empty of human life so that the desolate land (rejected by humanity as
worthless) becomes lush with vegetation.

The prophetic visions of a renewed creation have an affinity with the
stories of the first creation, in which human beings lived in a well-watered
garden and no living being ate the flesh of another.[110] The divine speeches do
not know of such a time. They instead describe a world that is created wild
and dangerous from its inception, a world not centered around humanity, and
indeed, not necessarily even hospitable to (or safe for) humanity. This vision
of creation in the divine speeches, while bearing some resemblance to other
biblical creation accounts, is unique in the Hebrew Bible.

The distinction between the creation theology of the divine speeches
and that of other biblical creation accounts could be discussed in terms
of theocentrism and anthropocentrism. The divine speeches are certainly
radically theocentric. Such terminology, however, is somewhat misleading,
as all of the biblical creation accounts can be said to be "theocentric." All
point to the awesome power of God in establishing creation. All lead to
praise of the Creator. What distinguishes the divine speeches from the other
biblical creation accounts is their view of the place of humanity in creation.
In this respect, as already noted, the divine speeches can be said to be
radically "nonanthropocentric," while many of the other creation accounts
are, to one degree or another, "anthropocentric." That is, the other creation
accounts (particularly Genesis 1–3 and Psalm 8) understand humanity as
the most important of God's creatures and as masters of the rest of creation,
masters particularly of the wild animals. The divine speeches emphatically
reject this view.

---

[108] Job 39:30. See discussion earlier in this chapter.

[109] See discussion in the appendix.

[110] See Gen 1:29–30; 2:10. Whether such prophetic visions reference a return to Eden
is a matter of debate amongst scholars. See discussion of Eliphaz's vision above in chapter
one.

Conclusions

I have explored in this chapter the creation theology of the divine speeches, articulating it in contrast to earlier chapters of Job and to other biblical creation accounts. The creation theology of the divine speeches, I argue, is unique in the book of Job and in the Bible as a whole. The speeches answer earlier statements and assumptions in Job about God's ordering of creation, about procreation, and about humanity's place in creation. In the divine speeches God negates Job's maledictions and stresses Job's inability to comprehend or master the world God has created. In other words, God puts Job in his place.

Given the striking absence of humanity from the divine speeches, one should note that the speeches still are addressed to a human being. Though designed to put Job "in his place," the speeches acknowledge that he does indeed *have* a place in creation; he is, after all, the sole passenger on this grand tour of the cosmos. He is privy to a God's-eye view of creation in all its beauty, in all its wildness. In this, God answers a view of creation articulated by the friends in the poetic dialogue. Frustrated with what they perceive as Job's intractable pride, both Eliphaz and Bildad at times denigrate all of creation, including humanity, as corrupt and impure. The heavens are not pure in God's sight, much less a human being, who is a "maggot" and a "worm."[111]

The divine speeches espouse a similar gulf between God and God's creation, particularly between God and humanity. In the process of asserting this radical distinction, however, the divine speeches do not impugn creation. To the contrary, they hold up creation in all its beauty and glory as a masterpiece of God. Humanity occupies only peripheral spaces in the divine speeches; but God does not call human beings "maggots" or "worms." Indeed, the recipient of this vision is a human being, and therefore, humanity is vouchsafed a position of some significance in the end.

What this particular human being learns about himself and his place in the world after seeing the vision of the divine speeches is articulated in his second and final response to that vision (Job 42:1–6). Job's response to the divine speeches (and the epilogue that follows that response) will be in part the subject of the next and final chapter of this book. That chapter will also explore the question of divine justice as it relates to the creation theology of the divine speeches. In other words, do the divine speeches provide an

---

[111] Job 4:17–21; 15:14–16; 25:4–6. See discussion above in chapter one.

"answer" not only to the views of creation espoused in the poetic dialogue but also to the concerns about justice and righteousness which comprise much of that dialogue?

The divine speeches occupy a climactic position in the book of Job, and they articulate a view of creation unique not only in Job but also in the rest of the Bible. It remains to be seen what that view of creation has to say to the problem of undeserved suffering articulated by the man from Uz.

CHAPTER 3

The Divine Speeches in the Context of the Book of Job

The previous chapter of this book examined the relationship of the divine speeches to what precedes them (namely, the prose prologue and the poetic dialogue between Job and his companions), with particular attention to the views of creation articulated in the different sections of the book. The divine speeches, however, are not the final section of the book of Job. In this chapter, therefore, I will examine the relationship of the divine speeches to what follows them: the second reply of Job and the prose epilogue. I will then examine the apparent disjunction between the dialogue, which is largely occupied with the question of undeserved suffering, and the divine speeches, which give little attention to the question. I will briefly summarize the findings of this study by offering suggestions as to how the divine speeches function in the final form of the book of Job. Finally, I will discuss how the creation theology of the divine speeches offers important implications for the environmental movement.

Job's Response and the Epilogue

If the divine speeches have engendered some discontent on the part of readers of the book of Job, the prose epilogue has likewise been a source of dissatisfaction. The restoration of Job's fortunes appears to contradict the theological perspective of much of the book, including that of the divine speeches. Pope, while acknowledging that the story could not satisfactorily end with anything other than Job's restoration, nevertheless says of that

restoration that it "appears to confirm the very doctrine of retribution which
Job had so effectively refuted in the Dialogue."[1] Francis Andersen comments,
"It is a wry touch that the Lord, like any thief who has been found out (Exod
22:4), repays Job double what he took away."[2] In the same vein, Newsom
acknowledges the apparent incongruity between the traditional worldview
of the epilogue and the radical perspective of the divine speeches:

> The entire world of the prose tale's discourse, aesthetic and moral,
> seems indigestible after the divine speeches. . . . [T]he conclusion of
> a work should serve to confirm and solidify the book's 'message,' the
> perspective for which it has argued. Yet as many commentators from
> Budde to Clines have noted, the prose conclusion seems morally at
> odds with the perspective implied in the divine speeches.[3]

The epilogue returns Job and the reader to the world of the prologue, with its
concern for Job's children, flocks, and herds. There is no place for the wild
things of creation in such a world. One is left to wonder then what relationship,
if any, the epilogue has to the divine speeches. To answer that question, it
is fruitful to examine the passage that connects the divine speeches and the
epilogue, namely, Job's final response to God (Job 42:1–6), which contains
the last words of Job in the book.

Job reacts to the revelation of YHWH in the divine speeches first with
silence and then, after the second speech, with the recognition of God's
power and his own lack of understanding (Job 40:4–5; 42:1–6). In what is
possibly an allusion to the story of the tower of Babel (Gen 11:6), Job says
to God, "I know that you are able to do all things, and that no plan of yours
can be thwarted" (Job 42:2).[4] Job thereby recognizes God's sovereignty in

---

[1] Pope, xxix. Pope blames the "incongruity" of the dialogue and the epilogue on the fact
that the author of Job is dealing with "prefabricated materials" in the prose tale, a "familiar
story" with which he could not take many liberties. Nevertheless, Pope considers the doubling
of Job's possessions to be "a highly artificial device and incompatible with Job's realistic
observations in the Dialogue" (xxx).

[2] Francis Andersen, *Job: An Introduction and Commentary* (Leicester, England: Inter-
Varsity Press, 1976) 293.

[3] Newsom, *Moral Imaginations*, 20. It is this incongruity between the divine speeches and
the epilogue that provides the primary grounds for Newsom's claim that the divine speeches
are not the climactic answer to Job's situation.

[4] The verb בצר is used in the niphal only in these two verses and is combined in both
with the root זמם. Michael Fishbane notes the same connection between this verse and the

contrast to any illusion of power held by prideful human beings. Job goes on to confess that he has uttered things he did not understand, wonderful things he did not know (Job 42:3).[5] Human beings cannot hope to attain to God's power; neither can they claim any knowledge comparable to God's—such was the thrust of much of the divine speeches.

Job responds to the divine speeches by "recanting" and "reconsidering about dust and ashes (עפר ואפר)" (Job 42:6). There is much debate about the translation of this verse. Many commentators contend that Job here repents *on* the ash heap mentioned earlier (Job 2:8).[6] Two points mitigate against such a translation, however.[7] First, the niphal of the root נחם, when used with the preposition על, as it is here, means "to reconsider; to change one's mind about something."[8] Job thus is not repenting *on* a literal heap of dust and ashes but has changed his mind *about* "dust and ashes." Second, the phrase "dust and ashes" does not refer to physical dust but rather to the mortal state of human beings. The phrase recalls Job's description of himself in his last speech in the dialogue: "I have become like dust and ashes (כעפר ואפר)" (Job 30:19). These two words are used in conjunction only three times in the Hebrew Bible, in these two verses in Job and once in Genesis 18:27, where, in the process of interceding with God for Sodom and Gomorrah, Abraham refers to himself as "dust and ashes."[9] The phrase עפר ואפר, then, is a way of referring

---

story of the tower of Babel ("The Book of Job," 91). See discussion of this verse in the appendix.

[5] Note the quotations of God's speech embedded in Job's final reply. See discussion of this verse in the appendix.

[6] Such is the translation of Pope, Gordis, Dhorme, and the translators of the NRSV. The twelfth century Jewish philosopher Maimonides also equates the "dust and ashes" of Job 42:6 with the ash heap on which Job sits in 2:8, but he understands the ash heap to be emblematic of a certain attitude Job used to hold. The verse thus means: "I abhor all that I used to desire and repent of my being in dust and ashes" (Maimonides, *The Guide to the Perplexed* [trans. Shlomo Pines; Chicago: Chicago University Press, 1963] 492–93). For Maimonides, Job's error consists of seeking happiness in health, wealth, and children, without knowing that true happiness lies in knowing God.

[7] The argument for the given translation of this verse is detailed in the appendix. I will summarize it here. It is based largely on the work of Janzen, 254–59.

[8] Cf. Ex 32:12, 14; 1 Chron 21:15; Ps 90:13; Jer 8:6; 18:8, 10; Ezek 14:22; 32:31; Joel 2:13; Jonah 3:10; 4:2; Amos 7:3, 6.

[9] The first Joban occurrence of the phrase (Job 30:19) differs from the other two occurrences in its use of the particle כ ("like"). I would argue that this is not a significant difference. Given the rarity of the phrase in the Bible, it seems likely that the author of Job is

to humanity's condition before God: such creatures are "dust and ashes" or,
less poetically stated, are mortal creatures. The fact that the author of Job
has already used this phrase once in its metaphorical sense argues against its
literal interpretation here. Job is not speaking about physical dust and ashes,
but about his own condition and that of humanity in general.

Given the vision of creation imparted to him in the divine speeches, Job
has to rethink his understanding of his own place (and thereby, humanity's
place) in that creation. The previous chapters of Job are filled with implicit
and explicit beliefs about humanity's place in creation, beliefs that place
human beings at the center of creation and at the center of God's attention.[10]
The divine speeches call these beliefs into question. They cause Job to
rethink his understanding of creation, and of humanity's place in it; in other
words, to "reconsider about dust and ashes." Job is merely a creature among
creatures, neither the center of creation nor its crown. He is not a chaos
monster threatening God's power; nor is he a king governing God's creation.
God is not inordinately concerned with him. The world was not created for
his sake and he cannot control or even understand it. God provides for all
his creatures, including human beings; but God also provides for creatures
indifferent (and even dangerous) to humanity.

Job is merely a creature among other creatures, yet a creature vouchsafed
a vision of God. "I had heard of you by the hearing of the ear, but now my
own eyes have seen you," Job says to YHWH (Job 42:5). After all the many
words spoken by Job and by his companions, after all the propositions
spoken about God, the divine speeches move Job from hearing to seeing. The
speeches, however, do not contain any detailed description of God. Therefore,
the "seeing" of God of which Job speaks must be a vision of the Almighty
as revealed in his creation of and care for the world. The Creator, Job has
learned, takes great pride and delight in his creation and makes a place in
that creation for creatures both wild and beautiful. Indeed, God seems to
take special delight in precisely those things that are most wild, particularly
in the chaos creatures Behemoth and Leviathan.[11]

---

deliberately referring to the Abraham story both times he uses it. In other words, the phrase
עפר ואפר in Job refers to humanity's condition before God, as it does in Genesis.

[10] See chapter one for a discussion of these beliefs about creation, and about humanity's
place in it.

[11] Brown develops this point in *Ethos of the Cosmos*, 360–72. Brown discusses at length
the vision of the animal kingdom contained in the divine speeches. God construes the wild
animals "as icons of freedom and dignity" (366). In reference to Leviathan, Brown asserts, "In

The second and final reply of Job to God is key to understanding the place of the divine speeches in the book of Job. The story does not end with Job's response, however. The narrative voice breaks in again at the end of the book to inform the reader what becomes of Job. God calls on Job to intercede on behalf of his three friends, to whom YHWH twice says, "[Y]ou have not spoken to me rightly, as has my servant Job" (Job 42:7, 8).[12] The three friends have been careful to advise and admonish the suffering Job on all manner of things *about* God. They have even advocated the practice of prayer, but they have never once in the dialogue taken their own advice and spoken *to* God, as has Job. They have never once interceded for their afflicted friend. As Davis writes, "[T]he final divine judgment on [the friends] is that they are totally off base, because they are trying to talk *about* God without engaging in the fearsome, always potentially disorienting business of talking directly *to* God. Therefore their words can only 'bloom like cut flowers.' When God speaks out of the whirlwind, they all blow away."[13] For their failings the three friends are ordered to offer sacrifices and Job intercedes for them.[14] God accepts Job's prayer on behalf of his three partners in the dialogue.

The epilogue goes on to speak of Job's restoration: Job's relatives come to comfort him and to give him gold; his wealth is doubled, and he begets

---

the flow of presentation, this monster of the deep progresses from being an object of abject terror to a specimen of beauty" (372). This vision is in contrast to that of ANE monarchs, whose inscriptions describe wild animals as enemies to be hunted or exploited (350–60).

[12] Most commentators translate the phrase, "You have not spoken *about* me what is right." [So Habel, Tur-Sinai, Fohrer, Gordis, the translators of the NRSV, et al.]. Such a translation has the difficulty of needing to account for how Job has spoken rightly *about* YHWH, when Job himself has just admitted that he has spoken what he did not understand. I prefer the translation "to me" because it points out the important fact that Job is the only human being in the book who speaks *to* God directly, rather than just *about* God. נכונה could still be translated "rightly" with this understanding of the preposition. The translation "to me" is supported by the use of the preposition אל two other times in 42:7 with verbs of speaking (אמר/דבר), meaning "to speak to."

[13] Davis, *Getting Involved*, 130. The phrase she quotes comes from Karl Barth, *Church Dogmatics* (Edinburgh: T&T Clark, 1961) 4:457.

[14] The problem with the translation "about me" can also be resolved by dividing the prose tale from the poetic dialogue, and then positing an original interlude between the prologue and epilogue wherein the friends spoke wrongly about God, and Job defended him (parallel to the interaction between Job and his wife in the prologue). In that scenario, Job could be said to speak rightly about God and the friends could be accused of improper speech. Such is the solution of Ginsberg ("Job the Patient and Job the Impatient"), among others. This is certainly a plausible solution to the problem and does not argue against the solution I have chosen, as each addresses a different stage in the compositional history of the book.

more children (again, seven sons and three daughters). The three daughters
(now named in the epilogue) are said to be the most beautiful women in the
land and are given an inheritance along with their brothers. Job lives 140
more years and sees four generations of his family. Then, like the patriarchs
of Genesis, he dies "old and sated with days" (Job 42:17).[15] Job once more
has returned to the comfortable world of the prologue, the world of family
and human community, surrounded by possessions and children.

The question remains how the epilogue is connected, if at all, with the
divine speeches. Davis suggests a reading of the epilogue that relates it to
the divine speeches by means of the motif of procreation.[16] In the prologue,
Job offers sacrifices on behalf of his children after their periodic feasts, for
"perhaps my children sinned and cursed God in their hearts" (Job 1:5). He
offers, as it were, preemptive sacrifices for his offspring. In the epilogue, by
contrast, Job behaves differently as a parent. He gives his daughters names
that are "unabashed celebrations of their loveliness: Dove, Cinnamon, and
Horn-of-Eyeshadow." Job also gives them an inheritance along with their
brothers, "apparently for no other reason than that they are exceptionally
beautiful."[17] According to Davis, Job in the epilogue has learned from the
divine speeches to be more like God in the way he exercises authority over
his children:

> The anxious patriarch who once feared the possibility of his children's
> sin now takes revolutionary delight in their beauty. These final odd
> details are far from gratuitous—or, in a deeper sense, they are entirely
> gratuitous, and that is exactly the point. In this unconventional style of
> parenting we see how deeply Job has comprehended and adopted as
> his own the principle that underlies God's מִשְׁפָּט: the freely bestowed
> delight that is in fact the highest form of causality in the universe,
> the generosity that brings another into free being.[18]

This interpretation of the procreation theme running throughout the book
of Job has the advantage of uniting three distinct sections of the book:
prologue, divine speeches, and epilogue. One might contest that it is based
on an argument from silence as the epilogue does not mention the children's
celebrations, much less Job's sacrifices for them. The epilogue, however,

---

[15] For the same phrase, see Gen 25:8; 35:29.
[16] Davis, "Job and Jacob," 119–20.
[17] Ibid., 120.
[18] Ibid.

does mention the sacrifice of the three friends and Job's prayer for them. Job's attention has shifted from an unnecessarily controlling and anxiety-ridden care for his children to a God-ordained, entirely proper intercession for his friends who have in truth offended God. The contrast between the two occasions of sacrifice provides support for Davis's interpretation, as do the "gratuitous" details of the daughters' names and the fact that they receive an inheritance along with their brothers.[19]

Davis's interpretation of the epilogue is also bolstered by the fact that procreation has been a recurring theme throughout the book of Job. Given the prevalence of this theme in the book, it is appropriate that Job's role as parent is highlighted in the epilogue. The description of his children, and the mention of his children's children, serves to emphasize his favored status as in the prologue. More importantly, this mention of Job's children also serves to connect him with the other elements of God's creation described in the divine speeches. The Sea, the rain, the ice, the constellations, numerous wild animals, and even Behemoth are all described in terms of procreation. Likewise, despite the huge losses Job has endured, he (presumably along with his wife) decides to risk having and loving children again. Job thus participates (along with the other creatures of the natural world) in the hopeful, life-renewing process of procreation.

The radical hope exhibited by such an act is portrayed poignantly in Archibald MacLeish's play *J.B.* At the end of this play-within-a-play, the two characters who play God and the Satan argue. The God-figure (Mr. Zuss) tells the Satan-figure (Nickles) that Job will get his wife back, and children will "follow":

> Nickles: *jeering*   Wife back! Balls! He wouldn't touch her.
> He wouldn't take her with a glove!
> After all that filth and blood and
> Fury to begin again!
> ....
> After life like his to take
> The seed up of the sad creation
> Planting the hopeful world again—

---

[19] William Brown offers a similar interpretation of Job's actions in the prose epilogue. He, too, notes the absence of any mention of Job's sacrifices for his children. Job in the epilogue is no longer the "obsessive patriarch" he was in the prologue. He gives his daughters their own inheritance and rules his household with the same freedom and "gratuitousness" that "sustains the cosmos" (*Ethos of the Cosmos*, 379).

He can't! . . . he won't! . . . he wouldn't
touch her!

Mr. Zuss: He does though.

Nickles: *raging* Live his life again? —
Not even the most ignorant, obstinate,
Stupid or degraded man
This filthy planet ever farrowed,
Offered the opportunity to live
His bodily life twice over, would accept
it—
Least of all Job, poor, trampled bastard!
....
It can't be borne twice over! Can't be!

Mr. Zuss: It is though. Time and again it is —
Every blessed generation . . .[20]

Job chooses to live his life again. He chooses, indeed, to risk having children again in spite of the potential for great pain such an act entails. But he has learned something from his ordeals and, in particular, from the revelation he is given in the divine speeches. He has learned to live in a world he cannot control. He has learned to live and participate in God's creation as a creature among other creatures. Job participates in creation not by inhabiting the wild realm of the divine speeches, but by joining again in human community. He intercedes for his friends and fathers more children, this time delighting in their beauty and giving them the freedom God gives his own creatures. In this way, the epilogue can be understood as a response to the extraordinary vision of the divine speeches.

The Problem of Divine Justice

Questions about the provenance of the divine speeches come up primarily because the speeches do not appear to address the concerns of the dialogue that precedes them: specifically, the problems of undeserved suffering and divine justice. Job maintains his innocence even in the face of his friends'

---

[20] MacLeish, *J.B.,* scene 10, lines 171–174, 184–198.

accusations that he must have done something wrong in order to deserve the suffering he experiences.[21] The divine speeches seem not to address Job's situation, mentioning neither his companions' accusations nor his own protestations of innocence. Job looks for a trial in a court of law; what he gets is a vision of the vastness of creation.

It is my contention that the divine speeches, contrary to first impressions, *do* contain an answer to the questions and problems of Job. The answer has to do (in part) with the issue of humanity's place in the natural world. God's description of creation reveals to Job that the world does not exist for the sake of humanity, but rather that humanity plays only a part in creation. The world exists for the sake of its Creator. The divine speeches, in other words, are radically theocentric.

Yet another aspect of God's answer to Job stems from this theocentric view of creation and has to do with the nature of justice. While it is true that the divine speeches do not address Job's situation directly, there is one passage that touches on matters of justice and wickedness. Like most of the rest of the divine speeches, this passage takes the form of questions that challenge Job to act with the knowledge and power of God. Unlike the rest of the divine speeches, however, the subject of this passage is humanity, a part of creation largely ignored in most of God's vision:

> Will you indeed annul my justice [מִשְׁפָּטִי]?
> Will you condemn me [תַּרְשִׁיעֵנִי] so that you may be justified [תִּצְדָּק]?
> Do you have an arm like God's,
> and can you thunder with a voice like his?
> Adorn yourself with pride and exaltation.
> Clothe yourself with splendor and majesty.
> Let loose your overflowing anger.
> See all who are proud and abase them.
> See all who are proud and humble them.
> Cast down the wicked [רְשָׁעִים] where they stand.
> Hide them in the dust together;
> bind their faces in darkness.
> Then even I will praise you
> because your right hand saves you. (Job 40:8–14)

---

[21] See, for instance, Eliphaz's speech in chapter 22, in which he has become so angry with Job that he accuses him of all kinds of wrongdoing. Job responds to all of his companions' accusations in 27:1–6, where he defends his integrity and his innocence. He does so consistently throughout the dialogue.

This is the only passage in the divine speeches to mention מִשְׁפָּט ("judgment, justice, order, case"). Yet מִשְׁפָּט is an important word in the rest of the book, especially in Job's own speeches. The man from Uz uses the word many times in the poetic dialogue. In contrast, the three friends use it only twice, chiding Job for doubting God's "justice," and speaking of the "judgment" into which God enters with Job.[22] Job's use of the word מִשְׁפָּט has to do most often with the legal case he seeks between God and himself.[23] For instance, in chapter 9, where he uses the word three times, he speaks of his "case," and wants God to come into "judgment" with him. He later complains that God has taken away his "right."[24] The same usage governs the appearance of מִשְׁפָּט in 13:18, 14:3, 23:4, 27:2, and 31:13.[25] Whether Job is speaking of his own case or that of his servants in former days, he almost always uses מִשְׁפָּט in the juridical sense.

The remaining two appearances of מִשְׁפָּט in Job's speeches are cases where the word is not used in a strictly juridical sense; in these verses it is better translated "justice" rather than "judgment" or "case." First, in 19:7, Job complains: "I cry out, 'Violence!' but I am not answered./I call out, but there is no justice."[26] The word מִשְׁפָּט in this instance could even be translated with a word like "order." Job's world has fallen into chaos, and he perceives no governing order or מִשְׁפָּט in it.[27] Then in his final defense, Job says of former days, "I put on righteousness and it clothed me/ My justice [מִשְׁפָּטִי] was like

---

[22] Job 8:3; 22:4. See, however, Elihu's many references to מִשְׁפָּט: 32:9; 34:4, 5, 6, 12, 17, 23; 35:2; 36:6, 17; 37:23. Elihu, like Job and the three friends, uses מִשְׁפָּט as a juridical term except in one instance, 37:23, where he combines it with "power" [כֹּחַ] as an attribute of God. Thus some hint of מִשְׁפָּט as sovereignty rather than simply justice or judgment can be read into this verse. So argues Scholnick, "The Meaning of *mishpat*," 525–26.

[23] Job 9:15, 19, 32; 13:18; 14:3; 19:7; 23:4; 27:2; 29:14; 31:13.

[24] Job 9:15, 19, 32; 27:2.

[25] Some of these usages are more obviously forensic than others, but all seem to have to do with legal "judgment," or the "case" or "right" of a litigant.

[26] Habel translates מִשְׁפָּט in this instance with "litigation." I disagree with his translation as there is no other reference to the legal process in the immediate context of the verse. Instead, the image is of a city under siege, which Habel notes (290, 295). Scholnick also interprets this verse in a legal sense: "I make a charge 'Lawlessness,' but I am not answered./I press charges, but there is no litigation" ("The Meaning of *mishpat*," 524). While such a translation is possible, it seems to me unlikely. Again, the immediate context is the image of a city under siege, not a courtroom. Also, both active verbs have the meaning "cry out (for help)," not "press charges."

[27] See Job 3:23; 7:12–21; 9:13–19; 10:14–22; 13:27; 14:1–6. See also discussion above in chapter one.

a cloak and a turban" (Job 29:14). Again, in this instance, the word מִשְׁפָּט is best translated "justice." Job in his former life was the source of justice and order in his community, the person who governed like a king and judged cases at the city gate. While the city gate was the court of law and Job himself was the judge, the use of מִשְׁפָּט in this instance has to do not with Job's litigation against God but with Job's just governance of his own world.

Given the many appearances of מִשְׁפָּט in Job's speeches, it is striking that God uses the word only once. After all Job's complaining about מִשְׁפָּט, God himself speaks and accuses Job of negating "my justice" or "my order" [מִשְׁפָּטִי]. Job's justice is a paltry thing compared to God's "justice" or "governance" of the cosmos. It is God's מִשְׁפָּט that is of the utmost significance, and Job stands accused of trying to annul it.

What it might mean to annul God's מִשְׁפָּט is illumined in the second stich of 40:8. Job condemns God [תַּרְשִׁיעֵנִי] so that he himself might be justified [תִּצְדָּק]. Again, both words have played a major role in the dialogue, but not here in the divine speeches. Job called on God not to condemn [לְהַרְשִׁיעַ] him, and further, he defended his own righteousness [צדק] on numerous occasions.[28] Likewise, both Job and his companions often referred to matters of condemnation, wickedness, and righteousness.[29] Given the prevalence of both roots throughout the dialogue, it is important to note that they are used together in the divine speeches only in this passage.[30] Here, God turns the tables on Job. Job had accused God of condemning him, when it is Job who is condemning God. Job had accused God of perverting justice, when it is Job who is doing so.

Scholnick translates מִשְׁפָּט in Job 40:8 as "my sovereignty" rather than "my justice" or "my order." She asserts that the Semitic root שׁפט/תפס has two meanings, one having to do with judging and the other having to do

---

[28] See Job 10:2; 13:18. God's challenge in 40:7–8 alludes directly to the former verse with its use of the words הוֹדִיעֵנִי and תַּרְשִׁיעֵנִי.

[29] The roots רשׁע and צדק are used numerous times in the dialogue: Job 3:17; 4:17; 6:29; 8:3, 6, 22; 9:2, 15, 20, 22, 24, 29; 10:2, 3, 7, 15; 11:2, 20; 12:4; 13:18; 15:6, 14, 20; 16:11; 17:9; 18:5; 20:5, 29; 21:7, 16, 17, 28; 22:3, 18, 19; 24:6; 25:4; 27:5, 6, 7, 13, 17; 29:14; 31:6. I do not even begin to include here the many appearances of the two roots in the Elihu speeches. The examples cited suffice to show the importance of the two words in the dialogue.

[30] The root רשׁע does appear in the divine speeches in one other passage, 38:13–15, to speak twice of "the wicked."

with ruling.[31] If she is correct in her interpretation, then the conventional understanding of justice (stemming from the realm of the law court) is not necessarily the understanding expressed by the author/redactor of Job in the divine speeches. His conception of justice instead has to do with what Scholnick calls "executive sovereignty, the prerogative of the ruler."[32] According to Scholnick's interpretation, Job has misunderstood the concept of divine justice, which has more to do with the royal court than with the court of law.

One of the primary images of God in the dialogue is that of judge. Job complains that God is judging him unfairly while the friends insist that Job must have done something wrong to deserve the punishment he is receiving from the Almighty.[33] The divine speeches, argues Scholnick, correct this image by showing Job that God's primary role in the universe is that of king, not judge. The reader should already have been aware of this fact, according to Scholnick: "The prologue enables the reader to understand that God is acting as Ruler to test His subject, not as Judge to punish him for wrongdoing."[34]

Scholnick's insights help to resolve the apparent incongruity between the divine speeches and the dialogue. Creation poetry does naturally lend itself to the motif of God as king.[35] God creates and sustains the world and continues to govern it. God's מִשְׁפָּט does not necessarily correspond to the juridical conception of justice. God's מִשְׁפָּט is larger than the human concept of "justice" or "judgment" as a strict system of punishment for wrongdoing

---

[31] Scholnick, "Poetry in the Courtroom," 194. Scholnick cites 1 Sam 8:9 as evidence for the "ruling" usage of the root. She argues that the divine speeches are God's testimony (i.e., the defendant's answer to Job's lawsuit against him) and not a change of venue from the courtroom to the realm of creation.

[32] Scholnick, "The Meaning of *mishpat*," 521. Scholnick argues that divine justice is presented in the divine speeches as magisterial right. Because God is sovereign over all creation, he has the right to take the property and family of his subjects as he deems necessary. Such is the right of kings according to 1 Sam 8.

[33] Job 9:19–24; 22:1–20.

[34] Scholnick, "The Meaning of *mishpat*," 523.

[35] See Ps 24; 29; 74:12–17; 93:1–2; 95:1–5; 96:10–13. See also Frank Moore Cross, *Canaanite Myth and Hebrew Epic* (Cambridge, Mass.: Harvard University Press, 1973) 91–111. Cross describes the joining of the motif of creation-kingship (illustrated in the Canaanite myth of Baal and the Sea) to the motif of Exodus-conquest in texts such as Ps 24 and Isa 51. God is hailed as king both because he created the world and because he acts in history to save Israel. There is no hint of the latter motif in the divine speeches of Job. There, divine kingship is based solely on God's creation of the world and his control of the chaotic elements Sea, Behemoth, and Leviathan.

and rewards for right behavior. God's מִשְׁפָּט has to do with the governance of the cosmos and the order God establishes in that cosmos, an order beyond human understanding.

Scholnick's insights are helpful, but they do not take into account two things: 1) the passage in the divine speeches in which the word מִשְׁפָּט appears;[36] and 2) the fact that the roles of king and judge are not as discrete in biblical thought as she seems to claim. First, although the term מִשְׁפָּט in Job 40:8 probably does have more to do with "sovereignty" than "justice," the rest of the passage (particularly verses 11–14) does indeed deal with matters of justice. Specifically, the passage deals with the punishment of the רְשָׁעִים ("wicked") and the גֵּאֶה ("proud"). Job has complained that the wicked are not punished while his friends have asserted that they are.[37] God responds that if Job can take on the attributes of God (his arm and his voice) and can destroy the wicked, then the Almighty will acknowledge that Job's right hand has given him victory.

Secondly, the roles of king and judge are more connected than Scholnick claims, as evidenced by this passage in Job 40. The assertion of sovereignty has to do with governance not just of the natural world, but of the human and moral sphere as well. Some illustrations from other biblical texts will serve to clarify this point. We look first at 1 Sam 8:9, the very passage Scholnick cites a number of times as justification for God's actions as king. The people of Israel have asked for a human king and, in response, God says to Samuel: "Now listen to their voice; but warn them and tell them about the way (מִשְׁפָּט) of the king who will rule over them." Scholnick writes of this verse:

> The use of this word in 1 Sam. 8:9 helps to illuminate its meaning in Job 40:8: the ruler has authority (*mishpat*) which attaches to his position of power. He may treat his people and their property according to his own interests without their prior consent. . . . God's actions are his prerogative as Ruler and a sign of His total control.[38]

---

[36] Scholnick mentions only in passing the rest of the passage, 40:11–13 ("Poetry in the Courtroom," 193). This is strange, given the emphasis she places on the verse that introduces that passage, 40:8. She acknowledges that 40:11–13, along with 38:12–13, speak briefly of God's responsibilities as divine judge of humanity; but asserts that the emphasis of the divine speeches is on God's role as king. While she is correct about the speeches' emphasis on sovereignty, it is significant that God's role as judge is described in the divine speeches at least once. That description deserves consideration.

[37] See Job 8:11–22; 15:17–35; 18; and Job's reply in chapter 21.

[38] Scholnick, "The Meaning of *mishpat*," 527–28. See also 522–23 and "Poetry in the

Scholnick takes the description of human kingship in 1 Samuel 8 to justify God's treatment of Job, especially the destruction of his property and family. Her translation of מִשְׁפַּט as "authority" in 1 Samuel 8:9, however, is problematic. A better translation would be "the way of [the king]," the king's *modus operandi*, one might say.[39] In this context, then, מִשְׁפַּט is not the God-given authority the king possesses, but simply an indication of how the human king will behave.

Scholnick's interpretation of 1 Samuel 8 neglects to mention that the passage takes a very negative view of human kingship. God says that the Israelites have rejected him as king in order to have a human king (1 Sam 8:7). One might assume that this explicit contrast between divine kingship and human kingship means that the despotic acts of the human king are not a reflection of the way in which God exercises sovereignty.[40] The human king will take his subjects' sons and daughters to be servants; he will take their wealth and he will make slaves of his subjects (1 Sam 8:11–17). Such things, the passage implies, did not happen when God was Israel's only king.

On the question of divine kingship, it is fruitful to look to the book of Psalms, where both human kingship and divine kingship are often the subjects of the psalmists' poetry. Psalm 10 and Psalm 96, for instance, speak of God as king, but they at the same time speak of God as judge.[41] The former describes at length the activities of the wicked and pleads for God, the king,

---

Courtroom," 194.

[39] Thanks to Jon Levenson and Ellen Davis for offering these suggestions (private communication). The NRSV, too, translates, "the ways of the king." Such a translation of מִשְׁפַּט in Job 40:8 is also possible although it is clear that God's *modus operandi* differs sharply from that of the human king in 1 Sam 8.

[40] There are, of course, numerous other biblical passages in which the human king is seen as a positive representative, even a "son" of the divine king, chosen and established by God. See 2 Sam 7:4–17; Ps 2; 18:50; 20:6; 89:27; etc. There is an abundance of scholarship on this subject of the conflicting views of kingship in Israel, a subject outside the scope of this study. For a sample of the scholarship, see John Bright, *A History of Israel* (4th ed.; Louisville: Westminster John Knox, 2000) 224–28.

[41] James L. Mays also notes this connection between the roles of king and judge in the Psalms (*The Lord Reigns* [Louisville: Westminster John Knox, 1994]). Mays considers the statement "*Yhwh mālāk*" to be the theological "center" of the Psalter. The statement implies many things, one of which is God's responsibility to execute justice in the earth: "Because the judgments of YHWH are acts to enforce his rule, the psalms give a prominent place to his work as judge" (15). Similarly, "The plea that YHWH 'judge' the one who prays is an appeal to the king as chief legal officer, who must hear the case of those whose cry for justice reaches him" (21).

to punish them. One can infer from these psalms that God's role as king necessitates his acting justly. Apparently that justice is not conspicuous in the psalmist's world, and he wishes to remind God of his duties as king: namely, to destroy the power of the wicked and to champion the cause of the oppressed. Moshe Weinfeld discusses at length this connection between sovereignty and justice or judgment in biblical and other ANE texts.⁴² In these texts the king (human or divine) "establish[es] justice [מִשְׁפָּט] and righteousness [צְדָקָה]."⁴³ This was true not just in Israel: "The notion that 'justice and righteousness' are essential for a reigning king was common throughout the Ancient Near East."⁴⁴ Weinfeld argues that the terms מִשְׁפָּט and צְדָקָה signify both juridical equity and social justice, i.e., taking care of the poor and needy.⁴⁵ The ideal king, then, is not the despotic sovereign described in 1 Samuel 8, but one who judges with equity and establishes justice for those who are oppressed, one who acts as both judge and king.

Psalm 96 calls on God's people to proclaim his rule: "Declare among the nations, 'YHWH is king!'/The world is established; it will not be moved./He will judge the peoples with equity" (Ps 96:10). In close juxtaposition, the roles of king and judge are both ascribed to YHWH. The psalmist goes on to describe a great symphony of praise arising from creation—the heavens, the earth, the sea, the fields, and everything in them—because YHWH is coming to judge the earth: "He will judge [יִשְׁפֹּט] the earth with righteousness, and the peoples with his faithfulness" (Ps 96:13). While God's coming in judgment might seem foreboding to human beings, it is seen by the rest of creation as a great and glorious event. Psalm 98 makes the same connection between the roles of king and judge and describes the same exuberant response of creation to the coming judgment of God. According to these texts, God's role as king is inextricably bound up with God's role as judge of the whole world, and his judgment is necessarily just.

Given the emphasis on God's sovereignty in Job and the Psalms, the question arises in both books why God's kingship does not lead to a universal

⁴² Moshe Weinfeld, *Social Justice in Ancient Israel and in the Ancient Near East* (Minneapolis: Fortress, 1995). See esp. 20–23; 45–74.

⁴³ See 2 Sam 8:15; 1 Kgs 10:9; Ps 72:1; Jer 22:3, 15; 23:5; 33:15; Ezek 45:9, etc. See also Job 29:14, where Job uses the same words to characterize his actions on behalf of the poor and the needy.

⁴⁴ Weinfeld, 59. He cites many examples of ANE texts that take up this same theme of the just and righteous king.

⁴⁵ Ibid., 44.

elimination of wickedness and injustice. Psalm 10, for instance, affirms both
the sovereignty of God and the ongoing existence of human evil, beliefs that
seem mutually exclusive. The psalmist holds the two realities in tension and
takes God to task for allowing evildoers to flourish:

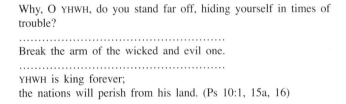

> Why, O YHWH, do you stand far off, hiding yourself in times of
> trouble?
>
> ....
>
> Break the arm of the wicked and evil one.
>
> ....
>
> YHWH is king forever;
> the nations will perish from his land. (Ps 10:1, 15a, 16)

Davis sees in the psalms the recurring idea that the world is ordered in such
a way as to leave room for human wickedness, as is apparent in the plea
for God to destroy the wicked at the very end of that great creation poem,
Psalm 104. God has established the world and provides for it, but there are
still wicked people in it. Davis notes, "So God may theoretically be able to
control the wicked, but that control is not fully evidenced on the ground. In
the Psalms, the praise offered by the non-human creatures is itself connected
with the expectation that God's מִשְׁפָּט will be more evident than it currently
is (see Ps 98)."[46]

This same awareness appears in the divine speeches. God has control
over everything in the cosmos, and this sovereignty is greatly extolled in
the speeches; but apparently, that sovereignty still leaves room for human
wickedness, as noted in Job 40:8–14.[47] This passage, however, is not an
admission of divine inability to control evil, as some scholars argue.[48]
Given the emphasis on God's power over everything else in creation, it
seems unlikely that this one passage admits divine weakness. Instead, this
passage distinguishes between the מִשְׁפָּט administered by Job in his own

---

[46] Ellen Davis, letter to author, 11 April, 2003. See Mays (21–22) for a similar discussion
of the place of the wicked in Psalms.

[47] As already noted, human beings have little place in the divine speeches, but the רְשָׁעִים
("wicked") and the גֵאֶה ("proud") are mentioned in Job 38:12–15 and 40:10–14. The latter term
is not used in 38:12–15, but the "uplifted arm," a symbol of pride or rebellion, is mentioned.
Both terms are used in 40:8–14. Given this correlation between the wicked and the proud,
one could interpret "wickedness" in the divine speeches as something close to "hubris." In
any case, God does not eliminate the רְשָׁעִים and the גֵאֶה, but he does limit them.

[48] Brenner, 133. See discussion above in chapter 2.

social world and the מִשְׁפָּט God establishes in the cosmos. As Habel argues, the מִשְׁפָּט Job himself espouses is one of "retributive justice;" but that principle does not apply in God's wider world. The Ruler of the universe does not abolish chaos and evil ("natural" and human), but he does establish limits for them.[49]

God's role as king is indeed emphasized in Job 40:8–14, as Scholnick argues; but God's sovereignty does not exclude his role as judge or his concern with the moral sphere. God's rule over the cosmos, God's מִשְׁפָּט, does not correspond with Job's or the friends' understanding of "retributive justice." It does, however, include some degree of control over human wickedness. God builds into the cycle of darkness and dawn a means of limiting human evil (Job 38:12–15). God describes with a series of challenging questions to Job how God's own powerful arm can abase the proud and trample the wicked (Job 40:9–13).[50]

Why God does not eliminate evil entirely is a question that is not answered in the divine speeches—or anywhere else in the Bible, for that matter. Levenson describes the creation theology of the divine speeches in relation to that of Psalm 104:

> In each case, the confinement of chaos rather than its elimination is the essence of creation, and the survival of ordered reality hangs only upon God's vigilance in ensuring that those cosmic dikes do not fail. . . . The world is not inherently safe; it is inherently unsafe. Only the magisterial intervention of God and his eternal vigilance prevent the cataclysm.[51]

Levenson goes on to argue that there is a tension in the theology of such passages. If the chaos monster is not destroyed, there is always the possibility that it might break its bonds and overwhelm the ordered world. Indeed, the psalms of lament exhibit just this tension. It is when God's historical foes seem to be gaining the victory—in other words, when chaos seems to be unloosed in the world—that the biblical writers most often invoke the story of God's defeat of chaos. Psalm 74 is a prime example of such a lament. It opens and closes with an extended plea for God to defeat his enemies and to

---

[49] See Habel, 564, and discussion above in chapter two.

[50] Like all the other questions to Job in the divine speeches, these questions show what Job is unable to do as contrasted with what God can do.

[51] Levenson, 17.

remember his chosen people. In the middle of the psalm is an affirmation of God's kingship, a description both of his defeat of the Sea and Leviathan and of his creation of the ordered world. The psalmist or redactor "acknowledges the reality of militant, triumphant, and persistent evil, but he steadfastly and resolutely refuses to accept this reality as final and absolute. Instead he challenges YHWH to act like the hero of old, to conform to his magisterial nature."[52]

The descriptions in the Psalms of the enduring place of human evil in the world correspond to the divine speeches' talk of the enduring existence of the "wicked" in God's world. The divine speeches, however, do not anticipate a coming judgment when God's משפט will be fully realized. Nor do the divine speeches contain or acknowledge any sort of plea for God to rise up as of old and conquer evil as in Psalm 74. Instead, the divine speeches simply assert that God has created the cosmos and establishes order within it and that God's משפט leaves a place for the Sea, Behemoth, Leviathan, and, by analogy, human wickedness. These forces of chaos are not annihilated, but neither are they allowed free sway over the world; they are limited by divine decree. They are given a place, but they are still controlled and circumscribed by God, the king and judge of the cosmos.

The divine speeches do not explicitly address Job's situation. They do, however, offer an answer to Job's concerns about divine justice. God is king; and like all good kings God establishes משפט in his kingdom, a משפט that operates not according to the principle of retributive justice, but according to the principles of freedom and gratuitousness. God is judge as well as king and he pays attention to and judges matters of wickedness and righteousness. But God also gives his human creatures the same freedom he gives the Sea and Leviathan. That freedom is a great gift; but it also has the potential for great harm. God therefore gives a place in the cosmos to the Sea, to Leviathan, and to human evil; but God also places boundaries on them. Such is the inexplicable but beautiful order God has placed in the world. Faced with such a vision of the cosmos, Job somehow has to learn to live in this tension between freedom and judgment, between chaos and order. In other words, Job has to learn to live under God's משפט.

---

[52] Ibid., 19. Levenson also discusses the use of the *Chaoskampf* myth in Isa 51:9–11 and Ps 89.

Conclusions

The book of Job with its discrete sections and disparate voices lends itself to scholarly deliberation about its literary integrity. The thematic and stylistic differences between the prose frame story, on the one hand, and the poetic core of the book, on the other, have given rise to speculation about the provenance of both.[53] Likewise, the provenance of the divine speeches has been a matter of scholarly speculation. Some scholars have argued that the original book of Job did not contain the divine speeches.[54] Most scholars, however, maintain that the answer of God is integral to the book of Job.[55] Job asks for such an encounter numerous times in the dialogue; and it is difficult to imagine any resolution to the book without it.[56] It is the content of the divine speeches and their apparent disregard for Job's concerns that have proved a conundrum for readers through the centuries. The speeches seem to address someone other than the suffering man from Uz. Accordingly, Levenson suggests the possibility that the divine speeches were composed for a different story in which the protagonist was not an innocent sufferer but "a Prometheus-like figure who challenged God's mastery of the world and claimed knowledge comparable to his."[57]

---

[53] Ginsberg, for instance, sees in the book an older story of "Job the Patient," used by a later author as the basis for his story of "Job the Impatient." (Ginsberg, 14–15). For the opposing argument, that the author of the prose and poetic sections of the book are one and the same, see Dhorme: "One and the same man can tell a story when necessary and sing when necessary" (lxv). See the introduction for a more extended discussion of the scholarship on Job.

[54] So Kuhl, 264-66, and D.B. MacDonald, *The Hebrew Literary Genius* (New York: Russell & Russell, 1933) 28–31. Jastrow, 67–77, considers the divine speeches an "appendix" to the original book of Job, which included only 2 cycles of speeches and the epilogue in 42:7–9. Norbert Peters (*Das Buch Job* [Münster: Verlag der Aschendorffschen, 1928]) argues that while the divine speeches were not original to the book, the poet of Job added them later himself.

[55] See, for instance, the commentaries of Habel, Newsom, Gordis, and Janzen. Fohrer also considers the first divine speech original to the book, but not the second ("Gottes Antwort," 4–10). Driver and Gray (351–53) and Rowley (14–15) agree with Fohrer that the second speech is not original to the book. Cf. Habel (526–27) for an outline of the parallels between the two divine speeches, the first addressing God's design of the universe, the second God's justice.

[56] See Job 9:32–35; 13:20–28; 14:13–17; 23:1–9; 31:35–37.

[57] Levenson, 155.

The question of the provenance of the divine speeches must remain an open one, as no alternate story has been found that incorporates the speeches or anything like them. What can be stated with certainty is that the divine speeches have been deliberately shaped to connect them with the other parts of the book of Job. As noted in the previous chapters of this book, there are many thematic and lexical links between the divine speeches and the rest of Job. Whether or not they were originally part of the book of Job, the speeches are now inextricably tied to the story of the innocent sufferer.

Given this evidence of deliberate shaping of the divine speeches and given their climactic position in the book, the question remains: What function do the divine speeches serve in the final form of the book of Job? Why would the author and/or redactor of Job use speeches about creation to address the plight of the unjustly afflicted Job?

In the final form of the book of Job, the divine speeches serve the function, first of all, of answering Job's many requests for an encounter with God, and of offering a means of resolving Job's situation. The dialogue between Job and his friends ends in confusion and discontent. The speech of Elihu does not elicit any response from Job. Without the appearance of God, Job is left sitting on the ash heap scratching his mutilated skin while his friends are reduced to silence. The appearance of God is a necessary component of the dramatic movement of the book and it does usher in a resolution to Job's situation even if some readers find that resolution unsatisfactory.

Why the author of Job chose to structure God's response in the form of a panoramic picture of creation is a question that has no definitive answer. Perhaps, as I've suggested already, the book was written to address the tragedy of the sixth century Babylonian Exile or some subsequent cataclysmic national event.[58] For the author of Job, the covenant relationship of YHWH and Israel was no longer an effective framework within which to understand such a tragedy so he reached back to a time before the Sinaitic covenant to find the setting for his story. Job, the non-Israelite patriarch, is tested like Abraham in Genesis 22, but this time God carries the test through to the end instead of calling it off at the last minute. Unlike Abraham, Job cannot rely on any covenant promises to know that everything will turn out all right in the end (Gen 22:15-19). Instead of making covenant promises, YHWH shows Job the beautiful, dangerous, but ordered world of creation and challenges him to live in it with freedom and faith. The author of Job does not or cannot find

---

[58] See the discussion in the introduction about the dating of Job.

answers to suffering in the covenant relationship of YHWH and Israel. Instead he finds answers in that which underlies God's relationship with every person (Israelite and non-Israelite alike): God's creation of and ongoing provision for the natural world. Creation, not covenant, is the basis of God's response to Job's anguish.

Such an answer to the interpretive problem of the divine speeches can only be speculative but it can be "fleshed out" by paying close attention to the content of the divine speeches and thereby seeing how they address the concerns of the rest of the book of Job. Realizing that no answer to the problem of the divine speeches can claim to be definitive, I will offer here some suggestions as to how the content of the divine speeches might address Job's situation. Much of what I will say has already been discussed in previous sections of this book; therefore, my conclusions will be offered here in summary fashion.

All biblical creation texts can be said to be theocentric; that is, to focus on God's actions in forming and maintaining the world. The creation theology implicit in the divine speeches, however, is unique in the Bible in its radical non-anthropocentricity. In other biblical texts, particularly in Genesis and Psalms, humanity is the crown of creation, its master or at least its caretaker. Much of the poetic dialogue among Job and his friends reflects just such an anthropocentric understanding of humanity's place in creation. In the divine speeches, though, humanity has almost no place except for passing references to the "wicked" and the "proud." Human beings are simply creatures alongside the other creatures in the natural world. They cannot control the wild animals, much less the cosmic and meteorological forces. Indeed, the wild animals laugh [שׂחק] at human attempts to control them or use them for their own purposes.[59] There even exist beings that are in many ways superior to humanity, the mythological creatures Behemoth and Leviathan. The natural world exists for the pleasure of God, not for the sake of humanity.

The author of the divine speeches, by removing human beings from the center of the created world, enlarges Job's (and the reader's) vision of that world. When Job was happy and prosperous, he was the center of his universe. Creation plays no role in the ordered, circumscribed world of the prologue—the same world Job describes in chapter 29—except as a threatening "other," lurking on the edges of Job's consciousness. He reigns as king among his peers and family, and he gives no thought to what exists

---

[59] Job 39:7, 18, 22; 41:21.

outside the boundaries of his fiefdom. This centrality of self continues in a different way after Job is struck by calamity, calamity that comes from outside Job's realm, from the wild forces of creation. Job's world implodes, and he becomes centered on his own despair and suffering.[60] He wishes for the grave, withdrawing from human relationship, light, and life into solitude, darkness, and death. Later, even as he stops wishing for death, as he defends his integrity and calls on God to answer him, Job understandably remains centered on himself. Stripped of goods, health, and family, Job dwells in the self-focused realm of despair, a situation not uncommon among those who suffer great loss.

The divine speeches answer this self-preoccupation by proclaiming to Job that he is not the center of the cosmos, that there exist realms and beings outside of himself that he never imagined. The vision of creation that is the divine speeches enlarges Job's own vision, so that he can move out of his self-centered despair and see the world from a God's-eye point of view. Indeed, the divine speeches enlarge Job's vision so much that he can even declare at the end of the book that he has seen God himself.

The divine speeches portray a creation that is fertile, bursting with new life. This motif of procreation in the divine speeches, however, has nothing to do with God's blessing or punishment of humanity, as it does in the rest of the book of Job. Procreation in the divine speeches is evidence of the ongoing, irrepressible force of life itself. Job's cursing of his own conception and birth in his first lament is not allowed to stand. He may wish to negate creation, but God ensures that creation will survive and thrive. The Sea comes gushing out of the primordial womb; the rain fructifies the barren wilderness; the wild animals bear and raise young. And all of this activity takes place without any regard to humanity. The wilderness is uninhabitable; the rain falls on desolate land where no person lives and causes it to sprout vegetation that no human will see. Unlike their domestic cousins, the wild animals will not serve humanity and their offspring will not increase humanity's wealth.

Life marches on, despite Job's maledictions, despite Job's and his friends' misunderstanding of the role of procreation. Procreation, according to the divine speeches, is not simply a means of blessing for humanity; it is a means of ensuring that life will continue for all of God's creatures. The

---

[60] See Alter, 96–97, for an eloquent description of the contrast between Job's inward-focused first lament in chapter 3 and the sweeping vision of the divine speeches.

blessing of fecundity, as God describes it, is for *all* of creation, and it cannot be negated.[61]

The divine speeches, as most readers note, do not address Job's specific situation. They do not explain why this righteous man suffers severe hardship. God does not acknowledge Job's innocence or explain the test he endures. Neither do the divine speeches explain why the wicked often go unpunished, one of Job's concerns in the dialogue. What the divine speeches do address are some of the assumptions underlying the views of both Job and his friends in the dialogue. One assumption has to do with the place of humanity in creation. Another concerns the role of procreation in the cosmos. Finally, and perhaps most significantly for the question of undeserved suffering, the divine speeches address assumptions about how God orders the universe.

Contrary to the view of a world ordered by a strict system of retributive justice (the view of Job's friends), the divine speeches paint a picture of a world governed with a certain freedom. In this vision of the cosmos, a place is given to things not traditionally associated with "order." Contrary to Job's vision of a world in chaos, a world where there is no perceptible order or מִשְׁפָּט, YHWH declares that he has indeed established מִשְׁפָּט in the cosmos. The Almighty describes the boundaries that he places in that world. He puts a fence not around Job, either for protection or for imprisonment, but around the Sea. God establishes the dawn and gives it the task of "shaking" the wicked out of the earth. God also controls Behemoth and that king of creatures, Leviathan.

In other words, according to the divine speeches, the order God establishes in creation is neither what the friends believed it was, nor what Job in his despair feared it was. The world is not a safe place, but it is indeed an ordered one. Forces of chaos and wildness are given a place in the world, but they are also given boundaries so that they cannot overwhelm it. There is a tension inherent in such a vision of the cosmos, a tension familiar from the psalms of lament. Job must acknowledge God's sovereignty; but he must also live with the knowledge that God's sovereignty does not exclude forces indifferent toward, and even dangerous to, humanity. Job must submit to God and learn to live in the untamed, dangerous, but stunningly beautiful world that is God's creation.

---

[61] See Gen 1:22, where the sea creatures and birds, not humanity, are the first recipients of the command to "be fruitful and multiply." Thanks to Prof. Ellen Davis for this observation.

There is a certain strange freedom in such submission, the freedom to be a creature along with all the other creatures of God's cosmos. The divine speeches teach Job that he cannot control nearly as much as he thought he could. He is not king; God is. Therefore, he does not have to carry the dead weight of self-imposed responsibility for everything in his life, a weight that he arguably bore in his former life. He can live with the same freedom God gives to all his creatures, a freedom to be what God created him to be while also acknowledging God's sovereignty and participating in God's care for his creation.

According to the final form of the book of Job, submission to God leads to blessing.[62] The epilogue finds Job restored to health, wealth, and community. All is not the same, however: there are hints that Job has learned from his encounter with God to live in the undomesticated cosmos that God has revealed to him and to take up his rightful responsibilities without striving for complete control of his "realm." Job "reconsiders" about what he thought was humanity's central place in the world (Job 42:6). He learns humility while not relinquishing responsibility. He offers proper sacrifices for his friends who have offended God, instead of "preemptive" sacrifices for his children. He takes the risk of fathering more children and thereby reinvests himself in the world. This time, however, he gives his daughters extravagant names to celebrate their beauty and he gives them an inheritance along with their brothers. Through the vision he has received in the divine speeches, it seems that Job has learned to govern his world with the same kind of מִשְׁפָּט with which God governs the cosmos, a מִשְׁפָּט that celebrates wildness and beauty, a מִשְׁפָּט that gives its subjects the freedom to become who they were created to be.

The divine speeches do not, and cannot, tell Job why he suffers. Job cannot know about the wager between God and the Satan or the test will be invalid. On a much more fundamental level, the divine speeches cannot tell Job why he suffers because there is, as the author of the book knows, no completely satisfactory "answer" to undeserved suffering. The divine speeches do most certainly, however, offer an answer to Job's assumptions and attitudes about creation, humanity's place in creation, and God's ordering of it. That answer enables Job once again to participate fully in the world, even with its acute, unexplained, and inexplicable suffering. That participation is finally the answer to the question that starts the whole drama, the Satan's challenge,

---

[62] See discussion in Levenson, 155–56.

"Does Job fear God for nothing?" (Job 1:9). Of all the boundaries God places in the world, there is one boundary that God himself cannot, or will not, cross. God will not force Job to serve him.[63] God gives Job the terrible freedom of deciding whether or not to serve God, even in the midst of Job's unexplained suffering. After his many struggles, Job chooses to do so, to serve God and to submit to God's sovereignty. Such a choice is testimony to the riskiest venture of all in God's perilous, beautiful creation: the adventure of faith, faith in a Creator who loves life, who delights in beauty and freedom, and who calls on his creatures to do the same. The divine speeches, with their magnificent vision of creation, lead Job to enter into that adventure of faith fully and freely. Such is the genius of the divine speeches and of the final form of the book of Job.

Postscript: Ecological Implications of Job's Creation Theology

The primary task of this book has been to explore the creation theology of the divine speeches in Job and to see how that creation theology addresses the situation of Job in the rest of the book. Though ecological concerns are not the primary focus of this book, I want to offer here some reflections on the implications of Job's creation theology for the faith-based environmental movement.[64] These reflections are offered merely as a starting point for further study, not as a comprehensive discussion of the topic.

---

[63] See Christopher Seitz, "Job: Full-Structure, Movement, and Interpretation," *Interpretation* 43 (1989) 3–17.

[64] The relationship between faith and environmental concerns seems to be a topic of growing interest in religious communities. Several recent books, for instance, have discussed the relationship between ecology and Christianity, including *Christianity and Ecology: Seeking the Well-Being of Earth and Humans* (ed. Dieter T. Hessel and Rosemary Radford Ruether; Cambridge, Mass.: Harvard University Press, 2000); *The Earth Bible* (ed. Norman Habel; 5 vols.; Sheffield: Sheffield Academic Press, 2000–2002); Sallie McFague, *Life Abundant: Rethinking Theology and Economy for a Planet in Peril* (Minneapolis: Fortress, 2001); Mark I. Wallace, *Finding God in the Singing River: Christianity, Spirit, Nature* (Minneapolis: Fortress, 2005); Roger S. Gottlieb, *A Greener Faith: Religious Environmentalism and Our Planet's Future* (Oxford: Oxford University Press, 2006); and Denis Edwards, *Ecology at the Heart of Faith* (Maryknoll, N.Y.: Orbis, 2006). There are numerous other books on the topic. Many of the books already cited in this volume also demonstrate a strong interest in environmental concerns. Note, too, the statement on global warming issued in February 2006, by eighty-six Christian evangelical leaders: "Climate Change: An Evangelical Call to Action." [Online: http://www.christiansandclimate.org]

The creation theology of the divine speeches lends itself to fruitful reflection on humanity's relationship with and responsibility for the rest of the natural world. In an age when we are becoming acutely aware of the effects of human consumption on the earth's climate, the book of Job speaks to us about the value of the nonhuman realm. In extraordinarily detailed and beautiful poetry, the divine speeches show Job that there exist wild places and animals whose value has nothing to do with their usefulness to humanity. The divine speeches articulate God's delight and pride in a world full of wild and beautiful things, and they call human beings to take such delight in the world, too. This creation theology is virtually unique in the Bible but it is not as well-known as the creation theologies of Genesis. Yet it can be a rich resource for theological reflection on the environment.

The unique voice of the divine speeches is best articulated in contrast to more well-known creation accounts in the Bible. As we have seen already, biblical passages like Genesis 1 and Psalm 8 depict humanity as the crown of creation. Humanity is created in the image of God and given a place only a little lower than God. God gives human beings dominion over the earth and over the nonhuman creatures of the earth. Such an understanding of humanity's place in creation can be and has been used as justification for misuse of the earth's resources.[65] If one understands human vocation in the world primarily in terms of "dominion" (Gen 1:26, 28), one might very well construe the relationship between humanity and the natural world as adversarial.[66]

In the divine speeches of the book of Job, humanity is neither the crown of creation nor its caretaker. Humanity is part of creation, along with the meteorological forces, the wild animals, and the mythological creatures Behemoth and Leviathan. Contrary to the assertions in Genesis 1 and Psalm

---

[65] The negative contributions of Christian theology to the environmental crisis are famously discussed by Lynn White in his 1967 essay, "On the Historical Roots of Our Ecological Crisis." The essay is reprinted in *This Sacred Earth: Religion, Nature, Environment* (ed. Roger Gottlieb; 2d ed.; New York: Routledge, 2004) 192–201. White has been justly criticized for, among other things, displaying "an ignorance of theological history" (Sallie McFague, "An Ecological Christology: Does Christianity Have It?" in *Christianity and Ecology*, 29). Nevertheless, Christian theology that appeals simplistically to the "dominion" command in Genesis 1 must indeed share some responsibility for the environmental crisis.

[66] The Genesis creation accounts need not and should not be read in such a way, of course. For a sympathetic and nuanced reading of the Genesis creation accounts, see Fretheim, *God and World*, 29–67, and Theodore Hiebert, "The Human Vocation: Origins and Transformations in Christian Traditions," in *Christianity and Ecology*, 135–54.

8, humanity does not and cannot have dominion over the nonhuman creatures. Job cannot use the wild ox to plow his field; the wild donkey does not pay heed to the voice of a taskmaster. Indeed, the wild animals laugh at humanity and its inventions. The psalmist asserts that humanity has dominion over all creatures, including everything that "passes through the paths of the seas" (Ps 8:9), but God proclaims that Job has no hope whatsoever of conquering that greatest of sea creatures, Leviathan. Leviathan cannot be used as food or a pet; he, too, laughs at humanity and its weapons. Job cannot even approach Leviathan's home, the Deep.

The concept of human dominion over the wild animals is refuted in the divine speeches. Instead, God holds up these denizens of the wilderness and the sea as examples of untamed beauty and freedom. God takes delight in these wild creatures and cares for them. Likewise, the wilderness and the sea themselves are depicted in the divine speeches as recipients of God's care and attention. God attends the birth of the Sea. God sends rain on the wilderness where no person lives. In the arid climate of the Near East, God is profligate with water, that most precious of resources, and with it fructifies the wasteland, useless to human beings.

The vision of creation in the divine speeches can fruitfully be used as a corrective to a consumerist view of the natural world. This worldview is fed by a nearly-constant barrage of advertising urging the average American to acquire more and more "stuff" without regard to how much of the earth's resources he or she is consuming. Such a consumerist culture encourages one to be focused on oneself or (at best) on one's family and friends, to the exclusion not only of the billions of people who live in "developing" countries but also of the nonhuman world, which suffers from human greed. A market-driven economy fueled by consumerism views the natural world primarily in terms of how it can be exploited by human beings. One has only to consider the proposal to drill for oil in the Arctic National Wildlife Refuge to see that worldview in action. To that consumerist culture, the divine speeches offer a radical vision. The speeches proclaim that humanity is not the center of the universe, that there exist creatures and places that have an intrinsic value quite apart from anything to do with human beings. The divine speeches assert that no creature or land can properly be called "God-forsaken." Indeed, God takes delight in all that God creates, especially those creatures and places that are unused and unusable by human beings.

The creation theology of the divine speeches calls humanity to a place of humility in relationship to the natural world. Human beings are not the center of creation, and they cannot control the natural world. Creation is not made for the sake of humanity; it comes into being for the pleasure of its Creator. Such a vision provides a necessary corrective to a creation theology that speaks of dominion and subduing the earth (Gen 1:28). According to this alternate biblical vision, humanity participates in creation as one kind of creature among many; it does not dominate the natural world.

That being said, it must also be noted that Job, and thereby humanity, is the sole passenger on this grand tour of the cosmos that is the divine speeches. Though human beings are almost non-existent in the divine speeches, they are granted a position of some prominence by virtue of Job's position as the recipient of the vision. Job is called to see the world from God's point of view and to take delight in its beauty just as God does. This position of humanity—as both observer and participant—is unique in the natural world and implies a certain status. Human beings are not the center of creation, but they are called to observe and appreciate the beauty of creation in a way akin to the Creator's delight in it.

We are aided today in such observation and appreciation by the tools of science and art. The questions that God puts to Job are unanswerable in Job's context: Do you know? Are you able? In today's world, however, we can answer at least a few of those questions. We do know the gestation period of the deer and the mountain goat. We have seen something of the depths of the sea. We understand to a certain extent how rain and snow are formed. Thanks to documentaries from National Geographic and similar organizations, we are able to observe and marvel in the wisdom and complexity woven into the natural world. The speed and grace of a leopard running, the intricate ecosystem of a tropical rainforest, the sense of smell that guides a Pacific salmon hundreds of miles back to its spawning ground—these details of the natural world that we are privileged to observe corroborate the sense of wonder and delight that permeate the divine speeches.

Those speeches set forth a vision of a world in which there exist creatures and forces that are beautiful and wild, inspiring wonder in the careful observer. These creatures and forces are also indifferent to and sometimes dangerous to human beings. The sea is both life-giving and death-dealing; meteorological forces—snow, tornadoes, hurricanes—play havoc with people's lives. Such a vision of a world dangerous to humanity is a challenge to those people, like the Job of the prologue, who wish to control the world around them. Davis puts the issue this way: "The great question that God's speech out of the whirlwind poses for Job and every other person of integrity is this: Can you love what you do not control?"[67] Can you love what you do not control: the sea, the wilderness, the wild animals? Can you appreciate and love those things and creatures simply because they are wild and beautiful and of great intrinsic value, and not because you can control them or make use of them in some way? The question is just as pertinent today as it was when the book of Job was written.

The divine speeches, with their unique biblical vision of creation, challenge people of faith—particularly Jews and Christians, the two faith communities that esteem the Hebrew Bible as Scripture—to understand their relationship with the natural world not as one of dominion or control, but as one of participation and appreciation. The divine speeches call humanity to a broad vision of the world, one not centered on human beings but instead cognizant of the vast and varied forms of life outside the human sphere. The divine speeches call human beings to see the cosmos from a God's-eye point of view and to love even that which they cannot control.

Such a vision does not imply that human beings are to give up responsibility for that which they can control. Job ceases to offer preemptive sacrifices for his children in the epilogue, but he does offer prayers for his companions who have in truth offended God. In a world where voracious human consumption of fossil fuels has begun to change the earth's climate, humanity must take responsibility for changing its own behavior so that life can continue for the countless species with whom we share this earth. With the call to observe and to love the world as God does comes the responsibility to care for and preserve the world for the other creatures that inhabit it and for our own children. "Stewardship," of course, is the word most often used for such care and preservation of the earth. Biblical texts such as Genesis 2:15 and Leviticus 25:23 speak more directly of stewardship than do the divine speeches in Job.[68] In the latter, "justice" might be the more appropriate word to use for humanity's relationship with the natural world. Because humanity is just

---

[67] Davis, *Getting Involved*, 140.

[68] In the Leviticus passage, the Israelites are reminded that the land is YHWH's and that they are tenants on it. In Genesis, Adam is told to "serve" and "keep" the garden. See below for more on the Genesis passage.

one sort of creature among many, human beings should act with justice in sharing the world's resources.

The two concepts—stewardship and justice—are not mutually exclusive, of course, nor are the biblical passages that speak of them. Both Adam in the garden and Job in the divine speeches are given privileged positions from which to observe and participate in God's beautiful creation. Adam is given responsibility to "serve" (עבד) and to "keep" (שׁמר) the garden (Gen 2:15). Job is taught humility in relationship to the natural world. In our current environmental crisis, both biblical voices should be heeded. According to Genesis 2, humanity is given responsibility to be stewards of the earth, serving it and keeping it as one keeps God's commandments.[69] According to the divine speeches, humanity is not the center of creation and should therefore learn humility. This humility that comes with the realization that the world was not made for the sake of humanity should result in a corresponding restraint and care in using the earth's resources, so that all God's creatures can live and thrive and become who they were created to be.

The divine speeches in Job are a biblical voice not as widely-known as the Genesis creation accounts, yet they offer a fruitful resource for people of faith who sense a call to care for creation. The church and the synagogue would do well to take up this biblical voice on creation and make it part of their preaching and teaching. The creation theology of the divine speeches can be used to broaden people's perspectives, to "de-center" humanity's focus on itself and to move that focus to the beauty and complexity of the natural world outside the human sphere. It can serve as a call to humility, to responsibility, to wonder, and to delight. "I had heard of you by the hearing of the ear," says Job to God at the end of the divine speeches, "But now my own eyes have seen you" (Job 42:5). Creation in its beauty, intricacy, wildness, freedom, and order shows forth its Creator. This magnificent vision of the divine speeches in Job is a vision that should be heeded as we struggle theologically with the issues of environmental degradation and humanity's relationship to the natural world. It is my hope that this book will contribute in some small way to that important conversation.

---

[69] The word שׁמר is used often in the Hebrew Bible to speak of "keeping" God's commandments or God's covenant. For more on Genesis 2, see the pieces by Fretheim and Hiebert mentioned in the footnote above.

Appendix: Translation and Commentary

Job 38

[1]YHWH answered Job from the whirlwind, saying,[1]

[2]"Who is this that darkens counsel with words lacking knowledge?

[3]Gird up your loins like a man. I will question you and you declare to me.

[4]Where were you when I established the earth? Speak, if you have discernment!

[5]Who took its measurements? Surely you know! Or who stretched out a measuring line upon it?

[6]Upon what were its bases sunk, or who laid its cornerstone,

[7]when the morning stars cried out together for joy, and all the sons of God raised a shout?

[8]And who fenced in Sea with doors when it came bursting out from the womb,

[9]when I made a cloud its clothing and thick darkness its swaddling clothes?

[10]I prescribed my boundary for it and set a bar and doors.

[11]And I said, 'Thus far you will come and no further. Here shall your proud waves be stopped.'

[12]Have you commanded Morning from your earliest days? Have you taught Dawn its place;

[13]to grasp the earth by its corners that the wicked might be shaken from it?

[14]It changes like clay under a seal, and they stand as those shamed.

---

[1] All translations of the biblical text are mine, unless otherwise noted. The translations are derived from the Hebrew text of *Biblica Hebraica Stuttgartensia* (ed. K. Elliger, et al.; Stuttgart: Deutsche Bibelgesellschaft, 1967–1977). I agree with the vast majority of scholars that the Masoretic Text remains the authoritative source for translations of the book of Job. I have noted, where appropriate, variants found in the LXX and other textual traditions, and have at times offered emendations based on those traditions. For a thorough discussion of text criticism of Job, see Pope, xliii–xlvii.

¹⁵Their light is withheld from the wicked, and the uplifted arm is broken.

¹⁶Have you come to the springs of Sea, or have you walked around in the depth of the Deep?

¹⁷Have the gates of Death been revealed to you? Have you seen the gates of deep darkness?

¹⁸Have you considered the breadth of the earth? Speak, if you know it all!

¹⁹Which is the way to the dwelling place of light, and where is the place of darkness?

²⁰Have you taken it to its territory? Do you know the paths to its home?

²¹You know, for you were born then, and the number of your days is great!

²²Have you entered the storehouses of snow? Have you seen the storehouses of hail

²³that I have stored up for the time of trouble, for the day of battle and war?

²⁴Which is the way to where lightning is apportioned, where the east wind is scattered upon the earth?

²⁵Who has cut for the flood a watercourse, and a way for the thunderbolt

²⁶to cause it to rain upon the uninhabited land, the wilderness where no person lives;

²⁷to satisfy the desolate and wasteland and to cause the parched land to sprout grass?

²⁸Does the rain have a father? Who begot the drops of dew?

²⁹From whose womb did the ice come forth, and who bore the hoarfrost of heaven?

³⁰Like a stone, the waters hide themselves, and the face of the Deep congeals.

³¹Have you bound the bonds of the Pleiades; or have you loosed the cords of Orion?

³²Have you brought forth Mazarot at its time; or have you guided the Bear with her children?

³³Do you know the statutes of the heavens? Have you established their rule on earth?

³⁴Have you raised your voice to the cloud so that a multitude of waters covers you?

³⁵Have you let loose lightning bolts so that they go forth? Have they said to you, 'At your service'?

³⁶Who set wisdom in the cloud cover or who gave understanding to my pavilion?

³⁷Who numbers the clouds in wisdom? Who tips over the water bottles of heaven

³⁸when dust runs together into a mass and clods of earth are joined together?

³⁹Have you hunted prey for the lioness? Have you filled the appetite of the young lions

⁴⁰when they crouch in dens, when they lie in a thicket as a lair?

⁴¹Who provides for the raven his food while his young ones wander about without food, crying to God for help?

Textual Notes

38:10 The literal translation of the first stich is, "I broke upon it my decree." This is an unusual use of the word שבר, which usually denotes either a physical breaking/shattering (of a piece of pottery, a door, weapons, etc.) or a metaphorical shattering (of a heart, pride, wickedness). How does one "break" a decree or boundary "upon" or "for" the Sea? Perhaps the allusion is to crushed stone at the seashore.[2] Various scholars have emended the verb.[3] This translation, however, follows Gordis and Habel in retaining שבר with the connotation of "decree" or "prescribe," based on a similar description in Prov 8:29 and the parallel verb in 10b.

38:11 The second half of the verse is a bit awkward. Scholars suggest that it is a scribal metathesis: ישבת גאון becoming ישית בגאון.[4] While such an error is possible, the phrase can be understood as written if the verb is taken as impersonal and passive: "Here shall be set the pride of your waves (i.e., your proud waves)."

38:12 I am reading the Ketiv in 12b, with the ה used as a mater lectionis, an anomalous use in the second person perfect. Though the definite article is often missing in Hebrew poetry, the Joban poet is particularly consistent in not using it for the various entities he describes. It is partly for that reason that I have capitalized references to those entities that are personified, to

² See Amos Hakham, *Sefer Iyov* (Jerusalem: Society for the Publication of the Bible, 1981) 292, and Driver and Gray, 300.

³ See Pope, 294, for the list of suggested emendations.

⁴ So suggests G. Gerlemann, the editor of Job in *Biblia Hebraica Stuttgartensia* (Stuttgart: Deutsche Bibelgesellschaft, 1977). Likewise Gordis, *Job*, 445.

emphasize their mythological roots.[5] Dawn (שחר), for instance, is found also in the Ugaritic poem about "The Birth of the Gracious Gods," where El begets the gods Dawn (*šḥr*) and Dusk (*šlm*).[6]

38:14 The subject of the second stich is difficult to determine. The only plural masculine noun in the previous verse is רשעים. Given the presence of the same word in the subsequent verse, it seems the only logical choice as the subject for the plural masculine verb in 14b. What can it mean, however, to say that the wicked "take their stand like a garment"? Some commentators suggest the emendation of ויתיצבו to ותצבע "to be dyed," which makes sense in a metaphor about clothing.[7] I prefer the less drastic emendation of לְבוּשׁ to לְבוֹשׁ "to be ashamed." The image is one of the wicked standing in judgment, their shameful deeds exposed by the light.[8]

38:16 נבכי, from an unknown root, is taken to mean something like "sources" or "depths," given its parallel חקר in the second stich of the verse. Commentators often relate it to the word in Job 28:11 revocalized as מִבְּכֵי, based on a Ugaritic cognate.[9]

38:24 The first stich is almost an exact echo of verse 19a. Here, however, the parallel to אור is not darkness, as one would expect, but the east wind. Commentators have been troubled by this apparent incongruity. They have therefore suggested various emendations, including רוח ("wind"), קטור ("smoke"), and אד ("mist"). Some suggest that אור here should be understood as "wind" or "air currents," based on Akkadian or Greek cognates.[10] All such emendations are unnecessary, as Norman Habel points out. אור here is to be understood not as "light," but as "lightning," as in 37:11 (where יפיץ is also employed).[11] Such a translation fits nicely with the following verse and its mention of thunderstorms.

---

[5] I have not capitalized references to every inanimate object, only those that are described in anthropomorphic terms or have obvious roots in ANE mythology (Sea, Death, Abyss, etc.).

[6] *CAT* 1.23. Simon Parker, ed. *Ugaritic Narrative Poetry* (trans. Mark S. Smith et al. Missoula, Mont.: Scholars, 1997).

[7] This emendation is suggested by Gerlemann in *BHS*, and by Pope, 295.

[8] See commentary below on 38:13. The emendation chosen here is suggested by Gordis, *Job*, 446. He makes further emendations to the verse that I consider unnecessary for obtaining a clear meaning.

[9] See Gordis, *Job*, 447.

[10] Ibid., 448.

[11] See Job 36:32; 37:3, 15. Habel, 522.

38:27 The second stich is awkward as it stands: "to cause to sprout the place where grass comes forth." It is preferable to read צָמֵא ("parched land") for מֹצָא.[12] The emendation reads smoothly, and צָמֵא provides a good parallel to שֹׁאָה ומשֹׁאָה.[13]

38:30 The verbs in this verse present some difficulty. Each would seem to fit better with the other's subject. Thus, the waters would "congeal," or "cling together" like a stone (cf. יתלכדו in 41:9), and the face of the deep would be "hidden" (with ice). Some commentators suggest that the verbs have been accidentally transposed. Habel argues that this is a deliberate poetic device, wherein two parallel verbs are each meant to be understood with the other's subject.[14] In any case, the progression of the description is natural, showing the effects of the "ice" mentioned in the previous verse.

38:32 The word מזרות is hapax, though the reference must be to a constellation, or perhaps to a number of unidentified "constellations," to which the similar word מזלות refers in 2 Kgs 23:5.[15] With many scholars, I am reading עיש as referring to the same constellation as עש in Job 9:9.[16]

38:33 The word משֹׁטר is hapax, though a noun from the same root, שֹׁטֵר ("officer"), is fairly common in biblical Hebrew. Both are derived from the root שֹׁטר ("to write"), a verb attested in Akkadian, and in the later Hebrew noun שְׁטָר ("document"). The noun here is cognate with Akkadian *maštāru* ("writing"). The sky full of stars is referred to in Akkadian as *šiṭir šamē* or *šiṭirtu šamāmi* ("heavenly writing").[17] משֹׁטר could be referring to the constellations described in the previous verses. Understood with its parallel משֹׁטר, חקות is, however, best translated "rule" or perhaps "law code."

38:34 The LXX has ὑπακούσεταί — "to listen to, to obey" instead of תְּכַסְךָ. It is unclear what the Hebrew original might have been. It is possible that the LXX translator might have changed the word to match the next verse better, where the lightning (potentially) obeys Job's voice.

---

[12] The adjective צָמֵא when used as a substantive almost always refers to people, though in Isaiah 44:3, צָמֵא is used as a parallel for יַבָּשָׁה ("dry ground"). It can, therefore, be understood as "parched land."

[13] The emendation is suggested by many commentators. See Driver and Gray, 305.

[14] Habel, 522. He offers no biblical parallel for such a poetic device. Driver and Gray argue that the transposition of the verbs is accidental (305).

[15] Pope, 301, identifies מַזָּרוֹת as a "dialectical variant" of מַזָּלוֹת.

[16] Ursa Major, or "the Bear," according to Pope, 71.

[17] Pope, 301.

38:36 The identification of טֻחוֹת and שֶׂכְוִי in this verse is a matter of debate amongst scholars both ancient and modern. The only other use of טֻחוֹת in the Bible occurs in Ps 51:8, where it is parallel with סָתֻם ("hidden"); hence the conjectured meaning: "inward parts." שֶׂכְוִי is hapax.

Gordis outlines four major lines of interpretation for these words. They may refer to: 1) the human spirit; 2) celestial phenomena; 3) Egyptian deities; or 4) birds associated with wisdom.[18]

It seems to me that the interpretation having to do with Egyptian deities is unlikely, given the complete absence of such references in the divine speeches. Likewise, a reference to the human spirit seems out of place both in the immediate context (a discussion of meteorological forces) and in the divine speeches in general, which do not credit humanity with much wisdom.[19] Since the speeches are concerned with creation, the most likely interpretations have to do with clouds or animals of some kind. Rabbinic tradition associates שֶׂכְוִי with the cock, hence the use of the word in the Jewish morning service: "who gave to the cock (לַשֶׂכְוִי) wisdom to distinguish between day and night."[20] No corresponding root for such a meaning is, however, attested. Therefore, it seems most likely that the reference is to clouds or other celestial phenomena.[21] The only problem with such a translation is that the divine speeches do not elsewhere ascribe wisdom to inanimate objects such as clouds.

Commentary

38:1 After everyone else in the dialogue has spoken—Job, his three friends, and Elihu—YHWH at last speaks. He addresses only the defiant sufferer, not the four men who have ostensibly defended him from Job's charges. Job is the only one of the human beings who has spoken directly to God, not just

---

[18] Gordis, *Job*, 452–53. Both Gordis and Tur-Sinai (533–35) opt for the last interpretation. Pope argues for the Egyptian deities. Habel asserts that the translation, "thick cloud cover," is most likely. Ibn Ezra and Rashi translate the words along the lines of "inward parts/heart." Driver and Gray list the options but do not choose one.

[19] Ps 51:8 is the best argument for this interpretation. Those who espouse this view derive טֻחוֹת from טִיחַ, "plaster, cover," hence, the reference is to the fat covering body organs. The same root, however, could be used to argue for the translation "cloud cover."

[20] Gordis, *Job*, 452.

[21] Following Habel, 523, I understand שֶׂכְוִי as שֻׂכִּי ("my booth/pavilion"), referring to a cloud canopy (cf. 36:29) and טֻחוֹת as "cloud cover."

about God.[22] Now, God speaks directly to Job. Job has demanded again and again that God appear and contend with him; therefore, the theophany marks the climax of the book. The content of the theophany, however, is not what Job anticipated. Rather than addressing Job's concerns about the justice of his suffering, God challenges Job with questions of his own.

The appearance of the tetragrammaton at the beginning of the divine speeches is striking. It appears 32 times in the book of Job, primarily in the prose prologue and epilogue, and only once in the dialogue.[23] Its use to introduce the divine speeches marks a distinct break with the dialogue which precedes it. The use of the tetragrammaton is one piece of evidence for a possible recontextualization of the divine speeches from another story.

Job has predicted God's use of a storm (שׂערה/סערה) in 9:17, though he asserts that God will crush him with it. Many biblical texts associate storms with theophanies.[24]

38:2 The first question of the many questions which make up the divine speeches addresses Job's right to challenge God: "Who is this?" "Who are you?" It is at once a question of identity and a question designed to put Job in his place. Human beings are largely absent from the description of creation in the divine speeches. It is significant, then, that the first question of the speeches is about the identity of humanity, in the person of Job. God accuses Job of obscuring understanding with his words. Both עצה and דעת are commonly found in wisdom texts.[25]

---

[22]Job starts to speak in the second person directly to God in 7:7. He continues to do so periodically in the rest of the dialogue, switching back and forth from third person to second person. The three friends and Elihu, on the other hand, never address God directly, though they advocate the practice of prayer.

[23] The tetragrammaton appears 18 times in the prologue (chapters 1–2), 8 times in the epilogue (42:7–17), 5 times in the divine speeches (38:1–42:6), and once in the dialogue, in 12:9. This last occurrence is not attested in some manuscripts, which instead use אלוה, the usual designation for God in the dialogue.

[24] סערה in Ezek 1:4 and Zech 9:14. See also Exod 19:16, 2 Sam 22:8–16, Isa 63:19–20, Nah 1:3, Ps 50:3, etc. In 2 Kgs 1, Elijah is taken up into heaven by a סערה.

[25] Proverbs contains 40 occurrences of the word דעת, by far the most of any biblical book. Job comes in second with 11 occurrences, while Ecclesiastes contains 8. The word עצה occurs most often in wisdom texts (10 times in Proverbs, 9 times in Job) and prophetic texts (18 times in Isaiah, 8 times in Jeremiah).

38:3 Job has questioned God numerous times in the dialogue, and now it is God's turn to question Job. Though Job claimed that he would "answer" God when he called,[26] Job expected nothing like what follows.

Many scholars have emended כְּגֶבֶר to כְּגִבֹּר "like a mighty hero." While the emendation is plausible, it seems unnecessary, particularly given the prevalence of the word גֶּבֶר in the book of Job.[27] Job and his companions have been largely concerned with the status of "men," particularly their relationship with God. Why should the divine speeches not pick up on this recurring word as they finally address the questions raised in the book? In fact, it is the question of being a "man," a human, that is one of the primary issues with which the divine speeches are concerned.

38:4–6 These verses mark the beginning of God's extended description of the natural world and its creation. They recount the initial act of creation: the foundation of the earth. This passage relies on the ancient Near Eastern correlation of creation with the building of a structure, specifically a temple, beginning with the laying of the foundation.[28] Temples were commonly understood in ancient Near Eastern literature as microcosms of the world.[29] Here in the divine speeches, creation itself is the temple, constructed by God for God's own glory.

"Where were you?" God asks Job, and it is again a question designed to put Job in his place. Job has neither the longevity nor the understanding to challenge God's ordering of creation. The questions in verse 5 are also rhetorical, since God has already claimed responsibility in the previous verse for laying the foundation of the earth. To "stretch out a measuring line" (נטה קו) can be an act of destruction[30] or of creation and restoration,[31] as it is here.

Given the many links between the creation of the tabernacle and the creation of the world in the Priestly narrative,[32] it is significant that אדן

---

[26] Job 13:22; 14:15.

[27] Job 3:3, 23; 4:17; 10:5; 14:10, 14; 16:21; as well as eight additional occurrences.

[28] See Ps 24:2–3; Ps 78:69.

[29] For a discussion of the connections between creation and temple/tabernacle building, see Levenson, *Creation and the Persistence of Evil*, 66–99; Peter Kearney, "Creation and Liturgy," *ZAW* 89 (1977) 375–87. For a discussion of this passage in Job as referring to a temple, see Brown, *Character in Crisis*, 92–93.

[30] Lam 2:8. I see no resonance of this meaning here.

[31] Zech 1:16.

[32] See Levenson and Kearney works cited above.

("foundation/base") in verse 6 is used almost exclusively in the Bible to refer to components of the tabernacle. The present verse and Cant 5:15 are the only exceptions. Likewise, the laying of a "cornerstone" (אבן פנתה) is referenced in other biblical texts that draw on temple language to describe restoration.[33]

38:7 God is not alone at the foundation of the world. The morning stars rejoice at its creation, as do the members of the heavenly court, the "sons of God."

The phrase בני (ה)אלהים is not a common one in the Bible. It occurs three times in Job, here and in 1:6 and 2:1, where the prologue describes God's heavenly court. It is used also twice in Genesis 6, the story of the "sons of God" who mated with human women. The imagery is that of a group of divine beings who co-exist with God. This imagery has obvious mythological roots, as one can compare it to the menagerie of divine beings found in virtually all extra-biblical ANE myths. It must be noted, however, that in Job the "sons of God" are obviously subordinate to God. In the prologue, they stand in attendance (התיצב) upon God; and in this verse, they rejoice in God's establishment of the earth.

The imagery of the "morning stars" and the "sons of God" can also be connected to the common epithet for God: "YHWH/God of hosts" (צבאות), found numerous times in the prophetic writings. Apparently, the title has its roots in a common motif of divine beings who serve God. More pertinent to our current text, the "host of heaven" (צבא השמים) are equated in legal and prophetic texts with the sun, the moon, and the stars, and the Israelites are warned against worshiping them.[34] Such a warning indicates that these celestial "hosts" were sometimes deified in ancient Israel, as in other ANE cultures. Here in Job, the morning stars appear to retain their status as divine beings. Nevertheless, they act positively as a chorus of praise for God's action in creation, not as illicit objects of worship.[35]

[33] Brown cites Ps 118:22 and Isa 28:16 (*Character in Crisis*, 93).

[34] Deut 4:19; 17:3. According to the first passage, it is all right for the nations to worship the "host of heaven," but not for Israel to do so, because Israel belongs solely to YHWH. Cf. 2 Kgs 17:16; 21:3, 5; 23:4; Jer. 8:2 for instances of the Israelites worshiping the hosts of heaven.

[35] See Neh 9:6 and 1 Kgs 22:19, where the "host of heaven" are also portrayed in a positive light. The latter text uses the imagery of the divine court which is found also in the Joban prologue.

38:8 The description moves from the foundation of the earth to the startling image of the birth of the Sea. The personification of the Sea is ubiquitous in ANE mythology. The Sea, whether Yamm in the Ugaritic Baal cycle or Tiamat in *Enuma Elish*, must be defeated before order can be established. Other biblical passages, including other passages in Job, allude to such myths.[36] Even the Priestly creation account, while not personifying the primordial waters, gives them a place *before* the foundation of the earth. In the divine speeches, however, the Sea is *born*. There is, therefore, presumably a time when it did not exist. It is not so much a primordial enemy of order as it is a rambunctious infant, albeit an awesomely powerful infant. God must "fence" it in as it comes bursting out of the womb.[37]

The use of the relatively rare verb שׂוך/סוך ("to fence in") in this verse echoes its two previous uses in the book of Job.[38] In 1:10, the Satan says to God, "Have you not put a fence (שַׂכְתָּ) around him and his house and all that he has?" In this case, "to fence in" is to protect someone from harm. Job uses the same word in 3:23 as he laments that he was born and wonders why light is given "to a man whose way is hidden, whom God has fenced in." In this case, the "fencing in" is a hostile act, a kind of suffocating and unwelcome attention.[39]

In this third usage, then, God uses סוך to denote a "fencing in" that has nothing to do with either the Satan's or Job's usage of the word. This "fencing in" is neither protective nor suffocating. It is an act designed to create order in the world, to contain a force that has the potential to run roughshod over God's

---

[36] Ps 29; 89; 114; Isa 51:9–10; Job 9:8; 26:12–13, etc. See John Day, *God's Conflict with the Dragon and the Sea* (Cambridge: Cambridge University Press, 1985).

[37] The writer of Job does not specify from whose womb the Sea is born. One could make comparisons to Tiamat, the mother of all the gods in *Enuma Elish*; however, Tiamat—the sea—is not herself born or begotten. She and her consort Apsu exist before anything else. See James Pritchard, ed., *Ancient Near Eastern Texts Relating to the Old Testament*, 3d ed. (Princeton: Princeton University Press, 1969) 61.

[38] Outside of these 3 occurrences in Job, שׂוך/סוך in the sense of "fence in" is used only one other time in the Hebrew Bible, in Hos 2:8. In its other occurrences, in Exod 40:21, Ps 5:12, Ps 91:4, and Lam 3:43, 44, it has the meaning "to cover." Given the allusion to the tabernacle in 38:6, it is interesting to note that the related word מָסָך refers almost always to the "veil" or "curtain" at the door of the tabernacle, or at the Holy of Holies (Exod 26:36; 35:15; 36:37; Num 3:31; etc.). The homonym סיך/סוך ("to anoint") is used more commonly than שׂוך/סוך.

[39] See Job 7:19: "Will you not turn your gaze from me? Will you not let me be until I swallow my spittle?"

ordered creation. Job has complained earlier that God is treating him like the Sea or a sea monster, setting a guard over him.[40] God corrects this assertion here; he does not "fence in" Job, either for protection or for correction. God "fences in" the Sea, and thereby creates order, albeit not the sort of order the Satan describes in the prologue, where the righteous are protected from any harm. The order that God builds into creation includes boundaries for the Sea, but it does not eliminate it. The Sea, a symbol of chaos, still has a place in God's ordered creation.[41]

38:9 The birthing imagery continues. God uses thick cloud to swaddle the newly-born Sea. Perhaps the imagery is that of clouds collecting on the horizon as one looks out to sea. This verse stands in sharp contrast to earlier verses in Job about God's relationship with the Sea. The image of God as divine warrior, treading on the back of the Sea,[42] has given way to that of God as midwife, swaddling the newborn (though powerful) infant. This verse is just one instance of the way in which the divine speeches reverse the images of creation found in earlier parts of Job.[43]

38:10–11 The birthing imagery gives way to more conventional language about the Sea. God sets a limit for the Sea, creating a bar and doors to contain it. The same motif is found in *Enuma Elish*, when Marduk, after slaying Tiamat and creating from her corpse the Sea and the firmament, places a bar and guards to keep the waters from escaping.[44] God also forbids the Sea to cross the boundary he has fixed for it: "Thus far you will come, and no further." God gives the Sea a place in creation, but he also sets limits on it.

38:12–15 The subject changes from the Sea to the dawn/morning. Though not quite as anthropomorphic as that of the Sea, the description of Dawn makes use of anthropomorphic images, particularly in verse 13, where Dawn grasps the corners of the earth and shakes "the wicked" out of it.

Aside from the presence of Job as the addressee, the mention of the "wicked" in this passage marks the first time that human beings are mentioned,

[40] Job 7:12.

[41] See further discussion in chapter two.

[42] Job 9:8; 26:12.

[43] This important point was discussed at length in chapter two. This rather benign image of the Sea contrasts with most biblical portrayals of the Sea, with the exception of the positive portrayal of Leviathan, the sea monster, in Ps 104:26. Usually portrayed as the enemy of God, in the psalm Leviathan is instead God's plaything. See commentary below on 40:25 for more on the figure of Leviathan.

[44] *ANET* 67, lines 135–40.

even peripherally, in the divine speeches. That the human beings in question are the "wicked" does not speak well of humankind's place in the order of things. By contrast, Dawn acts as God's agent, shaking the wicked out of the earth like so much dust out of a rug. This passage is the first confirmation in the divine speeches that God does have concern for the moral sphere, an issue raised again and again by Job in the dialogue. Earlier in the book, for instance, Job complains that the wicked are not punished, and he says much the same thing as these verses, that darkness is friend to the wicked, and light/dawn their enemy.[45]

The translation of verse 14 is difficult, but the image seems to be that of the approaching dawn bringing into definition the elements of a darkened landscape, as a seal forms images in a piece of moist clay. The wicked "stand shamed," as the light exposes their deeds. In verse 15, it is not clear whose light is withheld from the wicked. It could be the light of the wicked themselves, but it is more likely the light of בקר and שחר. God withholds light and life from the wicked and breaks their "uplifted (i.e., proud, rebellious) arm."

38:16 God challenges Job to find the sources of two primordial entities: the Sea and the Deep. The Deep (תהום) is the primordial ocean. The word is used a number of times in the Hebrew Bible, almost always without the definite article, which would suggest that it denotes an originally mythological being.[46] It is not explicitly personified here, as it is in other biblical passages. For example, in Gen 49:25 it is said—in a word usually reserved to describe animals—to "crouch (רבצת) beneath."

38:17–18 God continues to challenge Job to find the habitats of various entities—this time, death and darkness. The poetic parallelism is particularly

[45] Job 24:13–17. See also Job 34:22; Prov 7:9. G. R. Driver argues that "the wicked" here are not human beings at all, but part of the "heavenly host," in particular, the Dog-star Sirius ("the hairy one;" Arabic *šiʿra*), Canis Major and Canis Minor ("the two hairy ones;" Arabic *šiʿrayān*). (*JTS* 4 [1953] 208–12.) Such an interpretation is possible, given the mythological allusions in the divine speeches. It would not make sense, however, to say that the heavenly host are "shaken out" of the *earth*; and it seems unlikely that they would be portrayed in a negative light when in verse 7 they were part of the heavenly chorus of praise. In addition, the related passage in Job 24 argues for the interpretation offered here—that Dawn exposes the actions of wicked people and "shakes" them out of the earth, or at least sends them into hiding for the day.

[46] According to Day, 50. Day connects תהום to the Akkadian Tiamat and the Ugaritic root *thm/thmt*. He posits a Canaanite, rather than a Babylonian, origin to the mythology of the Dragon and the Sea.

striking in verse 17, with the alliteration of מָוֶת and צַלְמָוֶת. The latter word is
a favorite of the Joban poet. Of its 18 appearances in the Bible, 10 occur in
the book of Job. Its first appearance is in 3:5, where Job wishes that צלמות
and חֹשֶׁךְ would obliterate the day of his birth. In this verse and in 38:19, God
challenges Job's curse. Job has invoked צלמות and חֹשֶׁךְ, but he cannot even
claim to know their dwelling places. He has longed for death (מות) numerous
times (first in 3:21), but has never even been to its gates.[47]

In verse 18, the description moves from the depths of the earth to its
breadth. If Job cannot delve into the Deep, perhaps he can view the entire
expanse of earth.

38:19–20 Like חֹשֶׁךְ, מות, and צלמות, אור (light) is not in any way subject to
Job's wishes or knowledge. He tries to control it in his curse (3:9), but does
not even know the way to its dwelling place. These verses are one instance of
a recurring motif in the divine speeches, the motif of habitat. The homes of
the cosmological and zoological specimens described in the divine speeches
are inaccessible to human beings.[48]

38:21 The speech takes on a sarcastic tone, moving from questions to
statements: Surely you know the home of darkness, Job, for you have been
there. Your knowledge must be based on many years of experience. In fact,
you must have been born at the creation of the world.

In both the prose prologue and the poetic dialogue, Job has been portrayed
as an elder of the people, a man to whom other men come for counsel and
wisdom.[49] In the divine speeches, he is revealed as simply a human being,
lacking in power, lacking in wisdom. Behemoth, the "first of the acts of God,"
is ancient; Job, by contrast, is very young.[50] The argument that Job was not
present at the creation of the world, and therefore cannot judge God's actions,
echoes an earlier point made by Eliphaz.[51]

38:22–23 Meteorological forces enter the portrait of creation. The poet
imagines hail and snow gathered in storehouses, waiting for God's use. The
same image is used elsewhere of rain, wind, and the waters of the deep.[52]

[47] See the Mesopotamian myth of the descent of Ishtar into the Netherworld, where she
has to pass through seven gates (*ANET*, 107–9).

[48] See Job 38:16–17, 22, 24; 39:6, 27–28; 40:23; 41:23. See discussion below.

[49] Job 1:3; 29:7, 21–25.

[50] Job 40:19.

[51] Job 15:7.

[52] Deut 28:12; Jer 10:13; 51:16; Ps 33:7; 135:7.

Hail and snow are not simply natural phenomena, but weapons, stored up for God's use in time of war.[53]

38:24–27 This passage is in important one for understanding the view of humanity in the divine speeches. The passage describes thunderstorms, beginning with a reference to lightning and wind. Verse 25 echoes 28:26b, which also contains the answer to the question: God made a way for the thunderbolt, and God is the one who apportions the wind and rain.

The thunderstorm has a purpose. God causes the rain to fall on wilderness, on land uninhabited or abandoned by human beings. This pronouncement stands in contrast to an earlier statement by Elihu that God provides abundant rain for the sake of human beings. While the two statements are not in conflict, the one in the divine speeches could be understood to "correct" the other, to make it more accurate.[54] God indeed provides rain to humanity, but God also provides rain to a land unused and unusable by humanity. The divine speeches portray a universe that is radically theocentric, where things do not happen for the sake of human beings. Indeed, the rain is sent to the desolate land in order that the land itself might be satisfied and bring forth grass (דשא), just as the earth did at the beginning of creation.[55] This land is not just "wilderness;" it is שאה ומשאה (vs. 27). משאה, always paired with שאה, signifies total desolation.[56] Perhaps the connotation is one not just of desert or wilderness, but of land devastated by human warfare.

---

[53] See Joshua 10:11; Isa 28:17; Ezek 13:13.

[54] Job 36:27–28. It is widely accepted by modern scholars that the Elihu speech is not original to the book of Job, but was written and inserted by someone who was dissatisfied with the book as it stood. Elihu is mentioned neither before nor after his speech. The divine speeches follow most naturally not Elihu's speech, but Job's final defense (chapters 29–31), when Job challenges God to answer. It seems that the writer of the Elihu speech, like Elihu himself, was disturbed by the inadequacy of the three friends' arguments, and inserted his speech between Job's final speech and God's response. For a discussion of this issue, see Pope, xxvii–xxviii, and Gordis, *Job,* 546–53 (though note that Gordis believes Elihu's speech to be written by the same author as the rest of the book). This verse in the divine speeches, then, was not written originally to "correct" the statement by Elihu. In the final form of the book, however, it may be said to assume that function.

[55] Gen 1:11–12 features this rare word most prominently. The root is used 3 times in these two verses, once as a verb, which is a particularly rare occurrence.

[56] See Job 30:3 and Zeph 1:15, where the phrase refers to "the day of YHWH." See also Gordis, *Job,* 449.

APPENDIX

147

It is striking that verse 26 marks the first and only use in the divine speeches of the words אִישׁ and אָדָם ("man, humanity").[57] The word אֱנוֹשׁ appears not at all in the divine speeches. All three words are used numerous times throughout the rest of the book of Job. These usages range from simple description ("There was a man [אִישׁ] in the land of Uz") to profound reflection ("What is humanity [אֱנוֹשׁ], that you magnify them, that you set your mind on them?"). As noted above, human beings are almost nonexistent in the divine speeches, mentioned only peripherally to the rest of creation. In these verses, such inattention to humanity is made explicit: God sends rain not for the sake of human beings, but for the sake of creation itself.[58]

38:28–30 The divine speeches arc full of procreation images, of which these verses are prime examples. The sea is "born." The rain and dew have a father, and the ice a mother. Later, when the description turns to the wild animals, the speeches are filled with references to birth and offspring.

Robert Alter argues that this theme of procreation is an intentional link between the lament of Job in chapter 3 and the first of God's speeches.[59] In the former, Job has "uncreated" the night of his conception and the day of his birth. Job's life has become so unbearable to him that he wishes not just that he were dead, but that he had never been given life in the first place. The divine speeches apparently answer that challenge by reaffirming the power of procreation, applying its imagery even to things not normally associated with reproduction and birth. The Sea, that wild force, comes gushing out of the womb. The rain and ice are begotten and born. The wild animals bear and feed their young, ensuring that life will go on. Job cannot stop the powerful, life-affirming force of procreation. As Alter asserts, "Reproduction and nurturing are the very essence of a constantly self-renewing creation as the poet imagines it."[60]

Alter assumes, of course, that the writer of the divine speeches knows Job 3. The verbal and thematic links between the divine speeches and the rest of the book do indeed argue for some acquaintance with the book on the part of

[57] The word אִישׁ is used also in 41:9. There, however, it refers to Leviathan's scales, not to a human being.

[58] Contrast Isa 35:6–7, where waters break forth in the desert for the sake of the exiles who travel through it on their return to Israel. In the divine speeches, God also sends rain on the wilderness, but he does not do so for the sake of returning exiles, or for the sake of any other human being.

[59] Alter, *The Art of Biblical Poetry*. See especially Alter's discussion on 99–103.

[60] Ibid., 103.

the author and/or redactor of the divine speeches. In other words, even if the original setting of the divine speeches was outside the book of Job, the text of the speeches has undergone redaction in light of the rest of the book.

As in the metaphor of the birth of the Sea, the question of "whose womb" in verse 29 is an open one. Gregory Vall argues that the answer to the questions should be, "The rain does not have a father. No one gave birth to these things, but God is the source of them."[61] He asserts that the point of the passage is to distance Israel's God from the nature deities of the ANE.

It is possible that the divine speeches employ the language of birth because they come out of an ANE cosmology that uses the imagery of procreation rather than creation. Such a cosmology is largely unknown to us, except for passages in texts like *Enuma Elish*, where divine forces (including Marduk, the sun god, and the four winds) are born rather than made.[62] Likewise, in Egyptian texts, many of the gods are born or begotten of other gods.[63] To the extent that these divine beings are associated with natural phenomena—sun, moon, wind, sea—one could say that in these cosmologies the natural world is born rather than created. It must be noted, however, that in *Enuma Elish* the physical world—as distinct from the gods—is created from the corpse of Tiamat, the mother of the gods, rather than born of her living body.

The important point in these verses is not the literal answer to the questions—if one is even possible—but rather that God is in control of the meteorological forces, and understands them better than Job ever could.

38:31–33 The discussion moves to astronomy, but the force of the questions remains the same: Are you able to do what God can do? For the identification of the various constellations in these verses, see Pope's commentary on Job 9:9, where most of the same names appear.[64]

[61] Gregory Vall, " 'From Whose Womb Did the Ice Come Forth': Procreation Images in Job 38:28–29," *CBQ* 57 (1995) 504–13. Vall contends that the rhetorical question הֲיֵשׁ in the Hebrew Bible always anticipates the answer "no."

[62] *Enuma Elish* I, 1–20, 80–115. *ANET* 61–62.

[63] There appears to be a distinction in Egyptian texts between gods begotten through semen (the "Ennead of Atum") and those who come into being through a speech act (the "Ennead of Ptah"). The former are not the product of intercourse, but of masturbation. See "The Theology of Memphis" and "The Repulsing of the Dragon and the Creation" in *ANET*, 5 (line 55) and 6 (section xxvi 21). The former text, however, in an earlier passage mentions both mother and father, as well as "giving birth" (line 48).

[64] Pope, 70–71.

38:34–35 Again, Job is challenged to control the meteorological forces, an impossible task. The rain is not a servant to Job; neither is lightning. These elements serve only God.

The second stich of verse 34 is an exact echo of 22:11b, where Eliphaz is speaking about the punishment Job is experiencing because of the wicked acts Eliphaz assumes he has committed. In the divine speeches, the phrase refers not to punishment, but to control of the elements: Can you cause a flood of waters to cover you? The verse may also refer to Job's earlier attempt at self-annihilation in the lament of chapter three. Job has wished that he were never born, and/or that he would find death. God's reply: You do not have power over such things. You cannot cause a flood of waters to cover you. You cannot un-create yourself.

38:36 A difficult verse to translate (see textual notes above). Given the context, however, the verse is best understood as referring to celestial phenomena. What it might mean to set "wisdom" in the clouds is not clear. In any case, it is God who imparts (or withholds) wisdom.[65]

38:37–38 The description is of rainclouds, and what happens when it rains. Gordis and other scholars have difficulty with the first verb in verse 37, since it is not parallel to the second.[66] The problem, however, disappears if one gives up strict parallelism as a necessary characteristic of Hebrew poetry.[67] The meaning is clear: "Who can number the clouds? Who can tip over the waterskins of the heavens?"[68] Both stichs refer to rainclouds; there is parallelism enough to constitute poetry.

38:39–41 These verses mark a major turning point in the divine speeches. The subject hitherto has been the foundation of the earth, and a description of cosmological and meteorological forces. From these verses to the end of the first divine speech, the subject turns to the world of animals. Though occupied with different subjects, these two parts of the first divine speech

[65] Cf. the description of the ostrich, from whom God withholds wisdom, in 39:17.

[66] Gordis, *Job,* 453.

[67] See James L. Kugel, *The Idea of Biblical Poetry* (New Haven, Conn.: Yale University Press, 1981). Kugel argues against earlier scholars that the parallelism of Hebrew poetry does not consist of synonymity, but of continuity, often expressed as "A is so and, what is more, B." The parallelism of the verse in question can be understood to fit this formula. The two stichs are certainly parallel in their object: the rain clouds.

[68] The verb יַשְׁכִּיב is strange here. The literal translation is, "Who can cause the waterskins of heaven to lie down?" Such a translation, however, makes little sense. The subsequent verse seems to speak of the effects of rain, so some meaning like "tip over" is appropriate here.

are similar in some important ways. That is, in both parts of the speech, God shows Job that he has neither God's knowledge nor his power. Just as Job cannot control the meteorological forces, neither can he control the wild animals. The interrogative form of the speech continues into its discussion of the animal kingdom.

These last three verses of chapter 38 foreground in particular God's providence, his care for his creatures. They refer to God's providing food for the lion and the raven.[69] This theme will continue through the next chapter, in which God continues to describe a variety of wild animals, his knowledge of and provision for them, and humanity's inability to control them.

Verse 40 contains the two words מעונות and ארב, which are also paired in Elihu's speech in 37:8. The latter word is used in this form only in these two verses in Job; this is one of several pieces of evidence supporting the argument that the writer of Elihu's speech borrowed from the divine speeches.[70]

The answer to the question in verse 41 is contained in the question itself. The young ravens cry to God for food.[71] God is the one who provides. The alliteration of ארב and ערב has probably occasioned the juxtaposition of verses 40 and 41. Both assert the same thing: God the creator provides for God's creatures. The rest of the divine discourse will develop the theme, contrasting God's knowledge and control of the animals with humanity's knowledge and control of the same.

Job 39

[1]Do you know the time the mountain goats give birth? Have you observed the calving of the hinds?
[2]Do you count the months they fulfill? Do you know the time of their delivery?
[3]How they crouch, bringing forth their young, delivering their offspring?

[69] See Joel 1:20; Ps 104:21, 27–28; 145:15–16; 147:9 for similar motifs of creatures looking to God for sustenance, and God providing for them.

[70] See above on 38:26. There are many verbal and thematic links between Elihu's speech and the divine speeches. Evidence points to the former's borrowing from the latter. For a discussion of the issue, see Pope, xxvii–xxviii and Gordis, *Job*, 546–53. See also the discussion of the Elihu speeches above in chapter one.

[71] The same is true in Ps 147:9. These two verses are probably the source of the widespread legend that ravens are cruel to their young. This legend is found in *Leviticus Rabbah* 19:1 and other rabbinic sources, in Rashi, and even in modern German, where a cruel parent is called a *Rabenvater* or *Rabenmutter*. See Tur-Sinai, 537–39 for a detailed discussion of the legend.

[4]Their young grow strong; they grow up in the open field. They go forth and do not return to them.

[5]Who lets the wild ass go free? Who loosens the bonds of the wild ass?

[6]I made the steppe its home, and the salty waste its dwelling place.

[7]It scoffs at the tumult of the city; it does not hear the shouts of the taskmaster.

[8]It searches out the mountains for its pasture, and it seeks after every green thing.

[9]Will the wild ox be willing to serve you? Will it spend the night at your feeding-trough?

[10]Will you bind the wild ox in a furrow with your rope? Will it plow the lowlands after you?

[11]Will you trust it because its strength is great? Will you entrust your labor to it?

[12]Can you trust that it will return? Will it gather in your seed and your harvest?

[13]The wing of the ostrich rejoices. She has a gracious pinion and plumage.

[14]But she leaves her eggs on the ground and warms them in the dust.

[15]She forgets that a foot may crush them and a wild beast of the field may trample them.

[16]She treats her offspring harshly as though they were not hers. Though her labor is for nothing, she worries not.

[17]For God has withheld from her wisdom and has given her no portion in understanding.

[18]When she wings up on high, she scoffs at the horse and its rider.

[19]Have you given strength to the horse? Have you clothed his neck with thunder?

[20]Have you caused him to quiver like the locust? The majesty of his snorting is terrible.

[21]He paws mightily and rejoices as he goes out with power to meet the battle.

[22]He laughs at fear and is not dismayed. He does not turn back from the sword.

[23]Upon him rattle the quiver, the point of the spear, and the scimitar.

[24]With rushing and raging he swallows the ground. He does not stand still at the sound of the trumpet.

²⁵When the trumpet sounds, he says, "Aha!" And from a distance he smells the battle, the thunder of the captains, and the battle cry.
²⁶Is it by your understanding that the hawk flies, that he spreads his wings to the south wind?
²⁷Or is it at your command that the eagle mounts up, that he makes his nest on high?
²⁸On a cliff he dwells and abides; a rocky crag is his stronghold.
²⁹From there he seeks out food; his eyes search from a distance.
³⁰His young drink blood; and where the slain are, there he is."

Textual Notes

39:8 Given the other active verbs describing the onager, the noun יְתוּר is better vocalized as a verb, יְתוּר ("he roams").

39:12 Reading the Ketib (יָשׁוּב) rather than the Qere (יָשִׁיב). The second stich is a bit awkward grammatically unless one understands וְגָרְנְךָ as the product of the threshing floor (i.e., the harvest) rather than the threshing floor itself.[72]

39:13 This verse is particularly difficult to translate. What kind of bird is described, and what is being asserted about the bird? Most commentators follow the translation of the Vulgate and designate the bird as the ostrich, called רְנָנִים here because of its shrill cry.[73] Most translate the verb עלס ("to rejoice") as something like "flap joyously," "flap wildly." Nonetheless, to translate the simple meaning of the word—that is, "rejoice"—is sufficient in a poetic passage.[74]

The second stich has occasioned many different translations, as it lacks a verb, and one word could be either a noun or an adjective. Taken literally, it reads something like "if pinion stork/kind and plumage." Commentators are divided over whether חֲסִידָה is the adjective "kind" or the noun "stork."

---

[72] See Gordis, *Job,* 458. He cites Deut 15:14 as a similar instance of the use of גֹּרֶן.

[73] So Habel, Pope, Gordis, Driver and Gray. Tur-Sinai, however, argues that the reference here is not to the ostrich, but to two generic birds, characters in fables who are tricked by predators into abandoning their eggs and young. Tur-Sinai refers to similar fables found in Greek and Roman literature. Unfortunately, he has no ANE examples of such fables, but speculates that the classical authors derived them from ANE stories (Tur-Sinai, 544–47). This verse, then, would be a quotation of the fable. Such quotation in the divine speeches would be unusual, particularly since the fable in question is not extant except in literature of a later period and a different place. I find such speculation interesting, but unconvincing.

[74] עלס, though itself unknown with this meaning elsewhere in the Bible, is easily understood as a variant of the more common words עלץ and עלז, both of which mean "to rejoice."

Some see here a comparison of the ostrich and the stork, the latter having the reputation of being unusually devoted to its young.[75] Others emend the word to חסרה ("to lack"), asserting that the ostrich's wing lacks plumage.[76] One of the simpler emendations is that of Dhorme, who vocalizes אם ("with") as אֵם ("mother"), in the sense of "one who possesses a quality." He then translates the verse, "she possesses a gracious plumage and pinions."[77] This solution is attractive in its simplicity. One might also note the meaning of חסידה as "kind/loving," which suggests a deliberately ironic contrast with the rest of the description of the ostrich. Her plumage may be gracious, but she herself is anything but gracious and kind towards her offspring.

39:19 The word רעמה in 19b has occasioned some disagreement among scholars. A *hapax legomenon*, the word has been translated "mane" by some, referencing the Arabic term *umm ri'm* ("mother of the mane"), a designation for the hyena.[78] Such a translation, of course, makes sense, as the thing that "clothes" the horse's neck is the mane. On the other hand, רעמה appears to be from the root רעם, "to thunder." To say that a horse's neck is "clothed with thunder" is certainly acceptable in poetry.[79] It also fits with the rest of the passage, which speaks of "terror" (vs. 20), "raging" (vs. 24) and the "thunder" (רעם) of the captains" (v. 25). The poet is probably employing a word play, evoking both possible meanings of the word.

39:21 The first word of this verse is a plural verb which has no corresponding subject. Therefore, most translations (including the LXX and the Vulgate) emend it to a singular verb referring to the horse: "He digs/paws." The second word, traditionally translated "in the valley," can also be understood on the basis of Akkadian and Ugaritic cognates as "with strength."[80] Such a translation fits nicely with the parallel בכח ("with power") in the second stich of the verse. I have therefore adopted this emendation in my translation.

There is one other possibility for translating this verse. Could the first verb refer to those making preparations for the battle? "They dig in the valley and he [the war horse] rejoices. With power he goes out to meet the battle." The

---

[75] Gordis, *Job*, 459.

[76] Pope, 309. To the contrary, the ostrich's wings, while small, have abundant feathers.

[77] Dhorme, 603–4.

[78] Pope, 311, referencing L. Koehler and W. Baumgartner, *Lexicon in Veteris Testamenti Libros*, 1953.

[79] Habel calls such a translation "superior poetry," while the translation "mane" is "a prosaic leveling of the poetic language" (525).

[80] See Pope, 311, Habel, 525, and Michel, 291.

verb חפר is used for "digging" or "searching out/spying;" it does not normally describe preparation for battle. Those who prepare for battle, however, do so, by and large, in valleys—"encamping" in valleys, "spreading out" in valleys.[81] Such a situation gives the war horse reason to "rejoice," as he sees armies preparing for battle.

39:24 The verb יאמין in 24b is difficult to understand in this context. The horse does not "believe" or "trust" when the trumpet sounds? It seems best to follow Pope and take the verb in its most basic sense of "be firm, established," translating it as something like "stand firm."[82]

39:25 The word בדי is understood in the sense of the more common מדי, "as often as" or "when." האח is a cry of joy, as the war horse hears the sound of the trumpet calling him to battle.[83]

39:26 The root we saw in 39:13 as a noun is used here—for the only time in the Bible—as a verb: אבר ("to move pinions," i.e., "to fly/soar").

39:29 The verb that causes trouble in 39:21 (חפר) here has one of its usual meanings: "to search for."

39:30 The verb יעלעו is *hapax*. Various solutions have been proposed, the most common one being to derive the word from the root לוע or לעע ("to lick up, drink"), and emend it to read ילעלעו.[84] Whatever the emendation, the verb clearly refers to the ingesting of blood.

Commentary

39:1–4 This passage exemplifies the theme of procreation that figures so prominently in the divine speeches.[85] Whereas the previous verses had to do with the metaphorical "birth" of inanimate entities, however, these verses describe in detail the physical labor and delivery of wild animals. God continues to challenge Job, though in this passage the issue is not power, but knowledge. Does Job know when and how the wild animals give birth?

---

[81] Judg 6:33; 7:12; 1 Sam 17:2; 2 Sam 5:18; 23:13, etc.

[82] Pope, 313. Admittedly, the translation is not altogether satisfactory, as in the *hiphil* the verb always means "trust" or "believe." It makes more sense, however, to speak of the horse not standing still at the sound of the trumpet than to say that it does not "believe" (for joy) when it hears the trumpet call.

[83] See Isa 44:16; Ezek 25:3.

[84] See Judg 7:5–7. This emendation is proposed by Gerlemann, the editor of Job in BHS; by Gordis, *Job,* 464; and by Habel, 526, among others.

[85] See commentary on 38:28.

The phrase "count months," in verse 2 is found in the Ugaritic story of Aqhat, who "counts the months" (*[ls]pr yrḫ*) until his wife gives birth.[86] In verse 3, the process of birth is described in detail. The word חבליהם in Hebrew usually designates the pain of childbirth, although, in parallel with ילדיהן, the reference is obviously to the product of those pains (i.e., the offspring). The young animals grow strong and eventually leave their mothers to fend for themselves, never to return.

39:5–8 Another animal enters the picture: the wild ass, or onager. All other occurrences of the phrase in verse 5, שלח חפשי ("to set free") in the Bible refer to letting a slave go free.[87] The tendency of humankind is to see the onager as a potential beast of burden, but the wild animal is not a slave to any human being. In fact, the home of the onager is the desert and the salt plain, uninhabitable by human beings. God alone is its creator and provider.[88]

The onager scorns (שׂחק) the tumult of the city, the quintessential human domain. It does not listen to the voice of any human taskmaster. The phrase תשאות נוגש לא ישמע in verse 7 echoes in part an earlier verse in Job: קול נגש לא שמעו (3:18), where the subjects in question are the dead prisoners who no longer have to listen to their taskmasters.[89] Job wishes to be among them. God reveals to Job that freedom is not found in death, or at least, not only in death; freedom is part of the essential structure of the cosmos.

The word שׂחק ("to laugh, to scorn"), used here for the first time in the divine speeches, occurs a number of times later in the speeches, in reference to other creatures. The ostrich "scorns" the horse and horseman, while the horse itself "laughs" at fear.[90] God challenges Job to "sport" with Leviathan, that fiercest of all beings, the creature who "laughs" at the rattle of spears.[91] Earlier in the dialogue, Job uses שׂחק to describe his attitude towards his neighbors, those who waited for his word as eagerly as they awaited rain,

[86] Aqhat, tablet I, column II, line 43. Noted by Pope, 306, and Habel, 524.

[87] See Exod 21:26, 27; Deut 15:12, 13, 18; Isa 58:6; Jer 34:9,10, 11, 14, 16. The verse in Isaiah refers to letting "the oppressed" go free, which is not far from the idea of letting a slave go free.

[88] See Ps 104:11, where God provides the onager with water.

[89] These are the only two occurrences of the word נגשׂ in Job. Again, as discussed above, there are a number of connections between Job 3 and the divine speeches. These linkages are discussed at more length in chapter two.

[90] Job 39:18, 22.

[91] Job 40:29; 41:21. שׂחק is also used in 40:20. The wild beasts of the field "sport" on the mountains.

those among whom he sat as king.[92] In each instance, the word denotes the attitude of a superior to an inferior. In the case of the divine speeches, the animals appear to have the position of superiority over against the human beings who try to control them. At the very least, it can be said that these creatures are not in any way subject to humanity.

39:9–12 This passage paints a portrait of the wild ox. Like the wild ass, it has nothing to do with human beings. Both animals have domesticated cousins that are useful to human beings. Thus, the divine speeches contrast these two animals with their domesticated counterparts. The wild ass does not hear the driver's shouts; unlike the five hundred donkeys Job owned in his former life (1:3), the wild ass is not a beast of burden (39:7). Likewise, God asks Job pointed questions about the likelihood of the wild ox serving him as a domesticated ox would. Will it consent to serve him? The answer is obviously "no." Unlike the five hundred yoke of oxen Job owned in the prologue (1:3), the wild ox will not plow Job's fields or spend the night at his feeding-trough. It will not be used as a draft animal; it will not bring in the harvest. Its strength is its own and cannot be harnessed by humanity. Job cannot "entrust" his labor—and the fruits of said labor—to the wild ox (vv. 11–12). The wild ox is a symbol of power and danger in the Bible.[93] Like the rest of the animals described in the divine speeches, the wild ass and the wild ox cannot be used by humanity.[94]

39:13–18 This passage is omitted in the LXX. The description of the ostrich is not introduced by questions, as are descriptions of other animals in the divine speeches. The ostrich is not presented in a positive light, in contrast to the other animals in the speeches. Some commentators therefore argue that these verses are a later interpolation. As Habel asserts, however, it seems more likely that the LXX omitted these difficult verses than that someone later inserted them.[95] Keel also argues persuasively for the inclusion of this passage in the original form of the divine speeches, based on the literary pattern of the first divine speech, with its list of five pairs of animals. The ostrich is paired with the war horse in this pattern.[96]

---

[92] Job 29:23–25. A few verses later, the positions are reversed, and Job himself is the object of derision from those who are younger than he (30:1).

[93] Num 23:22; 24:8; Ps 22:21; 29:6; 92:10; Isa 34:7.

[94] The only possible exception is the war horse. See discussion below.

[95] Habel, 524.

[96] Keel, 61–125. See especially the example of ANE iconography on 79 (which depicts an ostrich and two horses!), and those on 103, 115 (which depict the king as "Lord of the

The description of the ostrich continues the emphasis in the divine speeches on the theme of procreation.[97] In this instance, however, the ostrich is depicted as a foolish and unloving mother. She abandons her eggs on the ground, not thinking and/or not caring that they might be trampled.[98] Nevertheless, by God's providence, her young survive.

The word יגיעה in verse 16 connects this passage about the ostrich with the previous one about the wild ox.[99] The verbal parallel may have occasioned the juxtaposition of two originally independent passages. On the other hand, the second passage may have been written to illuminate the first. In other words, if Job were to "abandon" or entrust his labor to the wild ox (39:11), he would be as foolish as the ostrich, who abandons her eggs to the ground, so that her labor is in vain (39:14,16).[100]

The reason that the ostrich is so foolish is that God has made her that way. He has withheld wisdom from her; or, more literally, "caused her to forget" wisdom (v. 17), and has given her no portion in understanding. The ostrich, too, is part of God's handiwork. To some creatures, he gives wisdom (38:36); to others, he does not. While the ostrich may not have been given wisdom, however, she has been granted other attributes. With her tremendous speed, or perhaps height, she scorns (שׂחק) the horse and its rider (v. 18).[101] This

---

Animals" holding two ostriches captive). It seems that the ostrich, like the other animals in Job 39, was indeed understood in ANE iconography as a symbol of chaos or danger, requiring subjugation by the king. It would, therefore, fit in with the other wild animals described in the first divine speech.

[97] See commentary on 38:28 and 39:1–4.

[98] If one follows *Leviticus Rabbah* 19:1 on Job 38:41, the ostrich in this chapter is parallel to the raven of the previous chapter; both are bad parents. Lam 4:3 also subscribes to the belief that the ostrich is a cruel parent. See discussion above on 38:41.

[99] The word is used three times in Job: 10:3, 39:11, and here. The verb עזב also connects the two passages (39:11, 14).

[100] This interpretation of the meaning behind the ostrich passage is similar to Tur-Sinai's interpretation (544), though with no reference to animal fables unattested in the extant literature.

[101] See commentary on 39:7. It is not clear what תמריא means. Tur-Sinai connects it to the *hapax legomenon* מראתו in Lev 1:16, which he translates "wing," and therefore, in the verb form, "to wing up" (547). The bird therefore cannot be the flightless ostrich, according to Tur-Sinai. Like Tur-Sinai, Pope connects the word with that in Lev. 1:16, but understands the latter as "the protuberance above the anus with the feathers which are cut off and tossed in the refuse" (310). He therefore understands the verb to refer to the ostrich spreading its tail feathers as it runs. In any case, the reference appears to be to the bird's speed, or perhaps height, as compared to that of the horse and its rider.

verse is one of the few in the divine speeches that mentions human beings, though here, as elsewhere, they appear only in a peripheral role.

39:19–25 Mentioned in the previous verse, the horse now becomes the subject of God's speech. After the series of declarative statements about the ostrich, the speech again takes the form of questions. Of the animals listed in the divine speeches, the horse is the only one that could be called domesticated. It is not, however, a beast of burden but of war, eager to do battle. It may be useful to humanity, but it is not what one would call "tame."

The description of the war horse is that of a majestic and terrifying animal. The verb הרעיש ("quaking") in verse 20 does not indicate fear but eagerness for the battle. It is interesting to note that the only time הוד is used in Job outside of the divine speeches, it describes God.[102] Likewise, אימה is used elsewhere in the book to describe the "terror" of God that falls upon Job and upon other evildoers.[103] Judging from such comparisons, the war horse is indeed a fierce animal.

Like the wild ass and the ostrich, the horse "scorns" or "laughs" (שׂחק) at adversaries; in this case, fear itself (v. 22).[104] He does not shy away even from the sword. The weapons of war do not prevail against the war horse. Like Leviathan later in the divine speeches, the war horse is impervious to such weapons.[105]

The noun רגז (v. 24) has been used previously by Job to designate the "trouble" with which human beings are afflicted. It is, in fact, the very last word of his first lament in chapter 3.[106] Here, the term applies to the "raging" of the war horse. Perhaps the divine speeches mean to set the "trouble/raging" of the human sphere within the larger context of creation, to enlarge Job's perspective.

---

[102] In Elihu's speech, 37:22. The third and last time הוד appears in Job, God uses it in a challenge to Job to clothe himself with "majesty" (40:10).

[103] Job 9:34; 13:21; 20:25. It is also used by Elihu to describe any "fear" Job may have of his young interlocutor (33:7), and, in the divine speeches, the "terror" that surrounds Leviathan's teeth (41:6).

[104] See commentary on 39:7.

[105] The language of war is used for both the horse and Leviathan. The words חנית, להב, and כידון each occur only two times in the book of Job—here in this verse and in the passage about Leviathan (41:13, 18, and 21, respectively). The same is true of רעש in the next verse, which is used also in 41:21.

[106] Job 3:26; see also Job 3:17; 14:1. See the discussion of this significant word in chapter one.

The description of the war horse ends with a series of words evoking the din of battle: שֹׁפָר ("trumpet"), רַעַם ("thunder"), תְּרוּעָה ("battle cry"). Such wording echoes that of the very beginning of the description of the war horse, where it is said that his neck is "clothed with thunder."[107]

39:26–30 In keeping with the predominant pattern in the divine speeches, when the subject changes, the description of the new object or animal is introduced by a question, or a series of questions.[108] The effect is to draw Job's attention to yet another illustration of the variety and grandeur of God's creation. The last animals described in the first divine speech are birds of prey. Pope speculates that 27b speaks of a vulture or falcon, paralleling the eagle of 27a. The LXX and Qumran Targum both introduce a second bird in the verse.[109] As the MT stands now, however, verses 27–30 all refer to the eagle.

Like many of the other entities or animals described thus far in the divine speeches, the eagle is discussed in terms of where it makes its home. It is known for building its nest in very high, inaccessible places, where predators cannot reach its young, and from where it can hunt prey.[110] By and large, the homes of the meteorological forces or animals described in the divine speeches are places inhospitable or inaccessible to human beings: the recesses of the Deep, the gates of Death, the homes of light and darkness, the storehouses of snow and hail, the "salt land" habitation of the wild ass, and the high rocky crag where the eagle dwells.[111] Again, humanity has no power over such beings and cannot even approach their dwellings.

The second stich of verse 30 is a proverbial saying, found in similar form in Matt 24:28 and Luke 17:37. The saying fits the context well, as the previous passage described a battle (vv. 21–25). The חֲלָלִים of this verse, then, are the slain human beings on the battlefield. The war horse and the eagle are something of a pair. The horse marches off to battle and facilitates the killing of human beings by other human beings. The eagle sits aloft and

[107] For the explanation of this translation, see discussion above in the textual notes on 39:19.

[108] The primary exception is the description of the ostrich in 39:13–18, which contains no questions. See discussion above on 39:13–18.

[109] Pope, 313–14.

[110] See Jer 49:16. It is interesting to note that סֶלַע and מְצוּדָה, together and individually, are used commonly in biblical poetry to describe God as the refuge of those who seek him (v. 28). See 2 Sam 22:2; Ps 18:3; 31:4; 71:3. See also Ps 42:10; 91:2; 144:2, where the words are used separately to describe God.

[111] Job 38:16–17, 19, 22; 39:6, 28. See also Job 40:23 and 41:23–24, where Behemoth dwells in the raging river and Leviathan in the Deep.

waits until the battle is over, then feeds on their corpses.[112] Wild birds of prey are not only uncontrolled by human beings; they even prey upon humanity! Such is the place of humanity in the description of creation found in the divine speeches.

Job 40

[1]YHWH answered Job, saying,

[2]"Shall a reprover contend with Shaddai? One who rebukes God must answer."

[3]Job answered YHWH, saying,

[4]"I am of little account. What shall I answer you? I put my hand to my mouth.

[5]Once I have spoken, and I will not answer; twice, and I will not do so again."

[6]YHWH answered Job from a whirlwind, saying,

[7]"Gird up your loins like a man. I will question you, and you declare to me.

[8]Will you indeed annul my justice? Will you condemn me so that you may be justified?

[9]Do you have an arm like God's, and can you thunder with a voice like his?

[10]Adorn yourself with pride and exaltation. Clothe yourself with splendor and majesty.

[11]Let loose your overflowing anger. See all who are proud and abase them.

[12]See all who are proud and humble them. Cast down the wicked where they stand.

[13]Hide them in the dust together; bind their faces in darkness.

[14]Then even I will praise you, because your right hand saves you.

[15]Behold now Behemoth, which I made with you. He eats grass like the ox.

[16]Behold now his strength in his loins, and his power in the muscles of his belly.

[17]He stiffens his tail like a cedar. The sinews of his thighs are knit together.

---

[112] Thanks to Prof. Gary Anderson for this observation (private communication). See Alter's comment that the lion and the raven at the end of ch. 38 and the eagle and hawk at the end of ch. 29, all violent beasts of prey, provide brackets for the whole list of wild animals (Alter, 102). Alter contends that there is a "peculiar beauty" in these violent creatures, and that they show Job that the animal world is a "nonmoral realm," making him see "the inadequacy of any merely human moral calculus."

¹⁸His bones are channels of bronze; his limbs like a rod of iron.

¹⁹He is the first of the works of God. Only his Maker can bring near his sword.

²⁰Indeed, the mountains bear grass for him; and all the beasts of the field frolic there.

²¹Under the lotuses he lies, under cover of reed and swamp.

²²The lotuses cover him as his shade; the willows of the wady surround him.

²³If the river bears down, he is not alarmed. He is confident even when a river gushes into his mouth.

²⁴Who will capture him by his eyes, or pierce his nose with hooks?

²⁵Can you draw out Leviathan with a hook? Can you thrust down his tongue with rope?

²⁶Will you place a cord in his nose? Will you pierce his jaw with a hook?

²⁷Will he plead for favor with you, or speak meekly to you?

²⁸Will he make a covenant with you, that you take him as a servant forever?

²⁹Can you play with him as with a bird? Will you leash him for your girls?

³⁰Will traders bargain over him? Will they divide him up among merchants?

³¹Can you fill his skin with harpoons or his head with fishing spears?

³²Lay your hand upon him, and you will not long remember the battle!

Textual Notes

40:16 The word שׂרירי is *hapax*. It is derived from the root שׂרר, "to be strong, healthy, firm." Given the context, it seems best to follow most commentators in translating it "muscles" or "sinews" of the belly.

40:17 The verb חפץ normally means "to desire." It cannot have that meaning here, however, as neither a tail nor a cedar can "desire." Commentators have suggested various options: "stiffen," "stand erect," "arch." If one takes the root meaning of חפץ to be something like "to strive hard for," then the translation "to stiffen" captures something of the same sense. This translation also fits with the common understanding of "tail" as a euphemism for "penis."[113]

---

[113] Such has been the understanding of translators from earliest times. The Peshitta and Vulgate render the parallel term פחדו as "testicles," which implies a sexual understanding of "tail." See Pope, 323–24 for similar interpretations by Albertus Magnus and Thomas Aquinas. Many modern commentators agree that זנב in this verse is a euphemism for the penis (Pope, 324; Habel, 566; Gordis, *Job*, 477, et al.).

40:1 The second stich has occasioned some difficulty for translators. Many emendations have been suggested.[114] The words themselves are not difficult, but the sense of the stich is uncertain. Adding "only" to the statement makes some sense of it: Only the one who made Behemoth can approach him with a sword (i.e., his creator alone has power over him).

40:20 The word בול is understood to be an abbreviation of יבול ("produce, tribute"). The subject of the first verb is unclear; it could be the same as the subject of the second verb (i.e., "all the beasts of the field") or it could be the mountains themselves. This translation opts for the second possibility, as the cantillation marks indicate. A more literal translation would be, "the mountains offer him tribute." The reference is clearly to food.

40:23 The verb עשק usually means "to oppress." Such a translation is awkward here, but one can derive a more literal meaning, "bear down," or perhaps something like "rage," which would fit with the parallel verb יגיח.[115]

The second stich does not refer to the Jordan River specifically. In every other occurrence of the name in the Bible, it appears with the definite article and/or in construct. In this verse, the poet has revealed his roots in the land of Israel by using the name as a generic term for "river."

40:24 There is no subject in this verse, and the first stich is unusually short. Some commentators, therefore, transfer אל-פיהו from the previous verse to the first stich of this verse, and find there a reference to El.[116] Others suggest the addition of the phrase מי-הו to the first stich, attributing its absence to haplography after פיהו.[117] This translation uses the latter emendation. It is not completely satisfactory, but it does fit the interrogative nature of the subsequent verses. One must also note the frequent use of מי ("who?") in the description of Leviathan in 41:2–6. If taken as a parallel to those verses,

---

[114] See Gordis, *Job,* 477, for a comprehensive list of suggested emendations.

[115] Cf. Gen 26:20, with the verb עשק, "to contend, argue." The Genesis verb is *hapax,* but it is used as a synonym of ריב. While ש and שׂ are two distinct phonemes in Hebrew, it is possible that the Masoretes incorrectly placed the diacritical mark in this case.

[116] Habel, 554, following in part a suggestion by Gunkel. Habel also then has to deal with references to two body parts (mouth and eyes) right next to each other. He takes up a suggestion by Gordis (*Job,* 480) to translate עיניו as "rings" or "cords." This suggestion, however, rests on a very speculative translation of עינותם in Hosea 10:10 as "rings." It makes a great deal more sense to retain the usual translation of עיניו as "eyes," especially given the context of this and the preceding verse, with their references to other parts of the face (פיהו and אף).

[117] Gordis, *Job,* 480; Pope, 327.

this verse asserts the ferocious nature of Behemoth, a creature who cannot be captured by mere mortals, but only by God.[118]

40:31 Both שֻּׁכּוֹת and צִלְצַל are *hapax*. The first is related to שִׂכִּים ("thorns") and the second to צָלַל ("to quiver, tingle"). The second word is in construct with דָּגִים, suggesting some sort of instrument used in fishing, perhaps a spear which vibrates in flight. Since thorns are not particularly useful for catching fish, שֻּׁכּוֹת must be something that sticks in the animal's flesh, hence "harpoons." The imagery is similar to that of the previous verses. God challenges Job to hunt Leviathan.

Commentary

40:1–2 These verses mark the end of the first speech. YHWH takes up words used a number of times in the dialogue: רִיב "to contend," and יכח "to rebuke, correct." He also uses the two most common names for himself in the book of Job, שַׁדַּי and אֱלוֹהַּ.[119] Both רִיב and יכח come from the realm of judicial proceedings.[120] The former is used only by Job, primarily to speak about the case between himself and God. For instance, in 10:2, Job says, "I will say to God (אֱלוֹהַּ), 'Do not condemn me; declare to me why you contend with me (תְּרִיבֵנִי).'"[121] The verb יכח, on the other hand, is used by both Job and his friends; but it also is employed primarily to speak about the argument between Job and God. In 13:15, Job cries, "He will kill me; I have no hope; but I will prove (אוֹכִיחַ) my ways to his face."[122]

Job pleads many times in the dialogue for his day in court, so to speak. Now God turns the tables on him, and declares that one who dares to contend with God must answer for himself. The setting, however, is not a judicial court, as Job expected, but the world that God created, an infinitely larger arena which encompasses much more than humanity. Such a setting changes the terms

---

[118] See 40:19: "Only his Maker can bring near his sword."

[119] God is referred to in the dialogue almost exclusively by these two names. The use of the tetragrammaton is reserved for prologue, epilogue, and divine speeches. See commentary on 38:1.

[120] See Ernst Jenni and Claus Westermann, *Theological Lexicon of the Old Testament* (trans. Mark E. Biddle; Peabody, Mass.: Hendrickson, 1997) 542–44, 1232–37.

[121] See Job 13:6, 8; 23:6; 31:35.

[122] See Job 6:25–26; 9:33; 13:3, 15; 16:21; 22:4; 23:7.

of the discourse and the understanding of what "justice" and "judgment" entail.[123] God takes up such concerns later in this same passage.

40:3–5 For the first time in the divine speeches, Job speaks. He acknowledges his own smallness in the face of God's creation. To "lay one's hand to one's mouth" seems to be a sign of dismay or deference.[124] Job cannot answer such an overwhelming display of power. His only recourse is to keep silent.

This first answer of Job's can be read as ambiguous, which would explain the need for God's second speech. Job may acknowledge that he is small, but he does not acknowledge God's power explicitly. Neither does he admit any wrongdoing or even any change of heart on his part, as he does in his second reply.[125]

40:6–7 Almost completely identical to 38:1 and 3, these two verses signify the beginning of the second divine speech.[126]

40:8 This is a significant verse in its use of three words having to do with justice, righteousness, and judgment: מִשְׁפָּט, צֶדֶק, and רשׁע. All three are used extensively in the dialogue of Job. It is only in this verse, however, that מִשְׁפָּט and צֶדֶק appear at all in the divine speeches, and it is only here that רשׁע is used as a verb (hiph., "to condemn").[127] This verse, then, and the passage it introduces seem to take up some of the concerns of the rest of the book more directly than the divine speeches have thus far.

The word מִשְׁפָּט ("justice, judgment, order, cause") plays a significant role in biblical discussions of law and justice.[128] In the book of Job, the word is used by almost every character, and particularly by Job himself: "I cry out, 'Violence,' but I am not answered; I call, but there is no justice (מִשְׁפָּט);" "As God lives, who has put aside my right (מִשְׁפָּט);" "I put on righteousness (צֶדֶק) and it clothed me; like a robe and a turban was my justice (מִשְׁפָּטִי)."[129] Job is

---

[123] See the commentary below on 40:8. Scholnick ("Poetry in the Courtroom") contends that the setting of the divine speeches is still, in a sense, the courtroom. The divine speeches, with their panoramic view of creation, are God's testimony in Job's case against him.

[124] See Job 21:5; 29:9

[125] See discussion below on 42:1–6.

[126] The only differences between the verses in the two chapters are insignificant: a missing ה in 40:6, and a missing ו in 40:7.

[127] רשׁע is used as a noun in 38:13, 15 and 40:12.

[128] It occurs 422 times in the Bible, distributed primarily in prophetic and legal texts (Isaiah, Jeremiah, Ezekiel, Deuteronomy, and Numbers) and in Psalms, Proverbs, and Job (Jenni and Westermann, 1392).

[129] Job 19:7; 27:2; 29:14.

concerned with מִשְׁפָּט as "justice" in general, and with his own מִשְׁפָּט — both
his "case" and his sense of his own righteousness. God has perverted מִשְׁפָּט
in all these senses, according to Job. The three friends and Elihu in turn
chide Job for doubting God's justice.[130] After such extensive usage in the
dialogue, then, it is noteworthy that the word is used for the first and only
time in the divine speeches in this verse, as God accuses Job of annulling
God's own מִשְׁפָּט.

What it means to annul God's מִשְׁפָּט is demonstrated in the second half
of the verse: "Will you put me in the wrong (תַּרְשִׁיעֵנִי) so that you might be
justified (תִּצְדָּק)?" Again, both words in question are used a number of times
in the dialogue, but only here in the divine speeches.[131] Job has pleaded
with God not to condemn (תַּרְשִׁיעֵנִי) him. He has defended his righteousness
(צדק) on numerous occasions.[132] He has, in Elihu's opinion, "justified (צדק)
himself rather than God."[133] Now God turns the tables on Job: Is he really
so convinced of his own righteousness that he would condemn God? Would
he thereby annul God's מִשְׁפָּט, God's "justice" or "order," the order God has
built into creation itself? The second speech begins, then, by dealing with
questions of justice and judgment, concerns of the dialogue but not thus far
of the divine speeches.[134]

40:9–10 The first speech has dealt primarily with Job's lack of knowledge
and control over creation. In these verses, God asks Job more directly whether
he has God's attributes: a powerful arm, a thundering voice, pride, exaltation,
splendor, and majesty.[135] Such is undoubtedly the thrust of these verses. It is
interesting to note, however, that the words in question also refer to various
entities and animals in the divine speeches. The Sea has "pride" (גָּאוֹן), the
horse has "splendor" (הוֹד), and Leviathan rules all who are "lofty" (גֹּבַהּ).[136]
Job cannot attain to the splendor of God; neither does he possess the glorious
attributes of some of his fellow creatures.

[130] Job 8:3; 22:4; 34:12, etc.

[131] In the case of רשע, only here in its verbal form.

[132] Job 9:20; 10:2; 13:18; 29:14, etc. See chapter three for a more comprehensive list of
the usages of צדק and רשע in the dialogue.

[133] Job 32:2.

[134] This whole passage, 40:8–14, is discussed at some length in chapter three. See the
two articles by Scholnick, "Poetry in the Courtroom," and "The Meaning of *mishpat* in the
Book of Job."

[135] See Job 22:12; 37:4, 22 for these words as attributes of God.

[136] Job 38:11; 39:20; 41:26.

40:11–13 Verses 11 and 12 have a chiastic structure, 12a echoing 11b, with
a different verb. Again, Job is challenged to act like God, to abase all who
are proud. Of course, it is God who usually humbles (שׁפל) the powerful, the
proud, and the wicked.[137] Again, as in previous verses, humanity appears
only in a peripheral role, as "the proud." Verse 12 expands the description of
the intended objects of wrath to include "the wicked," a group synonymous
with "the proud." Again, as in 38:13 and 15, "the wicked" are among the
sole representatives of humanity in the divine speeches.

Dust (עפר) (v. 13) is mentioned a number of times in the book of Job. In
this case, as in previous verses, it indicates death/Sheol.[138] Job is challenged
not only to abase the wicked and the proud, but to end their lives.

40:14 If Job is able to do all that God challenges him to do, then God himself
will acknowledge his power. The image of God "praising" a human being is
startling. Of course, the whole challenge (vv. 7–14) is ironic, for Job cannot
do such things.[139] Nevertheless, the passage is important, as it is one of the
only places in the divine speeches where the question of the wicked and their
fate is directly addressed. The implication is that God is able to do what he
challenges Job to do—abase the wicked and punish the proud—just as in every
other case in the divine speeches. Particularly in the description of Behemoth
and Leviathan, which immediately follows this passage, God asserts divine
sovereignty; God is the only one who can control the mythic beasts. Just so,
God is the only one who can abase the wicked.[140] Why God does not always
do so is another question, one that is not addressed in this passage.[141]

40:15 God's challenge to Job gives way to the description of a new creature,
one unlike any discussed before. The term בהמות is the plural of the word for
"cattle." The LXX therefore translates it θερια, "animals." It is clear, however,

---

[137] 1 Sam 2:7; Isa 13:11; 26:5; Ps 147:6, etc.

[138] Job 7:21; 20:11; 21:26; 34:15.

[139] Brenner argues that God himself cannot do such things. She asserts that the passage
is not ironic, but a "straightforward, although partial, admittance of divine failure." God is
admitting that he cannot vanquish evil, indeed, that he has "little or no control over evil"
(133). Given the description of God's control of Behemoth and Leviathan which immediately follows this passage, however, it seems implausible to read a divine confession of
weakness here.

[140] Note that Gregory and Aquinas view Behemoth and Leviathan as symbols of evil
and Satan (see discussion in the introduction). One can understand that connection, given
the proximity of this passage, which speaks of the wicked, to the descriptions of the two
mythic creatures.

[141] See the more extended discussion of this passage in chapter three.

from the subsequent description that the word refers to a single creature, perhaps "the Animal, the Beast."[142]

Behemoth is a mythological creature, bearing some resemblance to the hippopotamus. While a number of scholars designate Behemoth and its counterpart, Leviathan, as the hippopotamus and the crocodile, respectively, it is difficult to reconcile the descriptions of them with the characteristics of these two powerful but finite creatures.[143] This is particularly true of Leviathan, who is said to breathe fire, but Behemoth, too, possesses extraordinary traits. His strength is like that of iron or bronze, and he stands firm against raging rivers.[144]

Leviathan appears in other biblical texts, including Job 3, while Behemoth does not. Both creatures, however, are named together in post-biblical texts. In 1 Enoch 60:7–9, they are said to be separated, one to live in the ocean (Leviathan) and the other in the wilderness (Behemoth). They also appear in 2 Esdras 6:49–52 and the Apocalypse of Baruch 24:4. It is likely that these post-biblical references are derived from this passage in Job, but it is also possible that the writer of Job as well as the authors of the apocalyptic works are alluding to a common ANE myth.[145] In any case, the appearance of the two

---

[142] See Pope, 320. He notes this is the "plural of majesty" or the "intensive plural." Most modern commentators agree with the understanding of "Behemoth" as the name of a single creature. A notable exception is Tur-Sinai, who translates the word as a feminine plural, and argues that the subsequent passage refers to Leviathan, not to a second creature (556–63).

[143] Gordis argues at length that the two creatures are the hippopotamus and the crocodile (*Job*, 569–72). Keel, basing his argument on Egyptian iconography, also argues that Behemoth and Leviathan are a kind of "super-hippopotamus" and "super-crocodile" (127–56). Pope, on the other hand, cites Ugaritic texts to assert the mythological status of the two creatures (320–23). Alter falls in the middle, seeing the creatures as both natural and, in a poetic hyperbole, mythological (106–7). See Day, 65–68, for a review of the scholarly literature on the subject. Day himself argues for the mythological interpretation.

[144] While this study argues for the mythological status of Behemoth and Leviathan, it is interesting to note that even today crocodiles and hippopotamuses are known as fearsome and dangerous creatures. The story is told in a newsletter of the Evangelical Lutheran Church in America of young Sudanese refugees in Pennsylvania who react in fear when taken near the Susquehanna River. They ask, "Where are the crocodiles and the hippopotamuses?" The refugees had wandered across Sudan, Ethiopia, and Kenya for years and had seen many of their companions killed by these fierce river creatures. *Voices of Congregational Life*, 14:3 (2002) 7–8.

[145] See Pope, 320–22 for an extended discussion of the possible links between Behemoth and certain bovine mythological creatures called "Eaters" and "Devourers" in the Ugaritic texts. Pope also connects Behemoth with "the bull of heaven" in the Gilgamesh Epic (ANET, 83–85).

creatures as mythological beasts in later texts supports their mythological status in the divine speeches of Job.

The phrase "with you" (עִמָּךְ) compares Job to the creature Behemoth. Though the meaning of the comparison is not entirely clear, it implies something of an affinity between Job and Behemoth; the same Creator made them both.[146] Not only is Job incapable of controlling Behemoth; he also may have no greater importance than Behemoth in the sight of the God who created them both. This is a radical egalitarianism, even more than that espoused by Job in the dialogue, where he equates himself and his slaves: "Did not he who made me in the womb make them? One formed us in the womb."[147] In the dialogue, Job compares himself with fellow human beings, albeit slaves; in the divine speeches, God compares him with an animal, albeit an animal of extraordinary abilities.

40:16–17 Behemoth is a creature of immense strength. The מָתְנַיִם ("loins") and the בֶּטֶן ("belly, womb") are associated with physical and sexual power.[148] The זָנָב ("tail") in v. 17 is commonly understood by commentators as a euphemism for "penis."[149] The description of Behemoth, then, in these verses continues the emphasis in the divine speeches on procreation. While no mention is made of any offspring—indeed, Behemoth is a singular creature in all respects—the attention of the reader is drawn to its intense physical and sexual power.

40:18–19 Behemoth's enormous power resides not only in his muscles and sinews, but in his very bones, which are as strong as bronze and iron. Earlier in the dialogue, Job challenged God, "Is my strength the strength of stones? Is my flesh of bronze?"[150] This assertion about Behemoth may be a deliberate echo of the earlier verse, continuing the comparison of Job and Behemoth begun in 40:15. One should also note the description of Leviathan in 41:16: "His heart is as hard as stone." Job does not have the strength of these two creatures.

---

[146] See comments below on 40:19, where God states that Behemoth is the "first" of his ways. Such a statement, when combined with Eliphaz's question in 15:7 ("Are you the firstborn of humanity?"), implies that Behemoth is not equal to Job, but actually greater than him.

[147] Job 31:15; cf. 3:19 for another view of egalitarianism—that found in death.

[148] See Nah 2:2 and Mic 6:7. The word בֶּטֶן, when applied to a woman, always means "womb." In the verse from Micah, however, the word is associated with the power of procreation even in the undoubtedly male speaker.

[149] See the explanation for this translation above in the textual notes.

[150] Job 6:12.

Verse 19a reads literally, "He is the first of the ways of God." The term דרך
ראשית is an echo of Prov 8:22, where the subject is Wisdom. Behemoth is the
"first" or perhaps "greatest" of God's creations. Such a statement supports
Behemoth's mythological status. Pope translates freely but poetically, "He
is a primordial production of God."[151]

This statement also continues the comparison of Behemoth and Job. As
noted above, in the dialogue at 15:7 Eliphaz asks Job mockingly whether he
is the first (ראישון) human born, whether he was "brought forth before the
hills" (לפני גבעות חוללת). This last phrase is itself a direct echo of Proverbs
8:25, where again the subject is Wisdom. Both Behemoth and Job, then, are
likened subtly to Wisdom. While Behemoth is compared favorably with her,
however, Job is found wanting in comparison to both primordial creatures.

These two verses highlight what appears to be a subtle comparison of
Job with Behemoth and Leviathan, a comparison in which Job is found
lacking.[152] The differences between Job and the mythological creatures are
greater than those between Job and the animals of the first speech.[153] Once
again, humanity is given a rather low status.

40:20 The second stich of the verse employs the word שׂחק, which has already
played an important role in the first divine speech, and will appear again in
reference to Leviathan in 41:21.[154] In the other verses, the best translation
is "to scorn, laugh at," and the object of the verb is humanity or humanity's
tools. Here, however, the verb describes the "sport" of the wild beasts, who
have no need to fear the grass-eating Behemoth, even on his feeding ground.
Given the connection of Behemoth with Wisdom in the previous verse, it
is interesting to note that שׂחק is used also of Wisdom in Proverbs 8. She
is said to "play" before YHWH all the time, and to "delight" in the world
he created.[155] While Behemoth is not the subject of the verb in this verse,
perhaps the sense is the same: The wild beasts of the field "delight in" the
world God has created.

40:21–23 As in the first divine speech, the home of the animal in question
is described, and that home is inhospitable to humanity. Behemoth lives in

[151] Pope, 317.
[152] John G. Gammie finds similar parallels between Job and Leviathan. He argues, however,
that the comparison puts Job in a positive light ("Behemoth and Leviathan"). I find such a
reading implausible; the comparison seems to me obviously designed to humble Job.
[153] See the commentary on 39:7 and 40:10.
[154] See commentary on 39:7.
[155] Prov 8:30, 31.

marshy areas and near rivers. These verses are the source of the interpretation that links Behemoth with the hippopotamus. The image with which the description of Behemoth ends is one of the beast standing in a rushing river, steadfast and unafraid even as torrents surge into its mouth. One would expect as much of a mythological creature whose limbs have the strength of bronze and iron.

40:24 The description of Behemoth is composed completely of declarative statements except here at the end, where God asks Job whether he can capture the Beast. The question hearkens back to those of the first speech, and, as there, the answer is an emphatic "No!" Job is not able to master the mythic creature. The reference in this verse to capturing Behemoth serves as a link to the passage that follows, where God asks Job whether he can capture or make use of that even more formidable monster, Leviathan.

40:25[156] This verse introduces the second of the mythological creatures, Leviathan. While Behemoth is not known outside of Job and some post-biblical texts, Leviathan appears a number of times both in the Bible and in other ANE texts.

In the Ugaritic texts, Leviathan is known as Lotan (*ltn*), an aquatic monster with seven heads. In the Baal cycle, Mot says to Baal,

> When you killed Lotan, the fleeing serpent, annihilated the twisty serpent, the potentate with seven heads, the heavens grew hot, they withered.[157]

Again, in the Baal cycle, the goddess Anat proclaims,

> Surely I fought Yamm, the beloved of El, surely I finished off River, the great god, surely I bound Tunnan [*tnn*] and destroyed him. I fought the twisty serpent, the potentate with seven heads.[158]

Though Lotan is not mentioned by name in the latter passage, the identical language indicates that Lotan is the creature described. The word *tnn*,

---

[156] English 41:1.
[157] *KTU* 1.5, column I, lines 1–4. The Ugaritic translations are by Mark S. Smith in *Ugaritic Narrative Poetry*.
[158] *KTU* 1.3, column III, lines 38–42

transliterated here as a proper name, appears a number of times in the Bible (תנין/תנים) in reference to the sea monster.[159]

The sea monster, or Lotan/Leviathan, seems to have been a common ANE mythological figure. It appears not only textually, but also pictorially. There is, for instance, a Mesopotamian seal cylinder from Tell Asmar that depicts a seven-headed dragon with flames rising from its back being subdued by two divine beings. The cylinder dates from the early Akkadian period.[160]

The motif of the defeat of Leviathan/Lotan/the Dragon is part of the larger myth of the defeat of Sea, found not only in the Canaanite Baal cycle, but also in Mesopotamian texts, most notably in Marduk's victory over Tiamat in *Enuma Elish*.[161] Sea (Yamm in the Ugaritic texts) must be defeated before order can be established.

In the Bible, Leviathan appears by name in five passages, though there are a number of additional references to "the dragon" (תנין/תנים), "Rahab," or simply to God's control of the sea.[162] In Ps 74:14, God is said to have "crushed the heads" of Leviathan at creation. Though the number of Leviathan's heads is unspecified, the image has a clear connection to the description of Lotan in the Ugaritic texts. In Ps 104:26, Leviathan is described more benignly as a creature God creates in order to "sport" (לשחק) with it.[163] The sea monster appears in an eschatological context in Isa 27:1, where it is also called התנין. God will kill Leviathan, the "fleeing/twisting serpent," in the last days, just as he did at creation. Finally, Leviathan is mentioned by Job in 3:8, his first

---

[159] Gen 1:21; Job 7:12; Ps 74:13; 91:13; 148:7; Isa 27:1; 51:9; Ezek 29:3, etc. The word sometimes appears to refer to a single sea monster; at other times, it refers to many such "dragons." The name Rahab is also used for the sea monster.

[160] The seal cylinder is described by Pope (330–31). See J. B. Pritchard, *ANEP*, 691. Pope also mentions a small shell plaque of unknown provenance which depicts a seven-headed monster with flames rising from its back (331).

[161] *ANET*, 66–67. For an extended discussion of this ANE myth, and its influence on biblical texts, see Day, *God's Conflict with the Dragon and the Sea*. Day traces the biblical allusions to Canaanite myths, not Babylonian ones (1–7). He thus argues against Hermann Gunkel's stand in his seminal work *Schöpfung und Chaos in Urzeit und Endzeit* (Göttingen, 1895). Of course, Gunkel had no knowledge of the Ugaritic texts.

[162] For a complete list of biblical references to the myth of the defeat of the Sea and/or the sea monster, see Day, v–vii.

[163] The phrase could also be understood to refer to Leviathan's "playing" in the sea, or it could have both connotations.

lament. He wants those who are skilled to "rouse Leviathan" to curse the night of his conception.[164]

Such is the background of this description of Leviathan in the divine speeches. After the long list of cosmological, meteorological, and zoological features of creation, Leviathan is displayed last, and the description of the sea monster is the longest of any creature in the divine speeches. It is as if Leviathan is held up as the crowning achievement of God's creation, the creature most worthy of awe and admiration on the part of Job. The mythological character of the creature is clear simply from the use of the name "Leviathan," a name that evokes a rich history of myth. This mythological character is reinforced by the description that follows, a description that resembles that of the crocodile, but that attributes characteristics to Leviathan surpassing those of any mere earthly creature.

As with most of the descriptions of other animals, the description of Leviathan begins with a series of questions. God challenges Job to capture Leviathan with hook or rope, as if the sea monster were a fish or another aquatic animal. The mention of Leviathan's tongue connects this verse with the previous one and the one following, both of which mention facial features. The whole series of questions in 40:25–41:6 can be understood to refer to God's control of Leviathan. Job cannot capture the sea monster, make a covenant with it, or play with it, but God can and does.

40:26–27 The challenge continues: Can Job place a cord in the nose of Leviathan, to lead him around? Pope notes that "human as well as animal captives were held or led with hooks drawn through the nose, lips, or jaws."[165] Even if Job succeeded in capturing Leviathan, would the sea monster plead with him for mercy (literally: "multiply supplications to you"), as a captive pleads with his or her captor?

40:28 To "cut/make a covenant" (כרת ברית) is, of course, an important phrase in the Bible, usually referring to covenants between God and humanity. In the book of Job, however, there is no mention of any covenant between God and humanity, much less the specific Mosaic or Davidic covenants between God and Israel. Such is the nature of the book; it never explicitly links itself

---

[164] The myth of the defeat of the Sea/Dragon—though not specifically the name Leviathan—is mentioned also in Job 7:12 and 9:8.

[165] Pope, 332. See 2 Kgs 19:28; Isa 37:29; Ezek 29:4; 38:4. Pope also notes that Egyptian and Assyrian reliefs depict captives in such a position.

to Israel or Israel's history, aside from its use of the tetragrammaton. The link between this verse and an earlier passage, however, is instructive.

In 5:22–23, Eliphaz holds out the promise that life will be good once Job accepts the discipline of God. Job will "laugh" (שׂחק) at destruction and famine. He will not fear any wild animal, for his "covenant" (בריתך) will be with the stones of the field, and the beasts of the field will be at peace with him.[166]

In contrast to Eliphaz's vision, the divine speeches hold out no hope of a covenant between Job and the wild animals, much less between Job and that wildest of beasts, Leviathan. The sea monster will not make a covenant with Job; neither will he serve him. Job must find an alternate vision of his relationship with the rest of creation. This verse implies that God himself is the only one with whom Leviathan has made a covenant, the only one whom Leviathan serves.

40:29 Leviathan will not be Job's servant, and he will certainly not be a pet for either Job or his household. Job cannot "sport" or "play" with him (התשׂחק-בו). On the contrary, according to Psalm 104:26, Leviathan was created by God so that God himself could "play" with it (לשׂחק-בו).[167] Levenson suggests that this passage in Job and the one in Psalm 104 allude to a lost myth in which Leviathan is not killed by God, but defeated by him and made into a divine plaything.[168] Again, what Job cannot do, God has already done.

As in the rest of the divine speeches, the use of the word שׂחק is instructive. The one who "plays/laughs/scorns"—in other words, the one in the position of authority—is not in the end Job, as Eliphaz's vision would have it, but Leviathan, who later "laughs" at the weapons of humankind.[169] What was true of the rest of the wild animals is certainly true of Leviathan—they all scorn humanity and humanity's inventions.

40:30–31 God continues to suggest various ways in which Leviathan might be of use to Job. Leviathan will not be a servant for Job (v. 28); neither will he be a pet or plaything (v. 29). So perhaps Leviathan can be caught and then sold among merchants, divided like a large fish to be eaten? All these

---

[166] The word ברית is used only 3 times in the book of Job: in these two verses, and in 31:1, where Job "makes a covenant" with his eyes not to look on a "virgin," often understood by scholars as a reference to a goddess (Ishtar or Anat). See Pope, 229.

[167] The phrase can also be understood to mean Leviathan was created to play in the sea. For our purposes, the first translation is preferable.

[168] Levenson, 16–17

[169] Job 41:21. See 39:7, 18, 22; 40:20, and commentary on these verses.

suggestions mirror the ways in which human beings use animals: as beasts of burden, as pets, and as food.

40:32 The translation given follows that of Habel and Gordis: "If you lay your hand upon him, you will not long remember the battle!" (i.e., you will not survive it).[170] After the list of possible uses Job might have for Leviathan, God comes to the point: Job has no hope of capturing the sea monster or using him in any way. He would not survive an encounter with him. Job is no match for Leviathan.

Job 41

[1]Any hope of him is deceptive. One will be cast down at the very sight of him.

[2]Is he not cruel when one rouses him? But who is he that he can take a stand before me?

[3]Whoever confronts me I will repay. Under the whole heaven, he is mine.

[4]Did I not silence his boasting, his proud talk and his persuasive case?

[5]Who can take off his outer garment? Who can penetrate his double coat of armor?

[6]Who can open the doors of his face? Round about his teeth is terror.

[7]His back is made up of rows of shields, closed with a tight seal.

[8]One is pressed to another so that no air can come between them.

[9]Each is joined to the next; they cleave together and cannot be separated.

[10]His sneezes flash forth light; and his eyes are like the eyelids of dawn.

[11]From his mouth come forth flaming torches; sparks of fire escape.

[12]Smoke rises from his nostrils, as from a pot set aflame over reeds.

[13]His breath sets charcoal ablaze, and fire issues from his mouth.

[14]Power resides in his neck, and terror dances before him.

[15]The folds of his flesh cling together. Cast hard upon him, they will not be moved.

[16]His heart is cast hard as a stone, hard as the lower millstone.

[17]When he raises himself up, the gods are afraid. At his crashing, they are beside themselves.

---

[170] Habel, 552; Gordis, *Job*, 482. The NRSV translates, "Lay hands on it; think of the battle; you will not do it again!" Either translation is possible, but it seems unlikely that Job would survive any sort of fight with Leviathan.

[18]If one overtakes him with a sword, it will fail; likewise a spear, a dart, or a javelin.

[19]He regards iron as straw and bronze as rotten wood.

[20]The arrow does not cause him to flee. Slingstones are turned to stubble for him.

[21]Clubs are accounted as straw; and he laughs at the rattling of the javelin.

[22]His underparts are sharp shards; he spreads out, a threshing sledge upon the muck.

[23]He brings the Deep to a boil like a cooking pot. The Sea he makes like a pot of ointment.

[24]In his wake is a glowing path; one would think the Deep white-haired.

[25]There is no one on earth who is his master. He is formed without fear.

[26]He oversees all who are lofty. He is king over all proud beings."

Textual Notes

41:1–4 There are a number of translation issues in these verses. In many instances, the translation chosen is based on the context of the verses and has important implications for the meaning of the whole passage. Therefore, the textual issues in these verses are discussed in the commentary below, rather than treated separately here.

41:5 The word רסנו ("his bridle") is generally thought to be a scribal error for סרינו ("his coat of mail").[171] Such is the reading of the LXX, and it makes far more sense than speaking of a "double bridle." Both stichs, then, refer to Leviathan's scales, as do the following verses.

41:7 In 7a, I read with the LXX and most scholars, גֵּוֹה ("his back") instead of גאוה ("pride").

41:10 The word עטישתיו is a *hapax legomenon*, but it has cognates in Syriac, Arabic, and Ethiopic. It is obviously onomatopoetic. Some commentators understand the reference to be to sunlight refracted in the spray coming from the crocodile's nostrils as it sneezes. Such an image does not do justice to the description of the fire-breathing Leviathan in the following verses.

41:11 The word כידודי is a *hapax legomenon*. Dahood relates the word to Ugaritic *kdd*, "child, son," while Pope relates it to Arabic *k(w)d*, "to emit fire."[172] Both translations amount to the same thing, as כידודי אש ("sons

---

[171] So Gordis, *Job,* 484; Habel, 555; and Pope, 335.

[172] M. Dahood, *Biblica* 46 (1965) 327, as cited by Pope, 342.

of fire") would presumably be "sparks, fire," parallel to בְּנֵי־רֶשֶׁף ("sons of
fire") in Job 5:7.

41:12 The second stich is uncertain. The literal translation is "like a pot set
aflame and a reed." Tur-Sinai, Pope, and Habel, following Dhorme, emend
אַגְמֹן ("reed") to אָגֵם ("boiling, hot"), based on Akkadian *agāmu* ("be angry")
and Arabic *ajam* ("be hot").[173] While such an emendation is attractive, it
creates a *hapax legomenon*. Therefore, it is more desirable to retain אַגְמֹן and
understand the "reed(s)" as the fuel for the cooking fire.

41:13 The word נֶפֶשׁ is, of course, more literally translated "throat," but here it
is most easily understood as that which issues from the throat (i.e., breath).

41:14 The root of דאבה means "to languish." If one understands the noun as
"languishing," any parallelism with עֹז ("strength") is lost. If one understands
דאבה as that which produces languishing, however, one comes up with
something like "terror" or "dismay," which is an appropriate description of
the effect Leviathan has on those who encounter him.[174]

41:17 The meaning of the second stich of this verse is unclear. The noun
has been emended to מִשְׁבְּרֵי יָם ("waves of the sea") or understood as an
elliptical phrase for מִשְׁבַּר מתנים ("breaking of the loins;" i.e., "fear").[175] It
is difficult to understand, in the first instance, how "waves" are parallel to
"gods." While the second emendation provides good parallelism, מִשְׁבָּרִים
can also be understood without emendation, as something like "breaking,
crashing"—something that Leviathan, with his formidable body, might be
expected to do when he "rises up."

The meaning of יתחטאו is more difficult to ascertain. In the Priestly
writings, the *hithpael* of חטא means "to purify oneself."[176] The verb cannot
have that meaning here. Pope cites an Ethiopic word of the same root
meaning "to withdraw" and an Arabic root meaning "cast down."[177] Either
would make good sense. If one takes the most basic meaning of the root, "to
miss the mark," the BDB phrase "to be beside oneself" is also acceptable.
The verb is obviously parallel to יגורו, and must indicate consternation on
the part of the gods.

---

[173] Dhorme, 637; Tur-Sinai, 570; Pope, 342; Habel, 556.

[174] See Habel, 556 for a similar suggestion. Pope, following Frank Moore Cross, amends
the consonantal text to דבאה on the basis of a Ugaritic parallel, and translates "strength"
(343). In either case, the word cannot mean "languishing."

[175] See Gordis, *Job*, 487 and Pope, 345.

[176] See Num 19:12, 13, 20; 31:19.

[177] Pope, 345.

41:18 The identifications of the last two weapons mentioned in this verse are speculative, as שריה is *hapax* and מסע in a similar context is found only in 1 Kgs 6:7, associated with stones used for building the Temple. This translation follows Pope, Habel, and Gordis in the weapons' identification.[178]

41:21 The identifications of the weapons in this verse are also uncertain. תותח is *hapax*, but based on an Arabic root *wataḥa*, many commentators translate it as "club, cudgel." Likewise, כידון (also in 39:23) has traditionally been translated "javelin," though others have suggested "scimitar."[179]

Commentary

41:1 The antecedent of תחלתו is unclear, though the subject appears to be an unspecified assailant. In other words, any hope an assailant has of conquering Leviathan is in vain. The same subject can be understood in the second stich. The ה beginning the second stich may be deleted on the basis of dittography. It can also be understood, according to Gordis, as the phrase הלא גם, a rhetorical question expecting an affirmative answer: "Will he not indeed be overcome at the sight of him?"[180] Pope argues that the Masoretes changed אֵל to אֶל, obscuring an allusion to the motif of the gods being terrified of Sea and its emissaries.[181] Given the theocentric tone of the divine speeches, however, it is unlikely that the writer would now assert that God is afraid of Leviathan.

The antecedent of תחלתו could either be Leviathan ("hope of him") or the action in the previous verse ("hope of it") (40:32). That is, there is no hope for human beings of laying a hand on Leviathan and defeating him. Both translations produce the same basic meaning. Any mere human who lays a hand on Leviathan will have no hope; he will surely be overthrown at the very sight of the sea monster.

41:2 This translation reads יעירנו, and understands אכזר to refer to Leviathan, not to the one who rouses him.[182] It is interesting to note that Job himself has

---

[178] See Gordis, *Job,* 488 for Arabic cognates. It is clear that the words indicate weapons of some kind, but the translation is speculative.

[179] See L. Koehler and W. Baumgartner, *The Hebrew and Aramaic Lexicon of the Old Testament* (Study Edition, vol. I; Leiden: Brill, 2001) under the entry כידון.

[180] Gordis, *Job,* 483.

[181] Pope, 337. The gods are terrified of Tiamat in *Enuma Elish* (ANET, 64) and of Yamm and his messengers in the Ugaritic Baal cycle (*CAT* column I, lines 21–24).

[182] Gordis cites the variant יעירנו, found in *Minhat Shai*, though *BHS* does not cite it (Gordis, *Job*, 483).

already spoken in his first lament of those who "rouse" Leviathan.[183] In that instance, however, Job seems to affirm the possibility of such an act. In the divine speeches, such an act is the height of foolishness. There is disagreement over the reading of the second stich. The MT reads לפני ("before me") while multiple manuscripts and the LXX read "before him." The latter reading preserves the parallelism of the verse. Regardless, given the predominance of first person suffixes in the subsequent verse, the reading of the MT is preferable and negates the need for extensive emendation. The verse is understandable as written: Even though Leviathan is fierce when roused, he cannot take a stand against God himself. Indeed, no one can stand before God, not even, by inference, Job. Rowold connects the מי הוא of this verse with the similar question to Job in 38:2: מי זה, and argues that God is "placing in juxtaposition two creatures each of whom has raised himself up against God."[184] Such an interpretation fits in well with other verses that connect Job and Leviathan.[185]

41:3 This translation, unlike many, does not emend the first person suffixes to third person. This verse is a continuation of the argument in the previous verse: Leviathan is indeed fierce when roused, but he cannot take a stand against God. Anyone, including Leviathan, who tries to confront God will be punished. The allusion is to the myth of God's defeat of Leviathan.[186]

The second stich has been rendered: "Everything under the heavens is mine."[187] While such a translation is plausible, the more literal translation offered here argues for the sovereignty of God particularly over Leviathan: "Under the whole heaven, he is mine." Leviathan is, after all, the subject of the whole passage. Rowold argues convincingly that the question מי הוא of 41:2b is answered by the לי הוא of this verse: "Who is he to stand against me? . . . He is mine!"[188]

41:4 This verse presents several textual problems. It can legitimately be translated a very different way.[189] The word בדיו can mean either "limbs,

---

[183] Job 3:8.

[184] Rowold, "מי הוא לי הוא!?," 107.

[185] See discussion in chapter two.

[186] See Job 7:12; 9:8; Ps. 74:14; 89:10, and the commentary on 40:25.

[187] Habel, 551.

[188] Rowold, "מי הוא לי הוא!?," 107.

[189] See the translation of the NRSV: "I will not keep silence concerning its limbs, or its mighty strength, or its splendid frame." Gordis agrees with this translation (*Job,* 470). The

parts," as in Job 18:13, or "boasting," as in Job 11:3. The word דבר in the second stich, as well as the use of חרש in both this verse and 11:3, point to the latter translation. The verb in the *hiphil* usually has the sense of "be silent," but can also mean "make silent," as in 11:3. The sense is similar to that in the previous verse: God controls Leviathan, and silences his boasting.[190]

The primary translation problem in the second stich has to do with the word חִין. It is often understood as an anomalous form of the noun חֵן ("grace, favor"). Pope relates it to the name Hayyin, a title for the Canaanite deity Koshar in the Ugaritic texts, and argues that the reference is to incantations that Koshar prepares.[191] Such a reference to a foreign deity is farfetched, given the emphasis on YHWH's control of creation. It is preferable to relate the word to חֵן and translate it as something like "favorable." Habel notes that the root ערך in Job is used most often to speak of "arranging" words.[192] His translation "persuasive case" fits the context well, and so is adopted here.

The translation offered here fits in well with the translation of the previous verses. The whole passage speaks of God's control of Leviathan, an emphasis that is lacking in the rest of the Leviathan pericope. This translation also has the advantage of not resorting to many emendations, particularly of pronominal suffixes in verses 2 and 3.

41:5 God controls Leviathan. The same cannot be said of human beings, as this and the following verses make clear with their recurring question, "who?" Who would dare attack this awesome creature? Thus begins a detailed description of Leviathan's physical attributes, beginning with his "armor," or hide.

41:6 If Leviathan is indeed patterned in part after the crocodile, one can understand the force of this question. Who would dare pry open the mouth of a crocodile, with its many teeth and powerful jaws? Indeed, if אימה describes

---

advantage of such a translation is that it fits the context of the verses immediately following this one. The translation offered here, however, is also a legitimate one, and it has the advantage of forming a coherent thought with the preceding verses, which speak of God's control over all creatures, including Leviathan. My translation, moreover, does not require the emendation of the first person references in verses 2 and 3 to third person, as do the translations of Gordis and the NRSV.

[190] Both the Qere (לו) and the Ketiv (לא) can be understood in this way, the latter as a negative question expecting an affirmative answer.

[191] Pope, 338–39.

[192] Habel, 555. See Job 13:18; 23:4; 32:14; 33:5; 37:19.

the snorting of the war horse in 39:20, how much more does it describe the terror of Leviathan's teeth?

41:7–9 The divine speeches reach their climax in these and the following verses, moving from questions to declarative statements about Leviathan's powerful body and overwhelming strength. Leviathan is depicted as the crown of God's creation; indeed, the "king of all proud beings." The description of him is the longest and most elaborate in the divine speeches.[193]

Verses 7–9 all make the same point: Leviathan is covered with scales (or "shields") that do not allow for any penetration. Not even a breath of air can come between them; they are sealed up tight as with a seal. Such is the "armor" of which verse 5 spoke. Leviathan is invincible.

41:10 עפעפי־שׁחר ("eyelids of dawn") is a phrase that occurs only here and in Job 3:9. It is noteworthy that Leviathan is also mentioned by name immediately before that reference, in 3:8, suggesting that the phrase was associated with the mythological sea monster. In chapter 3, Job curses the night of his conception, wishing that it had never seen light. The phrase עפעפי־שׁחר appears to be a poetic reference to the breaking of dawn, or to the stars at dawn. It is used in 3:9 and in 41:10 as a parallel to אור ("light") and in the former verse as a parallel to כוכבי נשׁף ("stars of dawn").[194] The description is that of Leviathan as a dragon-like creature whose eyes and nostrils flash forth light, perhaps even lightning.[195]

41:11–13 These verses elaborate on the image introduced in verse 10 of light/lightning coming forth from Leviathan's face. Like the previous verses about Leviathan's scales, this passage reiterates the same point over and over. In this case, the point is that Leviathan breathes fire. Smoke rises from his nostrils and his very breath can ignite charcoal.

This passage is very difficult to reconcile with the view that Leviathan is the crocodile. While one can imagine a spray of water reflecting the sunlight like "sparks" as the crocodile rises to the surface (vv. 10–11), it is difficult to understand the image of "smoke" rising from the crocodile's nostrils (v. 12), and it is even harder to imagine what the poet might have meant by saying that the crocodile's breath ignites charcoal (v. 13). Taken as a whole, then,

[193] See further discussion below on 41:26.

[194] The latter phrase might also be translated "stars of twilight," though if one takes Job 7:4 as a guide, נשׁף is to be understood as the first light of dawn, not the last light of evening.

[195] אור in Job 37:3, 11, and 15 is best translated "lightning."

this passage reinforces the understanding of Leviathan as the mythological sea dragon, not the ordinary, if formidable, crocodile.

41:14–16   The description of Leviathan moves to his physical strength, which is evident in his powerful neck and his impenetrable flesh. As if his armor-like scales and fiery breath were not enough, he is also possessed of immense strength, so much so that terror "dances" before him. The verb יָצַק ("to pour"), used three times in vv. 15–16, can have the technical meaning of "casting" metal.[196] Such is the image here. Leviathan's flesh and heart are as hard as metal or stone. He cannot be moved.

As noted above, Job earlier challenged God: "Is my strength the strength of stones (אֲבָנִים) or is my flesh (בְשָׂרִי) bronze?"[197] The divine speeches take up this description and apply it to Leviathan, whose flesh (בְשָׂרוֹ) is indeed like cast bronze and stones (אֶבֶן). Behemoth was described in similar terms.[198] Both creatures are subtly compared with Job, and both are found to have characteristics no human being possesses.

41:17   The motif of gods being frightened by Yamm/Tiamat and their messengers is found in both Mesopotamian and Canaanite literature. In the Gilgamesh epic, the gods cower in fear when the deluge comes. In *Enuma Elish*, they are speechless and frightened at news of Tiamat and her monstrous servants. And in the Baal cycle, they lower their heads to their knees when they see Yamm's messengers.[199] This mythological motif appears to be behind this reference in the divine speeches. Even the gods are frightened when Leviathan rises up. Nevertheless, YHWH has already made it clear that no one can take a stand against him, not even Leviathan (vs. 2).

41:18–21   This passage lists various weapons, all of which fail to harm—or even affect—Leviathan. The weapons of humankind are no match for the sea monster. Even iron and bronze—used to describe Behemoth in 40:18—are as flimsy as straw compared to the sea dragon's body (v. 19). This allusion suggests that Behemoth is weaker than Leviathan, and is one of the sea monster's subjects.[200] Neither stones nor arrows can cause Leviathan to flee. Indeed, he "laughs" (שָׂחַק) at the rattle of such weapons (v. 21), as the onager

---

[196] See Exod 25:12; 26:37; 38:27; 1 Kgs 7:16, 23, 24, 30, 33, etc.

[197] Job 6:12.

[198] See commentary on 40:18.

[199] *ANET* 94 (lines 113–26); 63–64 (lines 11–30; 81–91); *CAT* column I, lines 21–24.

[200] See 41:26.

laughed at the tumult of the city. The inventions of humankind hold no terror for these wild creatures.[201]

41:22–24 These verses describe Leviathan's effect on his abode, that is, the Deep, the Sea, the mire. He does not have a weak spot; even his underside is like sharp shards, stirring up the mire like a threshing sledge. His movements cause the water to "boil" like a cauldron and he leaves in his wake luminous white foam.

The poet uses three words to designate Leviathan's home: מצולה ("the Deep"); ים ("Sea"); and תהום ("the Deep, the Abyss"). All three have resonance in other creation accounts in the Bible. One notes particularly the use of תהום in the creation stories of Genesis 1, Proverbs 8, and Psalm 104—the "Deep" is a primordial entity, the division of which is necessary in order to allow for the creation of the inhabitable world. "Yamm," of course, is the name of one of the Canaanite deities, and the word possesses mythological connotations in some biblical texts as well.[202]

The fact that Leviathan can have such a dramatic effect on these primordial entities indicates both his mythological status and his great power. No ordinary creature can cause the Deep to "boil." No mere crocodile can gild the Sea with white foam. Leviathan has extraordinary power, as evidenced by the effect he has on his domain. Again, as in previous verses, the habitat of the creatures in the divine speeches is inaccessible to human beings. This is especially true of the habitat of that greatest of creatures, Leviathan.

41:25 "On earth" is literally "on the dust." Dust, or עפר, is a recurring word in the book of Job, used some 26 times, more than in any other book of the Bible. In Job, as elsewhere, עפר is often used as a metaphor for mortality.[203] Job pleads with God in 10:9: "Remember that you formed me like clay; and will you return me to dust?" He complains of the common lot of the blessed and the cursed in 21:26: "They lie down together on the dust, and worms cover them." Such is the lot of human beings, as Job complains in 14:10–12—they die and do not rise again. He compares such a fate with that of a tree, which, even if it is cut down and its stump dies in the "dust," may sprout new branches at the scent of water (14:7–9).

---

[201] See commentary on 39:7, 18, 22; 40:20; and 40:29.

[202] See Job 7:12; 9:8; Ps 74:13; 89:10; 113:3.

[203] See particularly Gen 2:7, where God forms man out of the עפר, and Gen. 3:19: "You are dust (עפר) and to dust you will return."

The word עָפָר also serves in Job simply as a synonym for "earth." In 19:25, Job holds out the hope that his redeemer lives, and that in the end he will stand "on the dust/earth." In this verse, too, עָפָר is understood most easily as a word for "earth"—no one on earth is Leviathan's master. Given the extensive use of עָפָר in Job, however, and its association with mortality, one can discern an allusion to mortality in this verse as well. In other words, no one "on dust"—no one who will return to dust, as every mortal human being must—can master Leviathan. The word עָפָר is used again a few verses after this one in one of the most significant and difficult passages in the book of Job, so it is well to note its usage here.

41:26 The description of Leviathan, and the divine speeches themselves, end with a declaration of Leviathan's kingship. He surveys all who are "lofty" (גָּבֹהַּ). He is king over all "children of pride" (בְּנֵי-שָׁחַץ). The latter phrase is used elsewhere in the Bible only in Job 28:8, in parallel with שַׁחַל ("lion"). It is therefore often translated "proud beasts," referring only to the animal kingdom. It is worth noting, however, that earlier in the divine speeches, God challenged Job to clothe himself with גֹּבַהּ ("loftiness"). The "lofty" and the "children of pride" could, then, legitimately be understood to include human beings as well as animals. In any case, the translation "proud beings" encompasses both possibilities.

The designation "king" (מֶלֶךְ) is not a common one in the book of Job. The only other being besides Leviathan who lays claim to the title is Job himself, in his final lament: "I chose their way and sat as a chief. I dwelt as a king (מֶלֶךְ) among his troops, as one who comforts mourners" (29:25). The divine speeches do not give credence to such a claim; instead, they hold up Leviathan as the king over all who are proud.

The divine speeches end on this note of Leviathan's supremacy. The grandeur of creation has been surveyed, and the climax of the survey is the extended description of Leviathan, including the claim that this mythological sea dragon rules over all the proud beings of creation. One must remember, however, that God's mastery of Leviathan has already been emphasized (41:2–4). YHWH is not included among those who are "on the dust" (עַל-עָפָר). God, and God alone, is master of all creation, master even of Leviathan.

Job 42

¹Job answered YHWH, saying,

²"I know that you are able to do all things, and that no plan of yours can be thwarted.

³'Who is this that conceals counsel while lacking knowledge?' Therefore I declared what I did not understand; things too wonderful for me which I did not know.

⁴'Listen now and I will speak. I will question you, and you declare to me.'

⁵I had heard of you by the hearing of the ear, but now my own eyes have seen you.

⁶Therefore I recant and change my mind about dust and ashes."

Textual Notes

42:6 There is a great deal of disagreement among scholars as to the translation of this verse, and it has great bearing on the interpretation both of the divine speeches and of the book of Job as a whole. The textual issues will therefore be discussed in the commentary below instead of being treated separately here.

Commentary

42:1 No commentary on the divine speeches is complete without a discussion of Job's second, and final, reply. Just as he replied briefly to the first divine speech, so here he is given a chance to respond to the descriptions of Behemoth and Leviathan, and to the divine speeches as a whole.

42:2 Job's first answer (40:4–5) was ambiguous, acknowledging his own insignificance, but not ascribing anything to God. His second response begins with an unequivocal statement of God's power. YHWH can do anything, and no plan (מזמה) of his can be thwarted (יבצר). The second stich seems to be an echo of Gen 11:6, the only other place in the Bible where בצר in the *niphal* is used. In the former verse, God is speaking of the builders of Babel: "And now, nothing they plan (יזמו) to do will be thwarted (יבצר)."²⁰⁴ Perhaps the Joban poet is alluding to the *chutzpah* of the builders of Babel in order to contrast their view of humanity with that displayed in the divine speeches. In the latter, omnipotence is ascribed not to human beings, but to YHWH. It is significant that the statement is put in the mouth of Job, who himself has

---

²⁰⁴ Michael Fishbane notes the same connection between this verse and the story of the tower of Babel. "In the mouth of Job, the echo of God's ancient judgment of cultural pride is transformed into a humble confession" ("The Book of Job," 91).

displayed a certain amount of *chutzpah* in the dialogues, and now acknowledges God's omnipotence.

42:3 Some commentators consider the first stich misplaced from 38:2, which it obviously echoes. It is more likely, however, that Job is quoting YHWH, in order to answer his challenge in the second half of the verse.[205] The same pattern is seen in 21:19, where Job quotes his opponents' arguments in order to refute them.[206] The fact that the quotation in 42:3 is not identical in wording to the original question in 38:2 supports the view that it is a deliberate device of the poet, not a misplaced bit of text.

YHWH's original challenge to Job had to do with Job's "words lacking knowledge," words which obscured true understanding. In this verse, Job acknowledges the validity of that challenge, confessing that he spoke without knowledge or understanding about things too wonderful for him.

Whether the divine speeches and Job's answers are original to the book of Job, in their current context, the "words lacking knowledge" must be those Job uttered in the dialogue. The "wonders" Job did not understand are most naturally understood as the subject of the divine speeches just past; that is, the wonders of creation, and of God's ways in creation. The "words," therefore, are those Job spoke about creation, and God's ordering of it.[207] Of course, all of Job's speeches can be understood to fall into such a category, as he complains of lack of order in the world, and the injustice of God's dealings with him.

42:4 The second stich is again a quotation from earlier in the divine speeches, in 38:3 and 40:7. The first stich is not a direct quotation from earlier in the text, but it captures the sense of God's challenge to Job: It is God's turn to speak, and Job must listen.[208]

42:5 Job contrasts "hearing" of God (or "hearsay" about God) and actually "seeing" him. The statement begs the question as to how exactly Job

---

[205] For the first view, see Tur-Sinai, 577–78. For the "quotation" argument, see Gordis, *Job,* 492.

[206] Noted by Gordis, *Job,* 492. In 21:19, as in this verse, there is no "marker" for the quotation. One must understand its nature from the context. It must be noted that in 21:19 the quotation refers to a general argument of the friends, not to specific words in the text, as is the case in this verse.

[207] For examples of such "words" about creation and God's ordering of it, see Job 3; 7:12–21; 9:1–10; 12:1–10; 14:18–22; 21:1–26.

[208] There is a possibility, of course, that the first stich is a direct quotation of some original text that has since been lost. That it is a quotation, however, and not Job's words to God, is verified by the second stich of the verse which is parallel to it.

has "seen" God. The divine speeches, after all, are auditory, and there is no description of the visual aspects of the theophany, aside from the mention of a whirlwind out of which God speaks. Again, if the divine speeches are not in their original form, it is certainly possible that there was in the text a visual description of God that has since dropped out.[209] In their current context, however, the divine speeches visually describe not God, but God's creation. As the book now stands, it is in this sense that Job has "seen" God—through the creatures and phenomena of the world YHWH has created.

42:6 This verse, as evidenced by the phrase על-כן ("therefore"), is the conclusion of Job's reply, the statement of what he has learned or decided about his whole experience. It is unfortunate, then, that the statement has occasioned some disagreement among scholars as to its meaning.

The first problem with translating this verse has to do with the lack of an object for אמאס, literally "I reject" or "I despise." The verb almost always occurs with an object. The LXX supplies an object—"myself" (εμαυτον); as does the Targum, which reads "my wealth." It is interesting to note, however, that this verb is used three other times in Job without an object.[210] It may be, then, that the object is not missing, but is to be understood from the context. In 7:16, for instance, where Job is wishing for death, the object of the verb must be something like "my life" or "my body." In this verse, the object is more difficult to ascertain. It could certainly be "myself." Nonetheless, since Job's response has been concerned largely with words—his "speaking without understanding," the "hearsay" he has heard about God—it is just as likely that what Job is rejecting is such speech. That is, he is rejecting what he has heard previously about God and/or what he himself has said. Taking the latter as the object, the word "recant" is a suitable translation of מאס.[211]

The other problem in this verse has to do with translating על-עפר ואפר ונחמתי. Most commentators translate the phrase "and I repent on dust and ashes," making reference to the "ash heap" (האפר) in the midst of which Job sits in 2:8.[212]

There are two points which argue against such a translation.[213] First of all, נחם in the *niphal*, when followed by על, does not mean "repent on," but

[209] See Ezek 1:4–28 for such a visual description of a theophany.

[210] Job 7:16; 34:33; 36:5.

[211] So Pope, 347.

[212] So the NRSV, Pope, Gordis, and Dhorme.

[213] For an extended discussion of these points arguing against this translation of 42:6, see Janzen, 254–259. Janzen argues for the idiomatic understanding of the phrase נחם על

"repent about/concerning" or "change one's mind about."[214] The preposition in 2:8 is בְּתוֹךְ ("in the midst of"), which denotes a spatial understanding. The same is not true of נחם עַל. This idiom indicates instead a change of attitude. Job is not "repenting on" a literal heap of dust and ashes, but changing his mind *about* "dust and ashes."

We have already noted above the importance of "dust" (עָפָר) in the book of Job. It is most often used as a metaphor for mortality. When combined with אֵפֶר, its meaning is even more explicit. The phrase עָפָר וָאֵפֶר is found only three times in the Bible. In Genesis 18:27, Abraham dares to argue with God about the fate of Sodom: "Now I am resolved to speak to the Lord, even I who am dust and ashes." The phrase "dust and ashes" refers to Abraham's humanity as opposed to the Lord's divinity.[215]

In Job 30:19, the phrase "dust and ashes" serves a similar purpose. In the previous chapter, Job had extolled his former existence, when he sat as a king among his troops, when those with whom he spoke waited for his words as they waited for life-giving rain.[216] In 30:19, he is in the midst of a lament, describing his present state: "He has thrown me into the clay, and I have become like dust and ashes." No longer is Job the "king" or "chief" of humanity; he is now nothing but dust and ashes—a suffering, mortal human being.

The rarity of the phrase עָפָר וָאֵפֶר and the fact that the Joban author has already used it once in a metaphorical sense argue for the claim that the phrase as it appears in 42:6 is referring to something other than a literal heap of dust and ashes. The translators of the LXX and the Qumran Targum

---

chosen here. He also goes into great detail about the metaphorical understanding of "dust and ashes." The argument presented here is based largely on Janzen's work.

[214] See Exod 32:12, 14; 1 Chron 21:15; Ps 90:13; Jer 8:6; 18:8, 10; Ezek 14:22; Joel 2:13; Jonah 3:10; 4:2; Amos 7:3, 6. The occurrence in Ezek 32:31, which is commonly translated, "to be consoled about," has been shown by Ellen Davis to have the same meaning as the other instances: Pharaoh "will change his mind." " 'And Pharaoh Will Change His Mind . . .' (Ezekiel 32:31): Dismantling Mythical Discourse," in *Theological Exegesis* (ed. Christopher Seitz and Kathryn Greene-McCreight; Grand Rapids, Mich.: Eerdmans, 1999) 234. Of the many instances of this idiom in the Bible, then, the only exceptions to this translation are in 2 Sam 13:39 and Jer 31:15, where the better translation is "to be consoled about."

[215] Janzen notes the similar concerns of Abraham and Job for justice and says of the former, "What we see, then, is not one who is self-abased before God in repentance, but one who, fully conscious of being dust and ashes, boldly claims a hearing with God" (256). The same, of course, could be said of Job.

[216] Job 29:21–25

understood the Joban author's use of the phrase as metaphorical. The former reads "I esteem myself dust and ashes;" and the latter, "I . . . am become dust and ashes."[217]

Job, then, is not "repenting" on a heap of dust and ashes. Rather, he is "reconsidering" or "changing his mind" *about* "dust and ashes;" (i.e., about humanity). The divine speeches—with their startling view of humanity's place in creation—have caused Job to change his mind about humanity, and presumably about his own place in the cosmos.

---

[217] See Pope, 349–50. Neither text takes the phrase as literally referring to a pile of dust and ashes. Nor does either text understand נחמתי as "I reconsider." Instead, each supplies a new verb for the second stich of the verse.

Bibliography

Alter, Robert. *The Art of Biblical Poetry*. Edinburgh: T&T Clark, 1985.

Baskin, Judith R. *Pharaoh's Counselors: Job, Jethro, and Balaam in Rabbinic and Patristic Tradition*. Brown Judaic Series 47. Chico, Calif.: Scholars, 1983.

Batto, Bernard. "Creation Theology in Genesis." Pages 16–38 in *Creation in the Biblical Traditions*. Edited by Richard J. Clifford and John Collins. Washington, D.C.: Catholic Biblical Association of America, 1992.

Ben Joseph, Saadiah. *The Book of Theodicy*. Edited and translated by L. E. Goodman. New Haven: Yale University Press, 1988.

Brenner, Athalya. "God's Answer to Job." *Vetus Testamentum* 31 (1981) 129–37.

Brown, William P. *Character in Crisis*. Grand Rapids, Mich.: Eerdmans, 1996.

____. *The Ethos of the Cosmos: The Genesis of Moral Imagination in the Bible*. Grand Rapids, Mich.: Eerdmans, 1999.

Clifford, Richard J. "Creation in the Psalms." Pages 57–69 in *Creation in the Biblical Traditions*. Edited by Richard J. Clifford and John Collins. Washington, D.C.: Catholic Biblical Association of America, 1992.

Crenshaw, James L. "Job, Book of." Pages 858–68 in vol. 3 of *The Anchor Bible Dictionary*. Edited by David Noel Freedman et al. 6 vols. New York: Doubleday, 1992.

____. *Old Testament Wisdom*. Atlanta: John Knox, 1981.

____, ed. *Theodicy in the Old Testament*. Philadelphia: Fortress, 1983.

Cross, Frank M. *Canaanite Myth and Hebrew Epic*. Cambridge, Mass.: Harvard University Press, 1973.

Davis, Ellen F. "'And Pharaoh Will Change His Mind...' (Ezekiel 32:31): Dismantling Mythical Discourse." Pages 224–39 in *Theological Exegesis*. Edited by Christopher Seitz and Kathryn Greene-McCreight. Grand Rapids, Mich.: Eerdmans, 1999.

Davis, Ellen F. *Getting Involved With God: Rediscovering the Old Testament.* Cambridge, Mass.: Cowley, 2001.

_____. "Job and Jacob: The Integrity of Faith." Pages 100–20 in *The Whirlwind: Essays on Job, Hermeneutics and Theology in Memory of Jane Morse.* Edited by Stephen L. Cook et al. New York: Sheffield Academic, 2001.

Day, John. *God's Conflict with the Dragon and the Sea.* Cambridge: Cambridge University Press, 1985.

Dhorme, Edouard. *A Commentary on the Book of Job.* Translated by Harold Knight. London: Thomas Nelson, 1967.

Driver, Samuel R. and George B. Gray. *A Critical and Exegetical Commentary on the Book of Job.* Edinburgh: T&T Clark, 1921.

Fishbane, Michael. "The Book of Job and Inner-Biblical Discourse." Pages 86–98 in *The Voice From the Whirlwind: Interpreting the Book of Job.* Edited by Leo G. Perdue and W. Clark Gilpin. Nashville: Abingdon, 1992.

_____. "Jeremiah IV 23–26 and Job III 3–13: A Recovered Use of the Creation Pattern." *Vetus Testamentum* 21 (1971) 151–67.

Fohrer, Georg. *Das Buch Hiob.* Gütersloh: Gütersloher Verlagshaus Gerd Mohn, 1963.

_____. "Gottes Antwort aus dem Sturmwind." *Theologische Zeitschrift* 18 (1962) 1–24.

_____. *Studien zum Buche Hiob (1956–1979).* Berlin: Walter de Gruyter, 1983.

Foster, Benjamin. *Before the Muses: An Anthology of Akkadian Literature.* Bethesda, Md.: CDL Press, 1993.

Fox, Michael V. "Egyptian Onomastica and Biblical Wisdom." *Vetus Testamentum* 36 (1986) 302–10.

_____. "Job 38 and God's Rhetoric." *Semeia* 19 (1981) 53–61.

_____. "The Structure of Job 3." *Biblica* 49 (1968) 503–8.

Freedman, David Noel. "The Elihu Speeches in the Book of Job." *Harvard Theological Review* 61 (1968) 51–59.

Fretheim, Terence E. *God and World in the Old Testament: A Relational Theology of Creation.* Nashville: Abingdon, 2005.

_____. "Nature's Praise of God in the Psalms." *Ex Auditu* 3 (1987) 16–30.

Gammie, John G. "Behemoth and Leviathan: On the Didactic and Theological Significance of Job 40:15–41:26." Pages 217–31 in *Israelite Wisdom: Theological and Literary Essays in Honor of Samuel Terrien*. Edited by John G. Gammie et al. Missoula, Mont.: Scholars, 1978.

Ginsberg, H. L. "Job the Patient and Job the Impatient." *Conservative Judaism* 21 (1967) 12–28.

Gordis, Robert. *The Book of God and Man: A Study of Job*. Chicago: University of Chicago Press, 1965.

_____. *The Book of Job*. New York: The Jewish Theological Seminary of America, 1978.

Gordon, Cyrus H. "Leviathan: Symbol of Evil." Pages 1–9 in *Biblical Motifs: Origins and Transformations*. Edited by Alexander Altmann. Cambridge, Mass.: Harvard University Press, 1966.

Gottlieb, Roger, ed. *This Sacred Earth: Religion, Nature, and Environment*. 2d ed. New York: Routledge, 2004.

Greenstein, Edward L. "A Forensic Understanding of the Speech from the Whirlwind." Pages 241–58 in *Texts, Temples, and Traditions*. Edited by Michael V. Fox. Winona Lake, Ind.: Eisenbrauns, 1996.

Habel, Norman C. *The Book of Job*. London: SCM Press, 1985.

Hakham, Amos. *Sefer Iyov*. Jerusalem: The Society for the Publication of the Bible, 1981.

Hermisson, Hans-Jürgen. "Observations on the Creation Theology in Wisdom." Pages 118–34 in *Creation in the Old Testament*. Edited by Bernhard W. Anderson. Philadelphia: Fortress, 1984.

Hessel, Dieter T., and Rosemary Radford Ruether, eds. *Christianity and Ecology: Seeking the Well-Being of Earth and Humans*. Cambridge, Mass.: Harvard University Press, 2000.

Hurvitz, Avi. "The Date of the Prose-Tale of Job Linguistically Reconsidered." *Harvard Theological Review* 67 (1974) 17–34.

Jacobsen, Thorkild. *The Treasures of Darkness: A History of Mesopotamian Religion*. New Haven: Yale University Press, 1976.

Janzen, J. Gerald. "Creation and the Human Predicament in Job." *Ex Auditu* 3 (1987) 45–53.

_____. *Job*. Atlanta: John Knox, 1985.

_____. "On the Moral Nature of God's Power: Yahweh and the Sea in Job and Deutero-Isaiah." *Catholic Biblical Quarterly* 56 (1994) 458–78.

Jastrow, Morris. *The Book of Job*. Philadelphia: J. B. Lippincott Co., 1920.

Keel, Othmar. *Jahwes Entgegnung an Ijob. Eine Deutung von Ijob 38–41 vor dem Hintergrund der zeitgenossischen Bildkunst.* Göttingen: Vandenhoeck und Ruprecht, 1978.

Kugel, James. *The Idea of Biblical Poetry.* New Haven: Yale University Press, 1981.

Kuhl, C. "Neuere Literarkritik des Buches Hiob," *Theologische-Rundschau* 21 (1953) 163–317.

Levenson, Jon D. *Creation and the Persistence of Evil: The Jewish Drama of Divine Omnipotence.* 2d ed. Princeton: Princeton University Press, 1994.

Mays, James L. *The Lord Reigns.* Louisville: Westminster John Knox, 1994.

Meier, Sam. "Job I–II: A Reflection of Genesis I–III." *Vetus Testamentum* 39 (1989) 183–93.

Michel, Walter L. *Job in the Light of Northwest Semitic.* Vol. 1. Rome: Pontifical Biblical Institute, 1987.

Miller, James F. "Structure and Meaning of the Animal Discourse in the Theophany of Job (38,39 – 39,30)." *Zeitschrift für die alttestamentliche Wissenschaft* 103 (1991) 418–21.

Müller, Hans-Peter. *Hiob und seine Freunde. Traditionsgeschichtliches zum Verständis des Hiobbuches.* Zürich: EVZ-Verlag, 1970.

Murphy, Roland E. *The Tree of Life: An Exploration of Biblical Wisdom Literature.* Grand Rapids, Mich.: Eerdmans, 1996.

Newsom, Carol. *The Book of Job: A Contest of Moral Imaginations.* Oxford: Oxford University Press, 2003.

_____. "The Book of Job: Introduction, Commentary, and Reflections." Pages 317–637 in vol. 4 of *The New Interpreter's Bible.* 12 vols. Nashville: Abingdon, 1996.

Parker, Simon B., ed. *Ugaritic Narrative Poetry.* Translated by Mark S. Smith et al. Missoula, Mont.: Scholars, 1997.

Perdue, Leo G. "Job's Assault on Creation." *Hebrew Annual Review* 10 (1986) 295–315.

_____. *Wisdom in Revolt.* Sheffield: JSOT, 1991.

_____. and W. Clark Gilpin, eds. *The Voice from the Whirlwind: Interpreting the Book of Job.* Nashville: Abingdon, 1992.

Pope, Marvin H. *Job: Introduction, Translation, and Notes.* 3d ed. New York: Doubleday, 1973.

Pritchard, James B., ed. *Ancient Near Eastern Texts Relating to the Old Testament*. 3d ed. Princeton: Princeton University Press, 1969.

Rad, Gerhard von. "Job XXXVIII and Ancient Egyptian Wisdom." Pages 281–91 in *The Problem of the Hexateuch and Other Essays*. New York: McGraw-Hill, 1966.

_____. *Wisdom in Israel*. Translated by James D. Marton. London: SCM Press, 1972.

Roberts, J. J. M. "Job's Summons to Yahweh: The Exploitation of a Legal Metaphor." *Restoration Quarterly* 16 (1973) 159–65.

Rowley, H. H. *Job*. 2d ed. London: Marshall, Morgan, & Scott, 1976.

Rowold, Henry. "Yahweh's Challenge to Rival: The Form and Function of the Yahweh-Speech in Job 38–39." *Catholic Biblical Quarterly* 47 (1985) 199–211.

_____. "מי הוא? לי הוא! Leviathan and Job in Job 41:2–3." *Journal of Biblical Literature* 105 (1986) 104–9.

Safire, William. *The First Dissident: The Book of Job in Today's Politics*. New York: Random House, 1992.

Sarna, N. M. "Epic Substratum in the Prose of Job." *Journal of Biblical Literature* 76 (1957) 13–25.

Scholnick, Sylvia Huberman. "The Meaning of *mishpat* in the Book of Job." *Journal of Biblical Literature* 101 (1982) 521–29.

_____. "Poetry in the Courtroom: Job 38–41." Pages 185–204 in *Directions in Biblical Hebrew Poetry*. Edited by E. R. Follis. Sheffield: Journal for the Study of the Old Testament, 1987.

Schreiner, Susan E. *Where Shall Wisdom Be Found? Calvin's Exegesis of Job from Medieval and Modern Perspectives*. Chicago: University of Chicago Press, 1994.

Seitz, Christopher R. "Job: Full-Structure, Movement, and Interpretation." *Interpretation* 43 (1989) 5–17.

Simkins, Ronald A. *Creator and Creation: Nature in the Worldview of Ancient Israel*. Peabody, Mass.: Hendrickson, 1994.

Stone, Michael E. "Lists of Revealed Things in the Apocalyptic Literature." Pages 414–51 in *Magnalia Dei: The Mighty Acts of God*. Edited by Frank Moore Cross, et al. New York: Doubleday, 1976.

Terrien, Samuel. "Introduction and Exegesis of the Book of Job." Pages 875–1198 in vol. 3 of *The Interpreter's Bible*. Edited by George A. Buttrick, et al. 12 vols. New York: Abingdon, 1954.

_____. *Job: Poet of Existence*. New York: Bobbs-Merrill, 1957.

Tsevat, Matitiahu. "The Meaning of the Book of Job." *Hebrew Union College Annual* 37 (1966) 73–106.

Tur-Sinai, N. H. *The Book of Job.* Jerusalem: Turim, 1957.

Vall, Gregory. "'From Whose Womb Did the Ice Come Forth': Procreation Images in Job 38:28–29." *Catholic Biblical Quarterly* 57 (1995) 504–13.

Van der Toorn, Karel. "The Ancient Near Eastern Literary Dialogue as a Vehicle of Critical Reflection." Pages 59–75 in *Dispute Poems and Dialogues in the Ancient and Medieval Near East.* Edited by G. J. Reinink and H. L. J. Vanstiphout. Louvain: Uitgeverij Peeters, 1991.

Wagner, Siegfried. "'Schopfung' im Buche Hiob." *Die Zeichen der Zeit* 34 (1980) 93–96.

Weinfeld, Moshe. *Social Justice in Ancient Israel and in the Ancient Near East.* Minneapolis, Minn.: Fortress, 1995.

Welker, Michael. *Creation and Reality.* Translated by John Hoffmeyer. Minneapolis, Minn.: Fortress, 1999.

Westermann, Claus. *Creation.* Translated by John J. Scullion. Philadelphia: Fortress, 1974.

_____. *The Structure of the Book of Job.* Translated by Charles A. Muenchow. Philadelphia, Fortress, 1981.

Zuckerman, Bruce. *Job the Silent: A Study in Historical Counterpoint.* New York: Oxford University Press, 1991.

Index of Ancient Works

Index of Subjects

Abraham, 14, 17n59, 105, 122, 187

Adam, 96, 131n68, 132

Al-Fayyumi, Saadiah ben-Joseph, 3–4

Ancient Near Eastern mythology, 29n18, 47, 66n11, 72n28, 75, 77; cosmology and, 29n18, 143, 148, 181; in divine speeches, 64, 81, 136, 141, 142, 155; Job's evocation of, 51, 76–77. *See also* Behemoth; chaos; dragon; Leviathan; Rahab; Sea; Yamm

animals, 8, 25–26; 53–54, 82, 147, 154; deer, 79, 130; divine speeches and, 8, 72, 79, 84; donkey, 86; eagle, 72, 79, 81, 90, 159, 160n112; goat, 79, 80, 98, 130; hawk, 32, 72, 80n48, 160n112; horse, 72, 80, 85, 86, 153–54, 155, 156, 157–58; 165; lion, 98, 150; mocking of humanity, 85, 129; ostrich, 53, 80, 81, 152–53, 155, 156–57; ox, 86, 156, 157; raven, 72, 79, 150; stork, 152–53; wild ass, 72, 85, 90, 98, 155, 156. *See also* creation; Job

Aquinas, Thomas, 4, 161n113, 166n140

Babylonian Exile, 15, 16, 19, 20, 122

Behemoth, 4, 8, 63, 68, 72, 81, 87–89, 94, 97, 106, 109, 123, 167–70; God's limitation of, 120, 125; procreative powers of, 81; wisdom and, 169. *See also* chaos; Job

Bildad, 34, 35, 38, 43–45, 46; denigration of creation, 101

blessing, 26, 33, 35–37, 81–82; wicked and, 81, 182. *See also* creation; Job; procreation

Calvin, John, 4–5

Chaldeans, 26

chaos, 3, 8, 29–30, 46, 67–68, 74, 76, 125; God's limitation of, 8, 74–75, 94, 119–20. *See also* Behemoth; dragon; Leviathan; Rahab; Sea

cosmology, *See* Ancient Near Eastern mythology; divine speeches

covenant, 13, 20, 43, 122–23; between Job and Leviathan, 89–90, 172, 173

creation: biblical accounts of, 95–100; as agent of blessing/cursing, 35–37, 39, 51, 59; as answer to Job's problems, 12–13; establishment of, 67–76; God's delight in, 76, 106, 128 God's

Index of Modern Authors

Harvard Theological Studies

61. Schifferdecker, Kathryn. *Out of the Whirlwind: Creation Theology in the Book of Job*, 2008.

57. Hills, Julian V. *Tradition and Composition in the* Epistula Apostolorum, 2008.

56. Nickelsburg, George W. E. *Resurrection, Immortality, and Eternal Life in Intertestamental Judaism and Early Christianity*. Expanded Edition, 2006.

55. Johnson-DeBaufre, Melanie. *Jesus Among Her Children: Q, Eschatology, and the Construction of Christian Origins*, 2005.

54. Hall, David D. *The Faithful Shepherd: A History of the New England Ministry in the Seventeenth Century*, 2006.

53. Schowalter, Daniel N., and Steven J. Friesen, eds. *Urban Religion in Roman Corinth: Interdisciplinary Approaches*, 2004.

52. Nasrallah, Laura. *"An Ecstasy of Folly": Prophecy and Authority in Early Christianity*, 2003.

51. Brock, Ann Graham. *Mary Magdalene, The First Apostle: The Struggle for Authority*, 2003.

50. Trost, Theodore Louis. *Douglas Horton and the Ecumenical Impulse in American Religion*, 2002.

49. Huang, Yong. *Religious Goodness and Political Rightness: Beyond the Liberal-Communitarian Debate*, 2001.

48. Rossing, Barbara R. *The Choice between Two Cities: Whore, Bride, and Empire in the Apocalypse*, 1999.

47. Skedros, James Constantine. *Saint Demetrios of Thessaloniki: Civic Patron and Divine Protector, 4th–7th Centuries C.E.*, 1999.

46. Koester, Helmut, ed. *Pergamon, Citadel of the Gods: Archaeological Record, Literary Description, and Religious Development*, 1998.

45. Kittredge, Cynthia Briggs. *Community and Authority: The Rhetoric of Obedience in the Pauline Tradition*, 1998.

44. Lesses, Rebecca Macy. *Ritual Practices to Gain Power: Angels, Incantations, and Revelation in Early Jewish Mysticism*, 1998.

43. Guenther-Gleason, Patricia E. *On Schleiermacher and Gender Politics*, 1997.

42. White, L. Michael. *The Social Origins of Christian Architecture* (2 vols.), 1997.

41. Koester, Helmut, ed. *Ephesos, Metropolis of Asia: An Interdisciplinary Approach to its Archaeology, Religion, and Culture*, 1995.

40. Guider, Margaret Eletta. *Daughters of Rahab: Prostitution and the Church of Liberation in Brazil*, 1995.

39. Schenkel, Albert F. *The Rich Man and the Kingdom: John D. Rockefeller, Jr., and the Protestant Establishment*, 1995.

38. Hutchison, William R. and Hartmut Lehmann, eds. *Many Are Chosen: Divine Election and Western Nationalism*, 1994.

37. Lubieniecki, Stanislas. *History of the Polish Reformation and Nine Related Documents*. Translated and interpreted by George Huntston Williams, 1995.

– Davidovich, Adina. *Religion as a Province of Meaning: The Kantian Foundations of Modern Theology*, 1993.

36. Thiemann, Ronald F., ed. *The Legacy of H. Richard Niebuhr*, 1991.

35. Hobbs, Edward C., ed. *Bultmann, Retrospect and Prospect: The Centenary Symposium at Wellesley*, 1985.

34. Cameron, Ron. *Sayings Traditions in the Apocryphon of James*, 1984. Reprinted, 2004,

33. Blackwell, Albert L. *Schleiermacher's Early Philosophy of Life: Determinism, Freedom, and Phantasy*, 1982.

32. Gibson, Elsa. *The "Christians for Christians" Inscriptions of Phrygia: Greek Texts, Translation and Commentary*, 1978.

31. Bynum, Caroline Walker. Docere Verbo et Exemplo: *An Aspect of Twelfth-Century Spirituality*, 1979.

30. Williams, George Huntston, ed. *The Polish Brethren: Documentation of the History and Thought of Unitarianism in the Polish-Lithuanian Commonwealth and in the Diaspora 1601–1685*, 1980.

29. Attridge, Harold W. *First-Century Cynicism in the Epistles of Heraclitus*, 1976.

28. Williams, George Huntston, Norman Pettit, Winfried Herget, and Sargent Bush, Jr., eds. *Thomas Hooker: Writings in England and Holland, 1626–1633*, 1975.

27. Preus, James Samuel. *Carlstadt's* Ordinaciones *and Luther's Liberty: A Study of the Wittenberg Movement, 1521–22*, 1974.

26. Nickelsburg, George W. E. *Resurrection, Immortality, and Eternal Life in Inter-testamental Judaism*, 1972.

25. Worthley, Harold Field. *An Inventory of the Records of the Particular (Congregational) Churches of Massachusetts Gathered 1620–1805*, 1970.

24. Yamauchi, Edwin M. *Gnostic Ethics and Mandaean Origins*, 1970.

23. Yizhar, Michael. *Bibliography of Hebrew Publications on the Dead Sea Scrolls 1948–1964*, 1967.

22. Albright, William Foxwell. *The Proto-Sinaitic Inscriptions and Their Decipherment*, 1966.

21. Dow, Sterling, and Robert F. Healey. *A Sacred Calendar of Eleusis*, 1965.

20. Sundberg, Jr., Albert C. *The Old Testament of the Early Church*, 1964.

19. Cranz, Ferdinand Edward. *An Essay on the Development of Luther's Thought on Justice, Law, and Society*, 1959.

18. Williams, George Huntston, ed. *The Norman Anonymous of 1100 A.D.: Towards the Identification and Evaluation of the So-Called Anonymous of York*, 1951.

17. Lake, Kirsopp, and Silva New, eds. *Six Collations of New Testament Manuscripts*, 1932.

16. Wilbur, Earl Morse, trans. *The Two Treatises of Servetus on the Trinity: On the Errors of the Trinity, 7 Books, A.D. 1531. Dialogues on the Trinity, 2 Books. On the Righteousness of Christ's Kingdom, 4 Chapters, A.D. 1532*, 1932.

15. Casey, Robert Pierce, ed. Serapion of Thmuis's *Against the Manichees*, 1931.

14. Ropes, James Hardy. *The Singular Problem of the Epistles to the Galatians*, 1929.

13. Smith, Preserved. *A Key to the Colloquies of Erasmus*, 1927.

12. Spyridon of the Laura and Sophronios Eustratiades. *Catalogue of the Greek Manuscripts in the Library of the Laura on Mount Athos*, 1925.

11. Sophronios Eustratiades and Arcadios of Vatopedi. *Catalogue of the Greek Manuscripts in the Library of the Monastery of Vatopedi on Mt. Athos*, 1924.

10. Conybeare, Frederick C. *Russian Dissenters*, 1921.

9. Burrage, Champlin, ed. *An Answer to John Robinson of Leyden by a Puritan Friend: Now First Published from a Manuscript of A.D. 1609*, 1920.

8. Emerton, Ephraim. *The Defensor pacis of Marsiglio of Padua: A Critical Study*, 1920,

7. Bacon, Benjamin W. *Is Mark a Roman Gospel?* 1919.

6. Cadbury, Henry Joel. 2 vols. *The Style and Literary Method of Luke*, 1920.

5. Marriott, G. L., ed. Macarii Anecdota: *Seven Unpublished Homilies of Macarius*, 1918.

4. Edmunds, Charles Carroll and William Henry Paine Hatch. *The Gospel Manuscripts of the General Theological Seminary*, 1918.

3. Arnold, William Rosenzweig. *Ephod and Ark: A Study in the Records and Religion of the Ancient Hebrews*, 1917.

2. Hatch, William Henry Paine. *The Pauline Idea of Faith in its Relation to Jewish and Hellenistic Religion*, 1917.

1. Torrey, Charles Cutler. *The Composition and Date of Acts*, 1916.

Harvard Dissertations in Religion

In 1993, Harvard Theological Studies absorbed
the Harvard Dissertations in Religion series.

31. Baker-Fletcher, Garth. *Somebodyness: Martin Luther King, Jr. and the Theory of Dignity*, 1993.

30. Soneson, Jerome Paul. *Pragmatism and Pluralism: John Dewey's Significance for Theology*, 1993.

29. Crabtree, Harriet. *The Christian Life: The Traditional Metaphors and Contemporary Theologies*, 1991.

28. Schowalter, Daniel N. *The Emperor and the Gods: Images from the Time of Trajan*, 1993.

27. Valantasis, Richard. *Spiritual Guides of the Third Century: A Semiotic Study of the Guide-Disciple Relationship in Christianity, Neoplatonism, Hermetism, and Gnosticism*, 1991.

26. Wills, Lawrence Mitchell. *The Jews in the Court of the Foreign King: Ancient Jewish Court Legends*, 1990.

25. Massa, Mark Stephen. *Charles Augustus Briggs and the Crisis of Historical Criticism*, 1990.

24. Hills, Julian Victor. *Tradition and Composition in the* Epistula apostolorum, 1990.

23. Bowe, Barbara Ellen. *A Church in Crisis: Ecclesiology and Paraenesis in Clement of Rome*, 1988.

22. Bisbee, Gary A. *Pre-Decian Acts of Martyrs and* Commentarii, 1988.

21. Ray, Stephen Alan. *The Modern Soul: Michel Foucault and the Theological Discourse of Gordon Kaufman and David Tracy*, 1987.

20. MacDonald, Dennis Ronald. *There Is No Male and Female: The Fate of a Dominical Saying in Paul and Gnosticism*, 1987.

19. Davaney, Sheila Greeve. *Divine Power: A Study of Karl Barth and Charles Hartshorne*, 1986.

18. LaFargue, J. Michael. *Language and Gnosis: The Opening Scenes of the Acts of Thomas*, 1985.

12. Layton, Bentley, ed. *The Gnostic Treatise on Resurrection from Nag Hammadi*, 1979.

11. Ryan, Patrick J. *Imale: Yoruba Participation in the Muslim Tradition: A Study of Clerical Piety*, 1977.

10. Neevel, Jr., Walter G. *Yāmuna's* Vedānta and Pāñcarātra: *Integrating the Classical and the Popular*, 1977.

9. Yarbro Collins, Adela. *The Combat Myth in the Book of Revelation*, 1976.

8. Veatch, Robert M. *Value-Freedom in Science and Technology: A Study of the Importance of the Religious, Ethical, and Other Socio-Cultural Factors in Selected Medical Decisions Regarding Birth Control*, 1976.

7. Attridge, Harold W. *The Interpretation of Biblical History in the* Antiquitates judaicae *of Flavius Josephus*, 1976.

6. Trakatellis, Demetrios C. *The Pre-Existence of Christ in the Writings of Justin Martyr*, 1976.

5. Green, Ronald Michael. *Population Growth and Justice: An Examination of Moral Issues Raised by Rapid Population Growth*, 1975.

4. Schrader, Robert W. *The Nature of Theological Argument: A Study of Paul Tillich*, 1976.

3. Christensen, Duane L. *Transformations of the War Oracle in Old Testament Prophecy: Studies in the Oracles Against the Nations*, 1975.

2. Williams, Sam K. *Jesus' Death as Saving Event: The Background and Origin of a Concept*, 1972.

1. Smith, Jane I. *An Historical and Semantic Study of the Term "Islām" as Seen in a Sequence of Qur'an Commentaries*, 1970.